Heidegger's Phenomenology of Religion

Indiana Series in the Philosophy of Religion
Merold Westphal, general editor

Heidegger's Phenomenology of Religion

Realism and Cultural Criticism

Benjamin D. Crowe

INDIANA UNIVERSITY PRESS
BLOOMINGTON AND INDIANAPOLIS

This book is a publication of

Indiana University Press
601 North Morton Street
Bloomington, IN 47404-3797 USA

http://iupress.indiana.edu

Telephone orders	800-842-6796
Fax orders	812-855-7931
Orders by e-mail	iuporder@indiana.edu

Manufactured in the United States of America

Library of Congress Cataloging-in-Publication Data

Crowe, Benjamin D., date
  Heidegger's phenomenology of religion : realism and cultural criticism / Benjamin D. Crowe.
    p. cm. — (Indiana series in the philosophy of religion)
  Includes bibliographical references (p.   ) and index.
    ISBN 978-0-253-34955-2 (cloth : alk. paper) — ISBN 978-0-253-21939-8
(pbk. : alk. paper)   1. Heidegger, Martin, 1889–1976.   2. Religion—Philosophy.
3. Phenomenology. I. Title.
  B3279.H49C755 2008
  210.92 — dc22

                                                                        2007022612

                   1 2 3 4 5 13 12 11 10 09 08

For Kristin

Contents

Acknowledgments

This book has benefited from the insights and inputs of many people. I would like to acknowledge in particular Professor Iain D. Thomson (University of New Mexico), whose own work provided a paradigm and a stimulus for my own, and with whom I have shared many fruitful conversations both in person and through e-mail. I would also like to thank Professor Mark A. Wrathall (Brigham Young University) for sharing his own thoughts on Heidegger's "gods" with me during the formative stages of this book. Acknowledgment is also due to Professor Elijah Millgram (University of Utah), who provided me with useful criticisms and comments during the final stages of my work. Thanks are owed to Professor Charles B. Guignon (University of South Florida), and to Professor Steven G. Crowell (Rice University), for comments on an earlier paper on Heidegger and "Baden" Neo-Kantianism, which substantially helped in shaping the present work. I must extend my sincere gratitude to Professor Merold Westphal (Fordham University) and Professor Robert J. Dostal (Bryn Mawr College) for carefully reviewing earlier manuscripts and providing invaluable criticism and advice. Finally, thanks to Dee Mortensen and Laura MacLeod at Indiana University Press for their professionalism and advice.

During the many months of reading and writing, my wife, Kristin, gave me continual support and not a little guidance as I struggled to formulate my argument and to understand Heidegger's texts. In a very real sense, she made it possible for me to complete this project.

Abbreviations of Works by Heidegger

The following lists abbreviations of works cited in parentheses in the body of the text. The references are given to the original-language version and, where applicable, to the corresponding English translation. These two references are separated by a slash.

G3   *Gesamtausgabe*, vol. 3: *Kant und das Problem der Metaphysik* (Frankfurt am Main: Vittorio Klostermann, 1991) / Richard Taft, trans., *Kant and the Problem of Metaphysics*, 5th ed., enl. (Bloomington and Indianapolis: Indiana University Press, 1997).

G4   *Gesamtausgabe*, vol. 4: *Erläuterungen zu Hölderlins Dichtung* (Frankfurt am Main: Vittorio Klostermann, 1981) / Keith Hoeller, trans., *Elucidations of Hölderlin's Poetry* (Amherst, New York: Humanity, 2000).

G5   *Gesamtausgabe*, vol. 5: *Holzwege* (Frankfurt am Main: Vittorio Klostermann, 1977) / Julian Young and Kenneth Haynes, eds. and trans., *Off the Beaten Track* (Cambridge: Cambridge University Press, 2002).

G7   *Gesamtausgabe*, vol. 7: *Vorträge und Aufsätze* (Frankfurt am Main: Vittorio Klostermann, 2000).

G9   *Gesamtausgabe*, vol. 9: *Wegmarken* (Frankfurt am Main: Vittorio Klostermann, 1976) / William McNeill, ed., *Pathmarks* (Cambridge: Cambridge University Press, 1998).

G15   *Gesamtausgabe*, vol. 15: *Vier Seminare* (Frankfurt am Main: Vittorio Klostermann, 1986) / Andrew Mitchell and François Raffoul, trans., *Four Seminars* (Bloomington and Indianapolis: Indiana University Press, 2003). (Partial translation of the preceding volume.)

G16   *Gesamtausgabe*, vol. 16: *Reden und andere Zeugnisse eines Lebensweges* (Frankfurt am Main: Vittorio Klostermann, 2000).

G20   *Gesamtausgabe*, vol. 20: *Prolegomena zur Geschichte des Zeitbegriffs* (Frankfurt am Main: Vittorio Klostermann, 1979) / Theodore Kisiel, trans., *History of the Concept of Time: Prolegomena* (Bloomington and Indianapolis: Indiana University Press, 1985).

G26   *Gesamtausgabe*, vol. 26: *Metaphysische Anfangsgründe der Logik im Ausgang von Leibniz* (Frankfurt am Main: Vittorio Klostermann, 1978) / Michael Heim, trans., *The Metaphysical Foundations of Logic* (Bloomington and Indianapolis: Indiana University Press, 1984).

G29–30 *Gesamtausgabe*, vols. 29/30: *Die Grundbegriff der Metaphysik. Welt—Endlichkeit—Einsamkeit* (Frankfurt am Main: Vittorio Klostermann, 1983) / William McNeill and Nicholas Walker, trans., *The Fundamental Concepts of Metaphysics: World, Finitude, Solitude* (Bloomington and Indianapolis: Indiana University Press, 1995).

G39   *Gesamtausgabe*, vol. 39: *Hölderlins Hymnen »Germanien« und »Der Rhein«* (Frankfurt am Main: Vittorio Klostermann, 1980).

G40   *Gesamtausgabe*, vol. 40: *Einführung in die Metaphysik* (Frankfurt am Main: Vittorio Klostermann, 1983) / Gregory Fried and Richard Polt, trans., *Introduction to Metaphysics* (New Haven: Yale University Press, 2000).

G46   *Gesamtausgabe*, vol. 46: *Zur Auslegung von Nietzsches II. Unzeitgemäßiger Betrachtung »Vom Nutzen und Nachteil der Historie für das Leben«* (Frankfurt am Main: Vittorio Klostermann, 2003). Freiburg: Winter Semester 1938–1939.

G48   *Gesamtausgabe*, vol. 48: *Nietzsche: Der Europäische Nihilismus* (Frankfurt am Main: Vittorio Klostermann, 1986). Freiburg: Second Trimester 1940.

G50   *Gesamtausgabe*, vol. 50: *1. Nietzsches Metaphysik. 2. Einleitung in die Philosophie: Denken und Dichten* (Frankfurt am Main: Vittorio Klostermann, 1990). Freiburg: Winter Semester 1941–1942 (not held), Winter Semester 1944–1945.

G51   *Gesamtausgabe*, vol. 51: *Grundbegriffe* (Frankfurt am Main: Vittorio Klostermann, 1981) / Gary E. Aylesworth, trans., *Basic Concepts* (Bloomington and Indianapolis: Indiana University Press, 1993). Freiburg: Winter Semester 1941.

G52 *Gesamtausgabe*, vol. 52: *Hölderlins Hymne »Andenken«* (Frankfurt am Main: Vittorio Klostermann, 1982). Freiburg: Winter Semester 1941–1942.

G53 *Gesamtausgabe*, vol. 53: *Hölderlins Hymne »Der Ister«* (Frankfurt am Main: Vittorio Klostermann, 1984) / William McNeill and Julia Davis, trans., *Hölderlin's Hymn "The Ister"* (Bloomington and Indianapolis: Indiana University Press, 1996). Freiburg: Summer Semester 1942.

G54 *Gesamtausgabe*, vol. 54: *Parmenides* (Frankfurt am Main: Vittorio Klostermann, 1982) / André Schuwer and Richard Rojcewicz, trans., *Parmenides* (Bloomington and Indianapolis: Indiana University Press, 1992). Freiburg: Winter Semester 1942–1943.

G56–57 *Gesamtausgabe*, vols. 56/57: *Zur Bestimmung der Philosophie* (Frankfurt am Main: Vittorio Klostermann, 1987) / Ted Sadler, trans., *Towards the Definition of Philosophy* (London: Athlone, 2000).

G58 *Gesamtausgabe*, vol. 58: *Grundprobleme der Phänomenologie* (Frankfurt am Main: Vittorio Klosterman, 1993).

G59 *Gesamtausgabe*, vol. 59: *Phänomenologie der Anschauung und des Ausdrucks. Theorie der philosophischen Begriffsbildung* (Frankfurt am Main: Vittorio Klostermann, 1993).

G60 *Gesamtausgabe*, vol. 60: *Phänomenologie des religiösen Lebens* (Frankfurt am Main: Vittorio Klostermann, 1995) / Matthias Fritsch and Jennifer Anna Gosetti-Ferencei, trans., *The Phenomenology of Religious Life* (Bloomington and Indianapolis: Indiana University Press, 2004).

G61 *Gesamtausgabe*, vol. 61: *Phänomenologische Interpretationen zu Aristoteles. Einführung in die phänomenologische Forschung* (Frankfurt am Main: Vittorio Klostermann, 1985) / Richard Rojcewicz, trans., *Phenomenological Interpretations of Aristotle: Inititation into Phenomenological Research* (Bloomington and Indianapolis: Indiana University Press, 2001).

G63 *Gesamtausgabe*, vol. 63: *Ontologie (Hermeneutik der Faktizität)* (Frankfurt am Main: Vittorio Klostermann, 1988) / John Van Buren, trans., *Ontology—The Hermeneutics of Facticity* (Bloomington and Indianapolis: Indiana University Press, 1999).

G65   *Gesamtausgabe*, vol. 65: *Beiträge zur Philosophie (Vom Ereignis)* (Frankfurt am Main: Vittorio Klostermann, 1989) / Parvis Emad and Kenneth Maly, trans., *Contributions to Philosophy (From Enowning)* (Bloomington and Indianapolis: Indiana University Press, 1999).

G66   *Gesamtausgabe*, vol. 66: *Besinnung* (Frankfurt am Main: Vittorio Klostermann, 1997).

G67   *Gesamtausgabe*, vol. 67: *Metaphysik und Nihilismus* (Frankfurt am Main: Vittorio Klostermann, 1999).

G69   *Gesamtausgabe*, vol. 69: *Die Geschichte des Seyns: 1. Die Geschichte des Seyns (1938/40). 2. Koinon. Aus der Geschichte des Seyns (1939/40)* (Frankfurt am Main: Vittorio Klostermann, 1998).

G70   *Gesamtausgabe*, vol. 70: *Über den Anfang* (Frankfurt am Main: Vittorio Klostermann, 2005).

G75   *Gesamtausgabe*, vol. 75: *Zu Hölderlin. Griechenlandreisen* (Frankfurt am Main: Vittorio Klostermann, 2000).

G79   *Gesamtausgabe*, vol. 79: *Bremer und Freiburger Vorträge* (Frankfurt am Main: Vittorio Klostermann, 1994).

G87   *Gesamtausgabe*, vol. 87: *Nietzsche: Seminare 1937 und 1944* (Frankfurt am Main: Vittorio Klostermann, 2004).

HB   Martin Heidegger and Elisabeth Blochmann, *Briefwechsel, 1918–1969*, ed. Joachim W. Storck (Marbach am Neckar: Deutsche Schillergesellschaft, 1989).

HR   Alfred Denker, ed., *Martin Heidegger/Heinrich Rickert, Briefe 1912 bis 1933* (Frankfurt am Main: Vittorio Klostermann, 2002).

NB   "Phänomenologische Interpretationen zu Aristoteles (Anzeige der hermeneutischen Situation)," *Dilthey Jahrbuch für Philosophie und Geschichte der Geisteswissenschaften* 6 (1989): 228–274 / John Van Buren, trans., "Phenomenological Interpretations in Connection with Aristotle: An Indication of the Hermeneutical Situation (1922)," in John Van Buren, ed., *Supplements: From the Earliest Essays to* Being and Time *and Beyond* (Albany: SUNY Press, 2002): 111–146.

SZ   *Gesamtausgabe*, vol. 2: *Sein und Zeit* (Frankfurt am Main: Vittorio Klostermann, 1977) / John Macquarrie and Edward Robinson, trans., *Being and Time* (New York: Harper and Row, 1962).

ZSD   *Zur Sache des Denkens*, 2d ed. (Tübingen: Max Niemeyer, 1976).

Other Abbreviations

KNS	*Kriegsnotsemester* 1919
SS	Summer Semester
WS	Winter Semester

Heidegger's Phenomenology of Religion

Introduction

This is a book about Heidegger's phenomenology of religion. At the very least, it should be of interest to scholars of Heidegger's philosophy and to philosophers of religion. Here at the beginning, however, I would like to make some suggestions about why I think it also might be of more general interest. First, I'll say a few words about the importance of Heidegger's philosophy as a whole, and then I'll indicate why I think his philosophy of religion, in particular, is important.

Heidegger gives voice, in his own dramatic, idiosyncratic way to a sentiment that seems to be prominent among inhabitants of later modern civilization. I have in mind here the general sense of uneasiness, of the absence of something important or significant. One could say that, for many people, there is the sense that things don't really *matter* to us late moderns any more, that they don't have real, independent value of their own. This sentiment surely underlies an array of contemporary cultural phenomena, including, but not limited to, environmentalism, various counter-cultures, the rise of anti-globalization ideologies, and the notable resurgence of traditional expressions of religiosity. This sentiment also finds its way into philosophy, for example, in criticisms of the treatment of certain goods as commodity values and in debates about the value of living things and of ecosystems.[1]

---

1. See Anderson (1988) and (1993); Taylor (1986), and Callicott (1989).

Heidegger's famous worries about mass culture, about technology, and about the decline of humanistic education are of a piece with this more general sentiment of dissatisfaction. Heidegger can be read as part of a chorus of voices that question the subordination of value to preferences. He has, however, his own unique, and often mystifying voice which, whether or not it has anything helpful to say at the end of the day, should be listened to. It is, after all, often the case that what seems strange or idiosyncratic today can be viewed as insightful and prophetic in the future.

Part of the interest of Heidegger's philosophy of religion lies in the fact that it provides a focused case-study of what happens when value is made to depend upon preference or interest. At least historically, religion is distinctive at least partly because of its insistence on the claim that human preferences and interests should be responsive to, rather than constitutive of, values. Indeed, one need only look at Greek tragedy, at the Hebrew prophets, at Augustine's *Confessions*, at the *Bhagavad-Gita* to find this insistence clearly expressed. The late modern tendency to transform religion into a marketplace, into an empty system of preference-satisfaction, strikes one as particularly perverse. Heidegger's phenomenology of religion is concerned quite directly with exposing, diagnosing, and correcting this distortion. As such, it is exemplary of a careful philosophical response to the disenchantment of the world.

Still, this is first and foremost a book about Heidegger's philosophy of religion. As will become clear below, his treatment of religion parallels contemporary work in the phenomenology of religion, as well as debates in theology about the interpretation of religious discourse and practice. Heidegger's approach to religion is, like his approach to so many other issues of philosophical import, uniquely his own. Still, in order to understand more clearly the conversation that, as I am suggesting, Heidegger should be invited to join, some points of clarification are in order. First, as the reader may already have noticed, "philosophy of religion" is a label for an extraordinarily diverse collection of approaches, styles, problems, and debates. In order to understand Heidegger's philosophy of religion, it is first of all necessary to locate him within this domain.

As far as I can tell, there are five broad, and overlapping, senses of the phrase "philosophy of religion." I do not pretend to have strict definitions of these senses. Instead, they are best understood through well-known exemplars. Thus, one might talk here of "types" of the philosophy of religion. First, there is *systematic* philosophy of religion, exemplified historically by the German Idealists. This type of philosophy of religion tends to present itself as a theory about religion *as such*, about the entire history of religion, and about the place of religion within human culture. Second, there is an *apologetic* type of philosophy of religion, exemplified in this case by works like Joseph Butler's *Analogy of Religion* and Alvin Plantinga's *Warranted Christian Belief*. Third, there is a *historical* type of philosophy of religion, which is occupied mainly with explicating the interesting thoughts of an important figure in the history of philosophy. A good example of this kind of work is C. Stephen Evans's recent study, *Kierkegaard's Ethic of Love*. (The present study could also be fitted into this category.) Next, one might pick out a *topical* variety, by which I mean the kind of work that is dedicated to a very specific problem (e.g., the problem of evil) or a very specific concept (e.g., atonement). The majority of English-language work in the philosophy of religion falls into this type; this no doubt reflects the emphasis of the "analytic" tradition on precise, focused, "one-at-a-time" examination of arguments and ideas.

While one might locate Heidegger's work in any number of these categories (most plausibly the first, "systematic" one), I think that the best place to situate his thought on religion is within yet another category or type, the *phenomenological*. Phenomenological philosophy of religion, or, better, phenomenology of religion, is itself quite variegated. Again, classic examples are perhaps more instructive here than rigid definitions. It is safe to say that *the* classic of the genre is Schleiermacher's *On Religion* (1799), though Rudolf Otto's *Das Heilige* (1917) might steal the show in some circles. A more recent example is the work of Merold Westphal.[2] If forced to say what these exemplars have in common, I would first point to their *descriptive-analytic* nature. That is, the phenomenological project has more to do with determining what the subject matter, in this case religion, really *is*, than with determining whether religious beliefs are justified or what place religion has in human history. I will leave it at this, since my concern is with *Heidegger's* particular version of the phenomenology of religion, and not with phenomenology of religion in general.

That Heidegger engages in a project called the phenomenology of religion, at least from time to time, is undeniable. More debatable, of course, is what this phenomenology amounts to, what its significance might be, and how it fits in with Heidegger's overall philosophical project. My aim in this study is to address the latter sorts of questions. That is, I want to determine just what Heidegger's phenomenological account of religion *is*, and to understand why he thought it useful or important, and to understand why or why not we might want to agree with him in this estimation of the project. I cannot hope to get very far with any of this, however, without first of all clarifying what the word "phenomenology" means when speaking of Heidegger.

There is an important sense in which Heidegger's entire philosophical project can be understood as being *phenomenological*. There are no real doubts that this is true of his work between World War I and the 1930s. While it may be more controversial, it is also safe to say that what Heidegger calls "thinking"

---

2. Westphal (1987).

and "reflection [*Besinnung*]" in the years after 1935 is largely contiguous with this earlier work, at least in its basic aims, motives, and methods, regardless of differences of detail or emphasis. Hence, there is a sense in which the term "phenomenology" simply describes "Heidegger's philosophy." There is also, as a letter of 1919 to Elisabeth Blochmann indicates, a sense in which Heidegger uses "phenomenology" more narrowly to refer to a specific project, e.g., "the phenomenology of religious consciousness" (HB 16).[3] Phenomenology, then, is not the name of a particular theory or program, but rather of a way of doing philosophy. As he puts it in SS 1923, phenomenology is a "how of research" (G63 72/57). The point is made even more clearly in *Being and Time*:

> Thus our treatise does not subscribe to a "standpoint" or represent any special "direction"; for phenomenology is nothing of either sort, nor can it become so as long as it understands itself. The expression "phenomenology" signifies primarily a *methodological conception*. This expression does not characterize the *what* of the objects of philosophical research as subject-matter, but rather the *how* of that research. (SZ 27/50)

One can conclude from this that what Heidegger says about phenomenology *as such* also applies, other things being equal, to what he says about the "phenomenology of X," where X is a particular subject matter of philosophical interest such as, for example, religion. However, while "phenomenology" is a formal designation for a way of doing philosophy, it is also important to recognize a specific group of ideas that are characteristic of Heideggerian phenomenology. Throughout his career, Heidegger deploys a medley of terms aimed at capturing his primary, overriding philosophical preoccupation: "factical life," "life-experience," "Da-sein" or "being-here," "human Da-sein," the "worlding of the world," "being itself [*das Sein selbst*]," the "truth of being," or the "topos of being," to name but a few of the more familiar examples. These are all terms that Heidegger employs for the totality of the deep structural conditions that render human life as a whole intelligible. Beneath the surface-level realities of day-to-day life, of scientific inquiry, of cultural activities, there is a complex pattern of responses to a primal network of meaning or significance [*Bedeutung*]. Before human beings come to live their lives in a self-conscious way, before philosophers get around to asking their questions or scientists start conducting experiments, human beings are "always already" involved in and, indeed, tangled up in this pattern.

The basic premise of Heidegger's approach to this fundamental pattern is that, contrary to a significant stream in modern philosophy, human life, even at the most basic, pre-reflective level, is *already* meaningful or intelligible.

---

3. Heidegger also talks about his work in the area as "philosophy of religion" (HR 54).

One finds this conviction first expressed in KNS 1919: "Life as such is *not* irrational (which has nothing whatever to do with 'rationalism'!)" (G56–57 219/187). Two semesters later, Heidegger makes the point in this way: "Life is not a chaotic confusion of dark torrents, not a vague principle of power, not a limitless, all-consuming non-being [*Unwesen*], rather *it is what it is only as a concrete meaningful form [Gestalt]*" (G58 148). Another way of putting the point is to say that life, as we encounter it at the most immediate level, is *expressive*; like human speech or gestures, life itself "speaks to us," is meaningful to us in a quite direct, though very often unthematic, way.[4] Heidegger therefore, quite early on, calls his project *hermeneutics* (G56–57 117/99, 218/187; G63 15–16/12–13; NB 16/121; SZ 37–38/62). Perhaps one of the clearest explanations of this project can be found in the "Natorp Report" from late 1922. Here, Heidegger styles the "phenomenological hermeneutics of facticity" as a matter of "the interpretation of the sense of this being [*Seinsinn*] with respect to its basic categorial structures, i.e., the modes in which factical life temporalizes itself, unfolds itself, and *speaks* with itself (*kategorein*) in such temporalizing" (NB 16/121). In other words, because life is always already meaningful or intelligible, there is no need to construct the structures that explain this fact. Instead, they can be "read off," as it were, from certain characteristic patterns of thought and behavior that Heidegger sometimes calls "basic experiences [*Grunderfahrungen*]."

What Heidegger here calls "categorial structures," and which readers of *Being and Time* know as "existentials," are the structures that are *expressed* in life itself as it is lived through, such that the latter is intelligible to us. Heidegger stresses repeatedly that these "categories" are not *concepts* that we use to think about the world or our lives. Instead, as he puts it at one point, "they are *alive in life itself* in an original way: alive in order to 'form' life on themselves" (G61 88/66). Even though these structures are largely tacit, they remain for all of us "to some degree intelligible" in that we have an *understanding* of our lives, what *Being and Time* calls an "understanding of being" (G61 88/66). The philosophical task is to make these *explicit*, to articulate what it is that is being *expressed* in life. This general fact about the phenomenological project also holds in the case of the phenomenology of religion. In notes appended to the text of his WS 1920–1921 lecture course, Heidegger describes the project as one of "ex-plication" as opposed to pure description (G60 129). The goal is one of "extracting [*Herausnahme*]" the "structural nexus" of religious life (G60 129).[5]

---

4. For a recent discussion of Heidegger's "expressivism," see Rudd (2003): 161–168, 201–220.

5. In a later remark, Heidegger is at pains to distinguish "phenomenological explication" from all "psychologizing, spiritualizing, [and] rationalizing" (G60 136).

The key to Heidegger's whole methodology is what he calls *formal indication* [*formale Anzeige*].[6] In *Being and Time*, without explaining this term, Heidegger employs this crucial idea at a number of points (SZ 52–53, 114, 116–117, 179, 231, 313–315). In his later works, Heidegger deploys a similar vocabulary of "pointers," "hints," and "indications" (G67 25; G69 86, 88; G52 1, 27; G53 193/156; G75 299, 355). A "formal indication" is a way of trying to articulate "categories" that are embedded in life as it is lived at the most basic, pre-reflective level. "Formal indications" have two distinct, but closely interrelated, functions. First, they are *prohibitive*. This function derives from the phenomenological motto, "to the things themselves," which, for Heidegger, means that "the conceptuality of the object [. . .] must be drawn out of the mode *in which the object is originally accessible*" (G61 20/17). In SS 1923, he describes this aspect of his view as a "precautionary measure" of "rejecting certain positions of looking which are dominant in the situation of research at the particular time" (G63 80/62). In practice, this idea is reflected in Heidegger's difficult vocabulary, and in the fact that he spends a great deal of time trying to explain what he is *not* saying, rather than clarifying what he *is* saying. Here again, this shows up clearly in Heidegger's phenomenology of religion. As one reads through the text of his WS 1920–1921 lecture course, one is continually bombarded by warnings and prohibitions regarding how *not* to go about interpreting religious life (G60 28–29, 82, 134).

Second, formal indications are *transformative*.[7] Dahlstrom captures this sense particularly well: "The aim of formal indication is to lead us back to the genuine sense of life, not for the sake of comprehending or contemplating it, but as part of actually renewing that sense or, what is the same, living life in an original and authentic way."[8] Phenomenological concepts are hints, pointers, indicators of a new way of looking at things and a new way of living. Heidegger describes his goal as "calling something to the attention of others," "compelling" others to "reflection" (G9 6/5, 42/36). Phenomenological concepts, while certainly meant to explicate the "categories" of life, are not *purely* descriptive. Nor are they *prescriptive*, in the sense that they provide some formula for how to think or how to live. Instead, they are open-ended pointers designed to disrupt or call into question prevailing ways of thinking and acting. One cannot "make deductions" from a formal indication (G63 80/62). This is why these concepts are "formal"; they are somewhat indeterminate, but in such a way that they "lead" to a concrete "enactment" (G61 33/26). Heidegger calls this the "existentiell" sense of "formal": "Formal

---

6. For an excellent discussion of this concept, see Dahlstrom (2001): 243–249. My brief account here is indebted to Dahlstrom's careful and illuminating exegesis.

7. For a good account of this aspect of formal indication, see Van Buren (1995).

8. Dahlstrom (2001): 248.

refers to a way of 'approach' toward actualizing the maturation of an original fulfillment of what was indicated" (G61 34/27).

As with other elements of his general phenomenological approach, Heidegger also employs "formal indication" in his phenomenology of religion. For example, at the beginning of his explication of Pauline Christianity in WS 1920–1921, Heidegger writes:

> The uniqueness of understanding in the phenomenology of religion is that it achieves a pre-understanding for an original way of access. Theological method falls outside the scope of our consideration. A new way for theology is first opened up with phenomenological understanding. Formal indication renounces the ultimate understanding that can only be given in genuine religious experience. It merely intends to open up access to the New Testament. (G60 67)

A few semesters before this course, one can find Heidegger asserting that challenging the reigning conception of Christianity is *"one* of the innermost tendencies of phenomenology" (G58 61). In this same course, Heidegger again intimates the *religious* import of phenomenology: "The root of the fundamentally perverted starting points and directions of contemporary and earlier concept-formation lies in not seeing and not investigating this phenomenon, e.g., in aesthetics and *above all* in philosophy of religion, to say nothing of the pseudo-problems of theology and apologetics" (G58 158, emphasis added).

In 1927, Heidegger uses the concept of "formal indication" to specify the relation between his philosophy and the theological enterprise of articulating the self-understanding of faith (G9 64/52). Again, one finds the "existentiell" sense of "formal" at work here; Heidegger does not claim that philosophy dictates the *content* of faith or of theology. Instead, he states emphatically that

> In thus formally indicating the ontological region, there lies the directive not to calculate philosophically the specific theological content of the concept but rather to allow it to arise out of, and to present itself within, the specific existential dimension of faith thereby indicated. Thus, formally indicating the ontological concept does not serve to bind but, on the contrary, to release and point to the specific, i.e., creedal source of the disclosure of theological concepts. The function of ontology here is not to direct, but only, in "co-directing," to correct. (G9 65/52)

This way of conceiving of the relation between phenomenology and theology is not simply an artifact of Heidegger's early theological proclivities, allegedly jettisoned later in his career. To the contrary, Heidegger never tires of "formally indicating" ways in which Christian faith can improve its own self-understanding. In the preface (written in 1970) to the essay quoted above, Heidegger expresses his hope that this piece will "be able to occasion repeated reflection on the extent to which the Christianness of Christianity and its theology merit questioning" (G9 44/39). In 1946, he draws a polemical contrast between "Christendom [*Christentum*]" and the "present form" of theology, on the one hand, and "Christian life" on the other (G5 219–220/164). Heidegger seems to have thought that this aspect of his phenomenological project could best be achieved by suspending his own religious commitments to a certain degree, hence the famous "atheism" of philosophy (G61 197/148).[9]

This *critical* aspect of Heidegger's phenomenology of religion cannot be emphasized enough. Heidegger is not interested in merely *describing* religion, or giving a better *theory* about it, though the success of his project certainly depends, to some extent, on his ability to do just these things. Instead, Heidegger wants to "point out" or "indicate" the contours of a way of *being* religious. On his view, being religious is the ultimate ground and final court of appeal for any and all thinking about religion. As he puts it in a letter to Elisabeth Blochmann, "a path leads from the basic religious experience to theology, but it *must* not lead from theology to religious consciousness and its living actuality [*Lebendigkeit*]" (HB 11).

Beyond the prohibitive and provocative aspects of Heidegger's "formal indications," there is also an important sense in which his phenomenological task is oriented toward the religious consciousness of modernity. Phenomenology in general is, as he says in several places, a matter of coming to grips with the dominant cultural consciousness of the age, particularly as it is explicitly articulated in disciplines like *philosophy* (G63 17/14, 31/25; NB 20/124; G40 6–7/9).[10] Again, this is something that is true throughout Heidegger's entire career. Indeed, in the 1930s and 1940s, he devotes considerable attention to the cultural consciousness of modernity, including its *religious* consciousness (e.g., G5 76/58). Modernity is a "destitute time [*dürftiger Zeit*]" in which the "gods" have "fled," i.e., in which religion becomes just another cultural creation of human subjectivity, a private world-view. Besides serving to spur theological reflection and encourage deepened religious life, Heidegger's phenomenology of religion also aims to expose the religious situation of modernity and to confront its philosophical expressions.

Throughout a major portion of Heidegger's career, *the* philosophical expression of modernity in general is Neo-Kantianism. Neo-Kantianism, particularly of the "Baden" or "Heidelberg" or "Southwest German" school, was explicitly billed as a "philosophy of culture" by its representatives. People like

---

9. Lawrence Paul Hemming examines what he calls the "pedagogical" aspects of Heidegger's "holy" atheism in Hemming (2002).

10. This is an aspect of Heidegger's thought that I have examined in considerable detail in Crowe (2006).

Wilhelm Windelband and Heinrich Rickert self-consciously viewed themselves as the heirs of Kant and the German Idealists, whose aims had been
to place the self-consciousness of modernity on a sure philosophical ground.
Heidegger maintains that an essential element of his phenomenological
project consists in confronting Neo-Kantianism (and various fellow-travelers)
as *the* expression of what he calls the "today." This is *particularly* true
when it comes to the matter of the religious consciousness of modernity. As
Heidegger was well aware, much of the most important work in the philosophy of religion in the first half of the twentieth century was being done by
people like Windelband and Rickert, as well as by people like Simmel and
Troeltsch who were quite explicitly influenced by Baden Neo-Kantianism.
It is a strange fact that, in most of the literature on "Heidegger and religion,"
attention has been exclusively focused on his critical dialogue with medievals
(e.g., Aquinas), early moderns (e.g., Hegel), and mystics (e.g., Eckhart), with
no mention of his contemporaries.[11]

At the end of his lecture course in WS 1920–1921, Heidegger provides
a remark that shows the ultimate significance of his phenomenology of religion—i.e., its critical goal. He writes:

> Genuine philosophy of religion does not emerge from previously held
> concepts of philosophy and religion. Rather, the possibility of its philo-
> sophical comprehension is provided by a determinate religiosity—for us,
> the Christian. Why Christian religiosity lies immediately in the field of
> vision of our investigation is a difficult question; it can be answered only
> through the solution of the problem of historical contexts. The task is to
> achieve a genuine, original relation to history, which must be explicated
> from out of our own historical situation and facticity. What it all comes
> down to is what the sense of history can mean for us, and with that the
> "objectivity" of the historical "in itself" disappears. There is only a history
> on the basis of a present. Only in this way must the possibility of a philoso-
> phy of religion be grasped. (G60 124–125)

This passage expresses, first of all, Heidegger's overall philosophy of
history. For Heidegger, history is something that we *are*; that is, the self-
interpretations through which we constitute our own identities, both individually and communally, rest upon a penumbra of meaning that is embedded
within the processes of historical change. On Heidegger's view, it follows
that our individual and communal task of working out who we are and what
we stand for requires confronting our shared history. But such a confrontation occurs only "from out of our own historical situation and facticity," that

---

11. A refreshing exception to this neglect is Charles R. Bambach, who explores Heidegger's
reception of the "dialectical" theology of Barth, Gogarten, and Bultmann in Bambach (1995):
189–203.

is, from the perspective formed by the unique, unrepeatable confluence of influences and events that comprise our age. Thus, Heidegger draws the conclusion that the study of history is *not* the detached concern of the objective historical researcher, but rather is the existential concern of every individual and of every generation as a whole. For the phenomenology of religion, this means that the "hermeneutical situation" of the present provides the inescapable context of all inquiry, not simply because contemporary values and assumptions invisibly guide the inquiry (which, of course, they do), but more deeply, because such inquiry is ultimately concerned with finding our own way through the present age.

The "today," of which neo-Kantianism is the most prominent philosophical expression, is the ultimate target of Heidegger's phenomenology of religion. Rather than making a contribution to what he called the "business" of philosophy, his only real aspiration was to shake up the dominant cultural paradigms of the twentieth century. For Heidegger, these paradigms, as they are instantiated in different domains of culture, are all expressions of one *fundamental* perspective: subjectivism.[12] Subjectivism is a way of understanding "being," i.e., of understanding that in which the normative meaning and intelligibility of things consist. It is not a philosophical theory, but a historical event that shapes modern culture and finds its expression *in* particular philosophical theories.[13] All the same, the best way to get after what subjectivism means is to state it as if it were a philosophical theory. To be specific, subjectivism is the view (for the most part tacitly held) that the "being" of beings is grounded in human beings, taken as subjects of consciousness. As Heidegger puts it in a 1937 essay, the view is that human beings constitute the "referential center [*Bezugsmitte*] of beings as such" (G5 88/66–67). In other words, subjectivism is expressed by the idea that human interests are prior to various forms of meaning or significance. This is most apparent in the widespread assumption that something's value is measured against its appropriateness for the satisfaction of a preference. To say that, for late modern culture, human beings are the "referential center of beings as such" is to say that it is as if the entire universe is a system of preference-satisfaction.

The most obvious consequence of this tacit assumption, when it comes to religion, is *theological anti-realism*. Theological anti-realism, unlike subjectivism, *is* most definitely a philosophical position, or, rather, a family of similar positions. Theological anti-realists can be straightforward atheists, like Feuerbach or Freud, or they can claim to still be somehow within the theistic

---

12. One could just as well label the basic principle of modernity "anthropomorphism," as Heidegger does on occasion.

13. For an account of the view of intellectual history underlying this central aspect of Heidegger's thought, see Rosemann (2002).

fold, like Ritschl or Troeltsch. Theological anti-realism can involve semantic commitments about the meaningfulness of God-talk, or epistemological commitments about the cognitive status of religious claims, or ontological commitments about what can or cannot be said to "exist," or anthropological commitments about the nature of human religious practice. It may involve a mixture of all of these. For Heidegger, what is most interesting about this family of views is not so much their denial of the existence of God. Whether or not some particular metaphysical theory has it right, the question of how we are to orient ourselves, make judgments, and coherently pursue goals is still very much on the table. For anti-realists, the best way to respond to this pressing issue is to construct a theory that purports to derive meaning, value, and normativity from human interests. Given our interest in something, e.g., rational autonomy, certain norms or values that are meant to shape practical reasoning are supposed to follow. There are no norms or values that are prior to such interests; our interests are not responsive to values, but constitutive of them. When it comes to religion, this implies that specifically religious norms and values are also posterior to human interests. Thus, for example, Feuerbach argues in *The Essence of Christianity* (1841) that God matters to us because of our interest in ourselves as free, rational beings. Similarly, Freud maintains that God matters to us because of our interest in maintaining a coherent personality in the face of a harsh, unforgiving world.

Perhaps surprisingly, this kind of anti-realism even finds a home amongst theologians. In Heidegger's day, liberal Protestants like Ernst Troeltsch were in the business of deriving religious meaning from our interests. These days, one finds the "Sea of Faith Network," which has made the issue of realism a point of heated debate within recent Anglican theology.[14] Don Cupitt captures the essence of this position quite clearly when he asserts that "God *is* the religious requirement personified and his attributes are a kind of projection of its main features as we experience them."[15] David Boulton, speaking on behalf of "Sea of Faith," writes that "God is, and always was, a metaphor for the values which, though we understand them to be generated by human culture, we have come to think of as 'ultimate' and 'eternal.'"[16]

For Heidegger, of course, the opponents were the Baden Neo-Kantians (with various fellow-travelers) and neo-Nietzscheans. Neither were particularly interested in metaphysics, having largely accepted the post-Kantian consensus in German philosophy that such an enterprise no longer makes sense.

---

14. For critical discussions of, and rather strong arguments against, this manifestation of theological anti-realism, see the following: Hebblethwaite (1988), Williams (1995), Plantinga (2000), Moore (2003), and Byrne (2003).

15. Cupitt (1980): 85.

16. Boulton (1997): 9.

They were, however, supremely interested in why things are intelligible to us, and particularly with the kind of intelligibility characteristic of domains like art, morality, and history. The Baden Neo-Kantians started with the idea that human culture is just the totality of goal-directed, reason-responsive activities. The goals in question are the sources of the more local norms that play into evaluative judgments in these various domains. These goals, usually called "values [*Werte*]," are not functions of the idiosyncratic preferences of particular empirical individuals. Rather, in order to have the kind of normative weight required to preserve the authority of evaluative judgment, these values derive from the interest of "reason itself," of what Windelband called "normative consciousness [*Normalbewußtsein*]." The neo-Nietzscheans, often called "vitalists" by their opponents (who were, by and large, the Baden Neo-Kantians), shared the idea that evaluative judgments concern the relationship between a thing and some end. In their case, however, the relevant end is not the abstract "interest of reason," but rather the interest of life, conceived of in quasi-Darwinian terms as a combination of survival and of the enhancement of power.

Giving accounts of this sort set the agenda for German-speaking philosophy in the final decades of the nineteenth century and in the first decades of the twentieth. Inevitably, philosophers from both camps came around to the subject of religion. The Baden Neo-Kantians applied themselves to this project with particular zeal. On the accounts offered by Windelband, Rickert, and Jonas Cohn, religion is ultimately a way that people have for representing their values (i.e., the "interests of reason") to themselves. Religious discourse about God, about heaven, and about other metaphysical mysteries is simply a way of depicting the fact that the values that guide cultural activity are not derived from the particular, idiosyncratic, local preferences of some particular person, but rather from the abstract, universal interests of reason. Moreover, given their abstractness and universality, these goals are best understood as Kantian "ideas," as concepts that help people organize their activities in a rational way, but which never correspond to any empirical representation. From this, the Neo-Kantians derived the notion that concepts like God or heaven are designed, in part, to represent a possible coincidence of a priori value and empirical reality.

Following his initial enthusiasm for Baden Neo-Kantianism prior to World War I, Heidegger soon began to suspect that these views fail as interpretations of religion. On his view, religious meaning, like all meaning, derives from a *world*. In *Being and Time*, Heidegger famously argues that the intelligibility of an item such as a hammer (i.e., its equipmental meaning) derives from a network of relations of instrumentality that is particular to a workshop. That is, a hammer matters to us and makes sense to us *as a hammer* because of the "work-world" in terms of which it is understood ahead of time. In the case of religious meaning, Heidegger came to maintain that relations of instrumentality are not the primary focus. Instead, borrowing partly from Augustine's distinction between *uti* (use) and *frui* (enjoyment), and relying on the evidence provided by certain characteristic religious attitudes and activities like devotion, contemplative prayer, a sense of vocation or calling, and the "feeling of absolute dependence" that figures so prominently in the thought of Schleiermacher and Adolf Reinach, Heidegger came to hold that religious meaning, "sacredness," derives from a network of relations ordered to a reality of unsurpassable, incommensurable, and transcendent value.

On the basis of a phenomenological analysis of the deep structures of religious life, as revealed in certain characteristically religious attitudes and activities, Heidegger maintains that religion is a particularly clear instance of the more general fact that meaning does not derive from interests, and that the attitudes and activities that express our interests only make sense against the background of a network of meaning that is prior to these interests. In the 1920s, he makes this more general point by saying that human beings "assign" themselves some project, or rather, assign themselves to some project, from out of a pre-given world. In his later works, he makes this point a bit more darkly by punning on the German phrase *es gibt* (literally, "it gives"); in other words, the real sense of the claim that "there is meaning" is that "it gives meaning." Following a recent suggestion by Iain Thomson, I call this position "ontological realism." Certainly, describing Heidegger's view as "realism" might be potentially misleading. However, it captures well the idea that, in the case of religion in particular, intelligibility or meaning is an "outside in" affair, rather than an "inside out" one. Still, to foreclose any possible misunderstandings, some further clarification is required. (The points made below will be treated again, and more fully, in chapter 2.)

First, Heidegger's realism is *semantic* rather than *metaphysical.*[17] In other words, Heidegger offers us a view about the *meaning* (in the sense of the deep structures described above) of religious life. To adapt a pithy phrase from a recent study by Peter Byrne, Heidegger's position is that realism "brings out the meaning" of religious life. That is, religion positively *insists* on the idea that meaning is *given* rather than *constructed*. Religious activities like contemplative prayer and worship, and attitudes like devotion, simply make no sense on the assumption that religious meaning is derivative of personal interests. Instead, according to Heidegger anyway, they are intelligible as the distinctive attitudes and activities that they are because they are *responsive* to meaning and value of a particular sort. By Heidegger's lights, any other account fails to make sense of why people care so deeply about

---

17. This distinction is borrowed from Byrne (2003): 2–6.

religion; anti-realist accounts, of the sort outlined above, do not account for the claim that religion actually places upon people.

The second point of clarification is that Heidegger's realism is *phenomenological* rather than *theological*. This is a point that concerns the grounds for adopting the position in question. For some (and I am among them), the reason to be a realist in either the semantic or metaphysical senses described above is that there is reason to think that God exists and communicates with human beings. While Heidegger may (or may not) have held theological views of this sort, they do not provide the primary philosophical motive for his realism about religion. Instead, his realism is grounded in the *phenomenology* of religion—an enterprise that is largely independent of theological commitments. For Heidegger, the case rests upon the analysis and exposition of attitudes and activities that are recognizably religious. Heidegger would be the first to admit, of course, that phenomenology is only possible on the basis of assumptions about the sorts of attitudes and activities that are religious. One cannot, as it were, start in a vacuum and then proceed to construct what religion is. Heidegger's procedure, however, is based on the thought that certain attitudes and activities are particularly revealing about a domain of phenomenological inquiry (compare his discussion of tools in *Being and Time*, of Hölderlin as the paradigm of poetry, etc.).

The final point of clarification concerns a distinction that is more local to Heidegger's thought. His realism about religion is *ontological* rather than *ontic*. That is, what Heidegger is a realist about is the a priori domain of meaning that structures religious life, rather than about particular beings, e.g., the Greek gods. To be sure, the domain of meaning constitutive of religious life is anchored, one way or another, in divine reality. But what interests Heidegger is not so much the metaphysical status of the latter, but rather the nature and role of a pre-given horizon of meaning in religious life.

For Heidegger, the very heart of religious phenomena can be captured by an admittedly Christian concept, which, on his view, can be adapted to fit religion as such—i.e., *grace*. Religion is a relation to God, a "being-toward-God," as he puts it, which pervades the totality of one's life. This relation, tacitly grasped and lived through in all one's doings and sufferings, becomes internally unintelligible on the assumption that meaning is derivative of human interest. That is, religious attitudes (e.g., devotion) and religious activities (e.g., worship) stop making sense if they are taken to be fully explained by the requirements of realizing certain interests. One can draw an analogy here to debates in meta-ethics. According to some, many accounts of moral obligation are such that, if they were accepted—particularly by people actually engaged in moral life—they would render moral life pointless, unintelligible, or irrational. Indeed, this seems to be the paradox of much of modern moral philosophy, for which it is axiomatic that, in one way or another, our interests and preferences are the sources of normativity and value. For example, on a contractarian view, it is rational to undertake moral obligations in order to fulfill our interests through a cooperative system. On a Kantian view, on the other hand, we are beings who have an interest in forming our own identities, i.e., in autonomy, and this interest is ultimately what constrains our choices. But if either of these views were adopted as accounts of the meaning of moral life, moral precepts and moral judgments would be deprived of much of their force, for we would ultimately have no overriding reason beyond our own interests for obeying them. But moral life involves being put under a *claim* by something; if one's account of moral life is missing this "something," then it risks rendering moral life internally unintelligible.

Heidegger shares precisely this sort of worry. Indeed, commenting wryly on Neo-Kantian value theory, which, as I have already pointed out, derives normativity and value from the interests of reason, Heidegger writes that "'values' [...] are the powerless and threadbare mask of the objectification of beings, an objectification that has become flat and devoid of background. No one dies for mere values" (G5 102/77).

For Heidegger, the bankruptcy of modern philosophy, exposed so harshly in this passage, is particularly evident in accounts of religion. As in the case of moral philosophy, religion is no longer viewed as a responsive, "outside in" enterprise, but rather as a way of representing our interests to ourselves. On Heidegger's view, however, this renders religion internally unintelligible. Whether the aim of the theory is to preserve religion as a valuable element of culture (Baden Neo-Kantianism) or to replace it (neo-Nietzscheanism), the product of the theory bears little resemblance to the original. The attitudes and activities that are characteristically religious only make sense on the recognition that religious meaning and value are completely independent of human interests. Otherwise, what is lived as sacrifice gets understood as self-promotion. This situation would be a bit like saying that marriage is exhaustively explained by economics, and yet still expecting people to talk about love.

For Heidegger at least, there is a real sense of urgency about all of this. On his view, anti-realist theories of religion are simply one of the many symptoms of a diseased Zeitgeist, one that is characterized by the near-total absence of any sense for independent value and meaning. According to Heidegger, the relation constitutive of religion is a gift, grounded in a historical event (as in Christianity), or in an understanding of being that does not place the human subject at the center (as in ancient Greece). The perversity of subjectivism, in Heidegger's eyes, is nowhere more apparent than in theology and the religious consciousness of the age. When God becomes a human artifact, and when the official intellectual mouthpieces of "religion" proclaim this fact, then there is no chance that religion—now a self-enclosed sphere of human activity—can ever be called into question, disrupted, or fundamentally reoriented. To say, with Nietzsche, that we have "killed" God, is, for Heidegger, to say that we have conquered the last bastion of independent meaning in the name of subjectivism. It is against this background that Heidegger's philosophical project ultimately makes sense. At the end of the day, his views on religion are meant to be pieces of a revolution in the conceptual paradigms of late modernity.

The organization of this study is as follows. In chapter 1, I explain the larger philosophical framework in which Heidegger's phenomenology of religion can be most fruitfully located—namely, his persistent, insistent, and controversial criticism of modern culture. I first explain the conceptual machinery that underwrites Heidegger's critical project, and which makes it distinct from kindred projects like neo-Marxist critical theory. I then describe how Heidegger reads the macro-level religious situation of late modernity, as well as philosophical theories of religion, as related symptoms of a general tendency toward the subjectivizing of meaning.

In chapter 2, I explore Heidegger's early (ca. 1917–1922) phenomenology of religion. Here I introduce one my central claims, namely, that the basic framework developed during this period remains stable throughout the remainder of Heidegger's long career. I describe three crucial influences on the development of his interpretation of religion: Husserl, Schleiermacher, and Reinach. I then examine how, in loose notes, letters, and lectures, Heidegger attempts to challenge anti-realist (especially Neo-Kantian) theories of religion.

In chapter 3, I turn to Heidegger's later (ca. 1929–1965) phenomenology of religion. Contrary to a prominent view, I maintain that there is little evidence of a substantial shift in Heidegger's approach to religion during this period. Instead, I show how, partly in response to Ernst Cassirer's "philosophy of symbolic forms," Heidegger consolidates his earlier ideas into a full-blown account of religious meaning. I then describe how this account plays itself out in his examinations of ancient Greek religion, of Hölderlin's poetry, and, above all, in his enigmatic discussions of "the gods."

Finally, in the conclusion, I undertake an assessment of the strengths and weaknesses of Heidegger's phenomenology of religion. I argue that Heidegger succeeds in (1) raising a robust challenge to anti-realist theories of religion, and (2) develops a number of insightful ideas regarding the basic structure of religion as a pattern of life. However, I also point out some of the limitations of his position. I trace these limitations back to Heidegger's constitutional aversion to the historical tradition of so-called "natural theology." This attitude circumscribes quite narrowly the applicability of Heidegger's thought to some contemporary debates in theology and in the philosophy of religion. It also helps to perpetuate a worrying, and damaging, mutual ignorance between so-called "analytic" and "Continental" approaches to the philosophy of religion. Despite these limitations, Heidegger's phenomenology of religion deserves a serious hearing. Heidegger embraces a task that has been largely abdicated (particularly by Anglophones) in contemporary philosophy, namely, cultural criticism. His work shows the legitimacy and the urgency of this neglected philosophical activity. And, Heidegger succeeds in mounting an impressive challenge to prevailing accounts of meaning and normativity, particularly in the study of religion, by showing how, at the end of the day, because they ground all value on our interests, they deprive us of a firm practical orientation.

ONE

Religion and Cultural Criticism

Heidegger's ongoing investigations into the phenomenology of religion are framed by a much broader concern, one that in fact permeates his entire oeuvre: the criticism of modern culture. Indeed, this broad concern has proven to be one of the more consistently compelling aspects of his thought. Right at the very beginning of his career, students flocked to his lectures, seminars, and to more informal gatherings, where by all accounts they found his relentless unmasking of the platitudes of bourgeois culture electrifying. Some of these listeners, like Leo Strauss, Hannah Arendt, and Herbert Marcuse, carried the general program of cultural criticism further in their own work. After World War II, a new generation of intellectuals encountered Heidegger's critiques of mass culture and technology, which were appropriated by everyone from the existentialists to the early theorists of the environmental movement.[1]

---

1. For a good overview of Heidegger's impact on environmentalist movements, see Zimmerman (1994): 91–149. A more recent contribution to this discussion is Thomson (2004). For a recent assessment of Heidegger's philosophy of technology see Feenburg (2005). On the relationship between Heidegger's criticism of culture and his notorious politics, see Zimmerman (1990), Bambach (2003), and Thomson (2005).

The distinctiveness of Heidegger's criticism of modern culture lies less in the symptoms of cultural crisis that he enumerates than in the conceptual apparatus he uses in accounting for these symptoms. The general religious situation of late modernity, of which Heidegger is an unsparing critic, is for him a complex of such symptoms. Their source lies in the deep, pre-reflective framework of meaning that shapes the way things show up to the members of modern culture. On Heidegger's account, every age has such a deep framework operating in the background, a framework that he often calls the "metaphysics" of the age. The changes that this deep framework undergoes in the course of Western history is what Heidegger calls the "history of being [*Seinsgeschichte*]." The modern age, viewed "being-historically," i.e., with an eye to its own deep framework, is characterized by Heidegger as an age of "subjectivism." As the deep framework of modern culture as a whole, "subjectivism" remains largely in the background of macro-level events and cultural trends. Yet, precisely because it is mostly tacit, it exercises a powerful influence on the way people think and act in the modern age. On Heidegger's account, for moderns meaning [*Sinn*] or significance [*Bedeutsamkeit*], the kind of intelligibility things have or the way in which they "matter" to us, is tacitly understood to be a product of human subjectivity. As Heidegger puts it in a 1937 essay, modern human beings tacitly take themselves to be the "referential center [*Bezugsmitte*]" of reality as a whole. The resulting pattern, which unifies the various symptoms of modern culture, is an absence of *intrinsic* meaning and value.[2] To use Max Weber's time-worn terminology, the reality that shows up for modern human beings is fundamentally "disenchanted."

The religious situation of the age, which Heidegger characterizes variously as the "flight of the gods," the "loss of the gods [*Entgötterung*]," the "absence [*Fehl*] of God," and the "death of God" is a clear instantiation of this general pattern of "disenchantment." In the modern world, religion seems to have lost what Heidegger calls the power to "ordain history," i.e., the power to anchor an entire culture. Instead, as with other systems of values (e.g., moral and aesthetic), religion is transformed into a matter of subjective conviction, into a "world-view." Running parallel with this subjectivization of religion are various, resolutely anti-realist theories about the nature of religion. Anti-realist theories of religion, in the sense in which I use this designation in the present study, maintain that religious meaning, broadly construed,

---

2. It is important to note that the kind of meaning or value that is allegedly absent in the modern world is *intrinsic* meaning or value. Heidegger does not hold that, for moderns, everything is simply meaningless. Instead, the meaning that things have, the sense in which they *matter* to people in modern culture, derives not from the things themselves and their richer connections with one another, but from human subjectivity.

is derived from interests. An obvious proponent of such a theory, with whom Heidegger was deeply engaged for decades, is Nietzsche. On most readings of Nietzsche, he holds that God and the entirety of the "supersensible world" are mere fictions—products of sub-conscious drives that are momentarily use-ful in the struggle for power. A less dramatic theory, though one with which Heidegger was equally concerned, can be found in the work of the so-called Baden School of Neo-Kantianism. Philosophers like Windelband, Rickert, and Jonas Cohn hold that religious concepts have no empirical, and therefore no real metaphysical, content to them, but are instead "postulates" or "regu-lative ideas" necessitated by the structure of human reason. For Heidegger, such theories reflect not the actual "immanent sense" of religious discourse and religious practices, but instead the deep framework of modern culture.

The aim of this chapter is to examine this complex of ideas as the gen-eral framework within which Heidegger's efforts in the phenomenology of religion find their real home. I begin by explicating Heidegger's evolving conception of the way in which a deep framework of meaning undergirds the superstructure of any culture. I then turn to his account of the deep frame-work characteristic of modernity, which I call "subjectivism." Along the way, I briefly discuss various symptoms or expressions of this deep framework that form recurring themes in Heidegger's writings, with an eye particularly on *religious* symptoms. Next, I explore Heidegger's account of the way in which dominant trends in intellectual discourse at a given time are expressions of this same deep framework. In particular, I examine what Heidegger takes to be the two dominant voices in contemporary philosophy: those of the Neo-Kantians, and of Nietzsche. I show how Heidegger views both as offer-ing anti-realist theories of religion that are consonant with the paradigmatic subjectivism of the age. The ultimate goal of Heidegger's work as a whole is to effect a deep conceptual revolution, a "new beginning" that can lead beyond the aporiae of late modernity. His phenomenology of religion forms an integral element in this overall project.

The Conceptual Framework for Heidegger's Cultural Criticism

Heidegger is certainly not unique among twentieth-century philosophers in his concern with the criticism of culture. Indeed, his work helped directly and indirectly to inspire some of the leading critical theorists of the cen-tury. Heidegger's critical reflections on modern art, mass culture, politics, education, and technology often run parallel to the work of philosophers like Adorno, Horkheimer, and Marcuse. Looking at the opposite end of the political spectrum, one can locate Oswald Spengler and Ernst Jünger, both of whom Heidegger read closely, giving a sympathetic hearing to the ideas of their "Conservative Revolution."[3] All of these thinkers, Heidegger included, were occupied with the broad cultural situation of late modernity, particularly with characteristic phenomena like technology, industrialized warfare, and social dislocation. Each of them deploys a distinctive conceptual scheme in order to diagnose and analyze the major cultural trends of the day. For example, the members of the "Frankfurt School" tended to deploy Marxist and neo-Hegelian concepts in their analyses. Indeed, in a piece that appeared in a Swiss newspaper around his eightieth birthday, Heidegger makes explicit reference to this Hegelian conceptual framework that guides the critical theorists of the Frankfurt School and tries to distinguish his approach from theirs (G16 212). Spengler, on the other hand, uses an idiosyncratic neo-Nietzschean scheme in his epochal *Decline of the West*, which Heidegger frequently discusses in the 1920s and 1930s.[4]

In Heidegger's case, this abiding interest in cultural criticism is one of several features of his work that differentiates his philosophy of religion from that of more recent Anglo-American philosophers. The latter by and large focus on circumscribed problems such as the problem of evil or the problems connected with the rational justification of traditional theism, while broader cultural tendencies are either left undiscussed or remain in the background of their discussions. For Heidegger, however, the opposite situation prevails. He leaves many of the favorite puzzles of recent philosophers untouched, while the religious situation of late modernity is one of the more persistent subjects of his reflections.[5]

Heidegger's criticism of culture is also distinct from that of the Frankfurt School and the Conservative Revolution because of the uniquely Heideggerian

---

3. For general accounts of the intellectual and cultural movement known as the "Conservative Revolution," which was at its peak during the 1920s and early 1930s in Germany, see Breuer (1993), Travers (2001), and Woods (1996). On Spengler and Jünger in particular, see Herf (1986). For a discussion of Heidegger's relationship with this movement, and with Jünger in particular, see Zimmerman (1990). Another work that links Heidegger to the Conservative Revolution is Fritsche (1999). Fritsche's account is, however, flawed in its overemphasis on a narrow reading of certain words and a lack of familiarity with Heidegger's corpus as a whole.

4. Heidegger's discussions of Spengler's popular work can be found in WS 1920–1921 (G60 42–43), SS 1923 (G63 37/29, 55–57/43–45), and WS 1929–1930 (G29–30 104–105/70). On Heidegger's reception of Spengler, see Zimmerman (2001); and Thomson (2005): 94–98.

5. Heidegger did not leave more focused problems *completely* untouched, however, and he seems to have been quite conversant with contemporary debates in philosophy of religion and theology. In SS 1920, for example, Heidegger discusses the ongoing debate regarding the difficulties allegedly posed by the history of religion for the metaphysical claims of traditional Christian theism (G59 20–22). His familiarity with the then emergent "dialectical" or "neo-orthodox" theology of Karl Barth and others has also been amply documented. See Gadamer (1987) and Bambach (1995). In later years, he briefly touches on the discussion surrounding the implications of recent physics for religion (G54 248/166).

conceptual scheme that shapes his analyses.[6] This scheme undergoes a process of evolution during Heidegger's long career. It would be a mistake, for reasons to be described in more detail below, to regard this developmental process as one in which later views completely supplant earlier, incompatible, views. Instead, the scheme employed in the period prior to *Being and Time* (1927) undergoes refinement and development, such that the one familiar to readers of Heidegger's later works is a kind of natural outgrowth of his earlier thought. In any event, the evolving conceptual scheme that Heidegger employs in his cultural criticism is distinctive of his thought. While he shares many concerns with critical theorists on the left and the right, as well as with religious thinkers, Heidegger ultimately differs from everyone else in the concepts he uses to diagnose and explain the macro-level phenomena of modern culture.

Heidegger's work prior to *Being and Time*, while not lacking in discussions of such phenomena, does appear to lack an account of what makes these phenomena distinctively *modern*. At the same time, he provides an analysis of culture, and of the relation between intellectual discourse and culture, that lays the groundwork for later developments. The centerpiece of this analysis is the claim that people inherit conceptual schemes through tradition, and that this inheritance invisibly shapes the way people think and act. Tradition, for Heidegger, is the repository of a "having been interpreted [*Ausgelegtheit*]" that lays out in advance the "paths" on which human beings carry out their daily activities (NB 6/116). That is, before one is even explicitly aware of the fact, one has been acculturated to a certain general way of looking at things, to certain ways of dealing with the facts of life. This tacit understanding of a network of possible significance is "expressed" or "lived out" at the most basic level in making use of things for certain purposes. Beyond that, however, this tacit understanding is "expressed" more literally in linguistic communication or discourse. In *Being and Time*, Heidegger puts the matter thusly:

> For the most part, discourse [*Rede*] is expressed by being spoken out, and has always been so expressed; it is language [*Sprache*]. But, in that case understanding and interpretation already lie in what has thus been expressed. In language, as a way things have been expressed or spoken out [*Ausgesprochenheit*], there is hidden a way in which the understanding of Dasein has been interpreted. [. . .] The understanding which has thus already been "deposited" in the way things have been expressed, pertains just as much to any traditional discoveredness of entities which may have been reached, as it does to one's current understanding of being and to whatever possibilities and horizons for fresh interpretation and conceptual articulation may be available. (SZ 167–168/211)

---

6. For a powerful argument for the distinctiveness and ongoing importance of this conceptual scheme, see Thomson (2005).

In his lecture course for SS 1923, Heidegger calls the "having been interpreted" that dominates a particular culture at a particular time the "today [*das Heute*]." This is "the present of those initial givens which are closest to us, every-one, being-with-each-other—'our time'" (G63 30/24).[7] The "today" is an "open space of publicness," a kind of shared "comprehension" that human beings have in advance of both themselves and the world as a whole (G63 31/25). A human being lives "from out of" this tacit, public understanding. Analyzing the "today," for Heidegger, is not to be taken as an attempt to "provide entertaining *portraits* of the so-called 'most interesting tendencies' of the present" (G63 30/25). Instead, the goal is to *explicate* the "today," to articulate the largely invisible features of the tacit conceptual paradigm that dominates a particular culture. The surface phenomena of the "today" are less important to Heidegger than are the deep structures that these phenomena express. Furthermore, the "educated consciousness" of a particular age is, for Heidegger, the most significant expression of this tacit conceptual paradigm (G63 33/27).

With this framework in place, Heidegger can then embark upon the analysis and diagnosis of significant phenomena in contemporary culture. Even the most superficial glance at his lectures, essays, and correspondence from the 1920s shows Heidegger to be constantly engaged in this enterprise. He mines intellectual trends as diverse as Baden Neo-Kantianism, Husserl's phenomenology, and Spengler's metaphysics of history in an attempt to uncover the guiding presuppositions of the age. A constant theme during this period is the pervasive anxiety about culture itself. For Heidegger, what unites the diverse philosophical movements of the day is a concern with a crisis of culture.[8] A typical remark to this effect can be found in his lecture notes for WS 1919–1920:

> A pervasive helplessness lies over all contemporary life, because it has separated itself from its genuine primal sources and merely skirts the issue.

---

7. In his account of the conceptual scheme that underwrites Heidegger's criticism of modern culture, Thomson argues that, in his early works, Heidegger holds that there is one "constellation of intelligibility" that lies beneath the entire history of European culture from the Greeks to the present, and further, that Heidegger's later, more historicist conception of different "epochs of being" constitutes a significant departure from his earlier views. See Thomson (2005): 115–118. However, here in 1923, Heidegger attributes a kind of historical specificity and contingency to the deep framework of a culture of precisely the sort that Thomson locates only in his post-1937 writings. This historical specificity is clearly evident in Heidegger's remark that "A defining feature of the awhileness of temporal particularity [*Jeweiligkeit*] is the *today*—in each case whiling, tarrying for a while, in the present, in each case our own present. (Dasein as historical Dasein, its present. Being 'in' the world, beling lived 'from out of' the world–the present-everyday)" (G63 29/24). This specificity is reiterated later in the same lecture course (G63 35–36/28).

8. Charles R. Bambach has cogently articulated the nature of the contemporary discourse of "cultural crisis," as well as Heidegger's response to it. See Bambach (1995).

> Typical: scribbling about the meaning of culture and the problems of
> culture—on the basis of what one imagines to be a fresh perspective—as
> one must if one gets crazy ideas about the problem of culture, instead of
> actively and productively *creating* a new culture. (G58 20)

In a similar vein, in WS 1920–1921, Heidegger tries to expose the roots
of contemporary concern with "historical consciousness." Again, these roots
lie in an anxiety about the allegedly corrosive effects of historical consciousness on everything from the certainty of science to the absolute validity of
values (G60 37). The program of the journal *Logos*, which brought together
Husserl and the Neo-Kantians in a struggle against relativism and historicism, also expresses this pervasive preoccupation (G63 42/33). The demand
for a "world-view" that integrates theory and practice, science and morality, is
also typical of the times (G61 43–44/33–34). In regard to religion, late nineteenth-century debates about the "absoluteness of Christianity," sparked by
the early work of the "History of Religion" school, typify the same underlying
worries (G59 21). Following the rise of historical consciousness, the uncon-
ditional claim to truth on the part of traditional Christianity began to seem
less and less tenable. If Christianity were a product of history, like all other
aspects of culture, how could it claim to possess a timeless truth?

While Heidegger's early critical analyses of what he calls the "today"
constitute an integral element of his overall philosophical project, he never
quite succeeds in uncovering the basic "having been interpreted" that lies
beneath the surface phenomena of late modern culture. The situation is
entirely different in his work after about 1930. With the conceptual apparatus of *Being and Time* firmly in place, Heidegger is able to develop a more
precisely articulated framework for his philosophical investigations of history
and culture. This framework is familiar to students of Heidegger's later writings as the "history of being." It would, however, be a mistake to regard this
development as a rejection of the ideas advocated in the 1920s, such as the
"today." In *Besinnung*, an unpublished manuscript composed between 1938
and 1939, Heidegger explicitly links his earlier ideas with the newer concept of the "history of being." Commenting on the task of reflecting on the
nature of contemporary philosophical discourse, Heidegger writes: "It must
know the today, not as the state of a 'historical situation' for the purpose of practical advancement or change, but rather as the essential hint
[*Wesenswinke*] of the being-historical essence of the age of modernity"
(G66 46–47).

As in SS 1923, when the notion of the "today" is first introduced,
Heidegger is careful to distinguish the nature of his own critical reflections
on culture from other possibilities. The lens through which he views culture
is still *hermeneutical*; that is, Heidegger thinks that culture needs to be "read"
like a complicated text in order to uncover or explicate the fundamental

concepts and intuitions that are expressed in macro-level cultural phenomena, such as philosophical discourse. Heidegger is not interested in merely cataloguing dominant trends in culture, but in peering behind or beneath them in order to articulate the deep framework that ultimately grounds their intelligibility. Here, in *Besinnung*, he describes macro-level cultural phenomena, collectively termed the "today," as "hints" of precisely this sort of deep framework.

To understand what, in general terms, this deep framework of any age consists in, one must look to the conceptual apparatus developed in *Being and Time*, particularly to the idea that human existence or "Dasein" is ontologically determined as "being-in-the-world." This means that human beings "always already" inhabit a largely inherited network of meaning, a "clearing" or "world," which sketches out in advance the way things can show up as meaningful to individual human beings or to a culture as a whole. In the late 1920s, Heidegger shifts his vocabulary somewhat, borrowing the term "transcendence" from scholastic metaphysics in order to indicate this fundamental structure. By 1929, Heidegger begins to deploy this entire apparatus as a way of grounding a distinctive philosophy of history. In an essay originally written as a contribution to a Festschrift for Husserl, "On the Essence of Ground," Heidegger succinctly describes this apparatus as follows:

> "Dasein transcends" means: in the essence of its being it is *world-forming*, "forming [*bildend*]" in the multiple sense that it lets world occur, and through the world gives itself an original view (form [*Bild*]) that is not explicitly grasped, yet functions precisely as a paradigmatic form [*Vor-bild*] for all manifest beings, among which each respective Dasein itself belongs. (G9 158/123)

Human beings are "appropriated" by a network of meaning, a "world," and from this take their particular perspectives on beings as a whole.[9] This perspective, which Heidegger here calls an "original view," shapes how things show up as meaningful within human experience. Indeed, this structure of "transcendence" is the deep framework that allows beings to be intelligible at all. Beings become intelligible when they "enter" a world. This event, whereby human beings, appropriated by a world, are able to experience

---

9. In regards to the concept of "world," Heidegger's position might best be understood as a kind of *ontological realism*. That is, he argues from a phenomenological analysis to the claim that the network of meaning that grounds the intelligibility of everyday experience is something that is *discovered* or *given* rather than spontaneously *created* by human beings. See Thomson (2005): 63. This position betrays the influence of Husserl's theory of categorial intuition, which, for Heidegger, involves the disengagement of the concept of the a priori from subjectivity. On the importance of "categorial intuition" for Heidegger, see Dahlstrom (2001): 74–101.

beings as intelligible or meaningful, is what Heidegger now calls "primal history." He writes:

> Only if, amid beings in their totality, beings come to be "more in being" in the manner of the temporalizing of Dasein are there the hours and days of beings' entry into world. And only if this primordial history, namely, transcendence, occurs, i.e., only if beings having the character of being-in-the-world erupt into beings, is there the possibility of beings manifesting themselves. (G9 159/123)

Behind or beneath "history [*Historie*]," as a series of intelligible events, is the singular event that makes it possible for this series to be intelligible or meaningful for human beings in the first place.[10] Heidegger calls this "primal history [*Geschichte*]." This idea, growing out of the conceptuality developed in *Being and Time*, anchors Heidegger's mature philosophy of history and culture. Throughout the rest of the 1930s and 1940s, in lecture courses, unpublished manuscripts, and shorter essays, Heidegger attempts to work out the details of this conceptual framework and its implications for understanding history and culture.

In the 1930 essay, "On the Essence of Truth," Heidegger first employs this concept of "primal history" in order to provide a kind of synoptic account of the history of European philosophy. His basic claim here is that, in the earliest stages of Greek thought, one can detect the "paradigmatic form [*Vor-bild*] for all manifest beings" that guides not only Greek culture, but subsequent Western culture as a whole. Heidegger tries to articulate this schema in the following dense passage:

> Beings as a whole reveal themselves as *Phusis*, "nature," which here does not yet mean a particular sphere of beings but rather beings as such as a whole, specifically in the sense of upsurging presencing. History begins only when beings themselves are expressly drawn up into their unconcealment and conserved in it, only when this conservation is conceived on the basis of questioning regarding beings as such. The originary disclosure of beings as a whole, the question concerning beings as such, and the beginning of Western history are the same; they occur together in a "time" which, itself unmeasurable, first opens up the open region for every measure. (G9 189–190/145, translation modified)

---

10. In a footnote, to which Heidegger calls his readers' attention in the 1947 "Letter on Humanism," Heidegger indicates the significance of this concept of "primal history" for his philosophy of religion: "The ontological interpretation of Dasein as being-in-the-world decides neither positively nor negatively concerning a possible being toward God. Presumably, however, the elucidation of transcendence first achieves an *adequate concept* of *Dasein*, and with respect to this being it can then be *asked* how things stand ontologically concerning the relation of Dasein to God" (G9 159/371n62).

This passage contains Heidegger's first attempt to work out the relationship between the "primal history" described in "On the Essence of Ground" and the history of philosophy. On Heidegger's account, buried within the remains of Greek culture and thought, one can detect the fundamental, yet largely tacit, perspective in terms of which things showed up as meaningful. Heidegger's point is not simply the rather obvious one that Greek culture, and especially Greek philosophy, play a foundational role in the later development of Western civilization. Instead, Heidegger is interested in discovering the deep framework that supports the achievements of Greek culture. On his account, the "questioning," i.e. the philosophical discourse, of the ancient Greeks "conserves" the deep framework that ultimately makes Western civilization possible. This framework is nothing else than the "primal history" or original "time" which consists in the "unconcealment" of beings as a whole.

As these ideas continue to develop during the 1930s, Heidegger searches for other ways to express this basic conceptual scheme for the philosophy of history and culture. At the end of the decade, in an essay called "On the Essence and Concept of *Phusis* in Aristotle's *Physics* β, 1" (1939), he uses the term "metaphysics" to describe the deep framework that he had called "primal history" in 1929. One passage in particular provides substantial clarification of Heidegger's idea:

> The systematic articulation of the truth at any given time "about" beings as a whole is called "metaphysics." It make no difference whether or not this metaphysics is given expression in propositions, whether or not the expressions are formed into an explicit system. Metaphysics is that knowledge wherein Western historical humanity preserves the truth of its relations to beings as a whole, and the truth about these beings themselves. (G9 241/185)

"Metaphysics," in the sense that Heidegger is using the term here, does not refer to a philosophical discipline that investigates the basic categories of reality.[11] Nor is it used in the disparaging sense common in post-Kantian

---

11. In his own account of what he prefers to call "ontotheology," Thomson seems to come close to eliding the crucial distinction between the deep framework of a culture and its expressions in intellectual discourse. On his view, metaphysics as an explicitly philosophical mode of discourse is assigned a central role in the formation of culture. See Thomson (2005): 25–26. One difficulty with this reading is that it attributes to Heidegger an implausibly inflated view of the real influence of philosophers. In periods where literacy was the achievement of a small minority, the claim that complex metaphysical systems impacted the way "ordinary" people thought and acted seems *prima facie* dubious. Heidegger's actual view is that the very same deep framework invisibly shapes *both* ordinary people *and* intellectuals. Dreyfus, in a recent account of Heidegger's philosophy of art, comes closer to what I think is the correct reading when he clarifies how, for Heidegger, artworks *articulate* the deep framework of a culture. The same is true for intellectual discourse. See Dreyfus (2005).

thought, where it refers to inquiries that go beyond the limits of empirical reality and hence of the proper application of concepts. Instead, "metaphysics" is Heidegger's name for the "primal history" that governs the culture of an age. To say that metaphysics in this sense is concerned with the "truth" is not to say that it is a matter of accurately representing reality or with developing a coherent system of thought. The notion of truth that Heidegger is using here is one developed in *Being and Time* and later.[12] Truth in this sense is not a property of propositions. Instead, truth is the way in which things are uncovered or given in a meaningful way within the domain of human experience. "Truth" as a property of propositions presupposes this prior givenness.[13] Metaphysics, then, is the tacit perspective that guides in advance the way this truth happens, i.e., the way in which things can be meaningfully present to human experience. "Metaphysics" in the more familiar sense of a philosophical system is an *expression* or *articulation* of metaphysics in this more original sense.[14]

Why might Heidegger use "metaphysics" now to describe the deep framework that enables more macro-level cultural phenomena? Heidegger's general procedure is to utilize the expressive power of familiar words in order to indicate phenomena that are generally overlooked or misunderstood. In this case, the sense of the Greek preposition *meta*, in "meta-physics," provides a clue to Heidegger's choice of terminology. "Meta" has the connotation of "above" or "beyond," as evidenced in a host of philosophical neologisms like "meta-ethics" or "meta-language." For Heidegger, beings are intelligible to human beings because, "beyond" or "above" them, their "being" is given. "Being" is the basic meaningfulness or intelligibility of things in general, and it "is" itself neither a particular being nor the whole of beings. As he puts it in *Being and Time*, "being" is *transcendental*; it is the a priori structure the constitutes the givenness of any particular being and of beings as a whole. "Metaphysics," therefore, seems like a fitting name for the way in which this a priori structure is itself "given" to human beings.

We are now in a position to understand the basic conceptual scheme that is in play in Heidegger's cultural criticism. On his view, macro-level cultural phenomena, particularly intellectual discourse in disciplines like philosophy and theology, are "expressions" of the a priori structure of "being" that

---

12. For an excellent discussion of the way in which Heidegger's conception of "truth" figures into his critique of technology, see Thomson (2005): 144–146.

13. For a detailed account of this idiosyncratic use of the term "truth," see Dahlstrom (2001).

14. This conception of "metaphysics" is still operative in Heidegger's thought in the 1950s, as evidenced by a comment in "On the Question of Being": "The fact that, and the way that, the being of beings is 'given' is meta-physics in the sense designated" (G9 413/312).

governs a particular culture as a whole. Cultural criticism is, therefore, not simply a matter of cataloguing the ills of contemporary society. Instead, the project is to discern and explicate the deeper framework that, on Heidegger's account, enables these surface phenomena. Again, a comparison with other species of cultural criticism is instructive here. For a Marxist, the project of cultural criticism does not stop with pointing out the problematic nature of various institutions or social dynamics. Instead, Marxist criticism traces these surface-level phenomena back to deeper structures that are ultimately economic in nature. The intuition, shared by Marxist critics and by Heidegger, is that cultural problems need to be addressed at this more fundamental level. The deep difference between a Marxist critic and Heidegger can be found less on the level of their descriptive accounts of social ills than in their deep analysis of the roots of these ills. Indeed, in "Letter on Humanism," Heidegger more or less concurs with Marx's descriptive account (G9 339–340/258–259).

Modernity and Subjectivism

For Heidegger, cultural criticism is a matter of discovering, exposing, and explicating the deep framework that grounds the surface-level phenomena of a culture. More concretely, he deploys the general conceptual apparatus outlined in the previous section, to examine the cultural paradigms of late modernity. As I have indicated in the introduction, Heidegger's position is that the deep framework underlying modernity is a specific configuration of intelligibility that might be called "subjectivism." Macro-level cultural phenomena, of both a religious and secular nature, are expressions of this deep framework. The same holds, on Heidegger's account, of philosophical and theological discourse. The project that these ideas are meant to support is presented quite clearly at the outset of the 1938 piece, "The Age of the World-Picture." Heidegger writes:

> In metaphysics, reflection on the essence of beings and a decision concerning the essence of truth is accomplished. Metaphysics grounds an age in that, through a particular interpretation of beings and through a particular comprehension of truth, it provides that age with the ground of its essential shape. This ground comprehensively governs all decisions distinctive of the age. Conversely, in order for there to be adequate reflection on these phenomena [*Erscheinungen*], their metaphysical ground must allow itself to be recognized in them. (G5 75/57)

Heidegger's claim is that, when placed under the microscope of his own conceptual scheme, an age reveals its "ground" as an understanding of being. For modernity, as Heidegger makes clear in "The Age of the

World-Picture" and elsewhere, this ground is what I am calling "subjectiv-ism." What is truly distinctive for modernity, according to Heidegger, is that human beings are conceived of as *subjects* (G5 88/66). The understanding of being grounded in this conception is one on which humanity "becomes that being upon which every being, in its way of being and its truth, is founded. The human being becomes the referential center [*Bezugsmitte*] of beings as such" (G5 88/66–67). In the age of subjectivity, "a being is first and only in being insofar as it is set in place by representing-producing [*vorstellend-herstellenden*] humanity" (G5 89–90/67–68). Human subjectivity is the "norm-giving domain" that governs all beings (G5 91/69). Human subjectivity is the "scene" within which beings must present themselves in order to be evaluated and comprehended.

In a contemporaneous lecture course (WS 1938–1939), Heidegger pro-vides a parallel description of the essential ground of modernity:

> "*Subjectivism*" in the strict sense is any interpretation of the human being that posits him as *subjectum* in an outstanding sense—in such a way that all beings are defined as such in a regressive grounding upon this *sub-jectum* (about "objectivism" as a mirror-image). With this, the human being, as *subjectum*, can be conceived of as consciousness, as person-ality, as "body," as "life," and this once again as "I"-hood or as *we-hood* [*Wirheit*], individual, community. In general, subjectivism is still not merely preserved, but expanded and sharpened; the definition of the human being as I-consciousness is only *one* special instance of subjectiv-ism. Subjectivism—*the pure revolving of the human being around himself, as the being in relation to which all other beings are determined in their beingness.* "Anthropomorphism" in the metaphysical sense. (G46 165)

What, then, is "subjectivism"? First, subjectivism is definitely not a phil-osophical theory, though, as the above passage suggests, various philosophical theories can be *expressions* of it. Second, subjectivism is not what Heidegger would call an *ontic* claim. That is, it is not a claim about the causal deri-vation of reality from human beings. Instead, subjectivism is a largely tacit *ontological* stance or perspective that can be detected in macro-level cultural phenomena and in intellectual discourse. More precisely, subjectivism is an a priori configuration of meaningfulness or intelligibility that shapes in advance the way things show up in human experience. In an age defined by subjectivism, the meaningfulness that things have in human experience is taken to be somehow or other *grounded* in human beings themselves. As Heidegger puts it in "The Age of the World-Picture," human subjectivity is the "norm-giving domain" that determines the possible meaningfulness of beings ahead of time. Beings are only meaningful for human beings to the extent that they have been (or can be) subjected to technological procedures or subsumed under human concepts.

Heidegger is here articulating the thought that what is characteristic of modernity is the subordination of meaning, value, and normativity to interests. For moderns, things matter because they figure into a system of preference-satisfaction. It is as if all of reality is a reflection of the contemporary real estate industry. The value that a piece of property has depends upon the going market rate for property of that sort, which bottoms out in what people are willing to pay for it in order to satisfy interests like being close to work, being distant from one's in-laws, etc. On Heidegger's view, this is more or less how everything gets evaluated by modern people. Things only make sense to us instrumentally; they only matter to us because of our antecedent preferences. Thus, it is not that preferences and interests are responsive to value, but rather that value—along with every other type of meaning and intelligibility—is derivative of our interests. "Reality" itself, as a basic mode of intelligibility, depends upon the position of something within a complicated web of command and control procedures that serve interests.

As Heidegger suggests in WS 1938–1939, "subjectivism" can be expressed in a plurality of articulate philosophical views. According to the sense of the term used by Heidegger, "subjectivism" is not synonymous or coextentional with an "anything goes" type of relativism. Scientific naturalism, for example, holds that the "real" is what is capable of being analyzed and predicted by means of established scientific methods. Putative "realities" that fall outside of this domain are to be explained away as epiphenomena. Kantian or Neo-Kantian idealism, while different in significant ways from scientific naturalism, would still have it that a "thing" is a representation that has been shaped beforehand by the a priori conditions of consciousness. Moral, religious, and aesthetic values have no empirical content, but are instead "ideas" of reason. Finally, another view that expresses what Heidegger calls "subjectivism" might be termed "neo-Nietzscheanism." On this view, nothing has any inherent intelligibility or meaning to it. "Reality," however defined, is a human construction all the way down. Again, while this view has little in the way of obvious affinities with the previous two views, on Heidegger's account it, too, stems from the metaphysical "ground" of modernity.

For Heidegger, macro-level cultural phenomena are symptoms of this underlying ground. What ties these together is the larger phenomenon of *meaninglessness*. In an unpublished manuscript, "Die Geschichte des Seyns" (1938–1940), Heidegger argues that a general loss of meaning is characteristic of the modern age (G69 45), a trend that he rather dramatically calls "devastation" or "desertification [*Verwüstung*]" (G69 48). In the late 1940s, he prefers the term "decrepitude [*Verwahrlosung*]" (G75 355). This term shows up in an address delivered at Bremen in 1949 called "Die Gefahr," "The Danger." Here, "decrepitude" means that things are torn away from "world," from a richer network of meaningfulness, and are instead substitutable, indifferent items in the technological ordering of reality (G79 46–47). At its most extreme, this situation means that nothing has any *intrinsic* normative force to it any longer (G65 121/84; G5 291–292/218).[15] In other words, the meaning and value of things is determined by their position in a system of preference-satisfaction. There are no longer any limits on human self-assertion, as Heidegger dramatically argues in "Die Geschichte des Seyns." "Annihilation" and "violence" become ends in themselves, and "criminality" on a colossal scale becomes a real possibility (G69 76–77). In 1944, Heidegger redescribes this situation as one in which "nothing is preserved with awe [. . .] 'indiscretion' holds sway [. . .] no awe and no reverence" (G75 299). Humanity rises up against reality as the master of all it surveys:

> This will determines the essence of modern man, without his having known anything at first about its far-reaching consequences, and without his being able to know even today the will which, as the being of beings, is the source of this will that is willed. In such willing, modern man turns out to be the one who surges up—in every relation to everything that is and therefore also to himself—as the producer who asserts himself and establishes this insurgency as absolute mastery. (G5 289/216)

Like Weber and some of his own neo-Marxist contemporaries, Heidegger views the modern condition as one in which technical rationality has triumphed over all intrinsic value or worth. The meaning that things have—if they still have any—is determined entirely by their place within the economy of human technical control. As Heidegger puts it in the 1946 essay "Wozu Dichter?": "everything, already in advance and therefore in the consequence, is relentlessly turned into the material of self-asserting production" (G5 289/217). In place of the void once occupied by intrinsic value, meaning now becomes *merely* a matter of subjective conviction. In *Beiträge zur Philosophie*, Heidegger points out how "as a substitute for the foundations that have disappeared, the 'world-view' of individuals was in a weak sort of way to continue to hold 'values' and 'ideals' together" (G65 37/26). The watchwords of the day—"world-view," "personality," "culture"—are so many "decorations" affixed to a life devoid of any substantive normative horizon (G65 53/38).

This general move toward the "subjectivizing" of normativity can be seen in the various non-religious symptoms of modernity that Heidegger

---

15. Julian Young argues that Heidegger's diagnosis of the modern age in terms of the loss of meaning is actually incompatible with his considered position on the relation between "Being" and value. See Young (1995). This is, however, a misreading of Heidegger's position. Heidegger does not hold that things are devoid of all "value," that they no longer matter *at all* to modern human beings. Rather, his contention is that, in the modern age, nothing has any *intrinsic* value any longer.

enumerates in "The Age of the World-Picture." He describes, for example, "the process of art's moving into the purview of aesthetics. This means the artwork becomes an object of experience [*Erlebnis*] and consequently is considered to be an expression of human life" (G5 75/57). In SS 1942, Heidegger reiterates this point by noting that, in the age of technical production, art is little more than an adornment designed to produce "sentimental values" (G52 142/114). Unlike, for example, the art of the medieval world, which served to express the guiding normative horizon of an entire culture, art is now reduced to one element in the overall "culture business."[16]

The prevalence of the notion of "culture" itself is, by Heidegger's lights, another symptom of modernity. In the modern age, the "age of the world-picture," human activity "is understood and practiced as culture. Culture then becomes the realization of the highest values through the care and cultivation [*Pflege*] of man's highest goods" (G5 75–76/57). That is, "culture" is the collective name of human activities that are defined by certain interests. Beyond these interests themselves, there are no norms or values to which these activities are answerable. Culture is a kind of catch-all concept for goals set by human beings; culture, he argues, "is that in which all development of all capacities is calculated and regulated" (G46 53; cf. G67 116). "Culture," and its associated concepts of "value" and "world-view," become masks worn by human self-assertion and the drive toward the complete "machination" of all beings. In notes from 1945 and 1946, Heidegger argues that the vaunted ideals of "enlightenment," "humanity," "progress," and "socialism" collectively constitute "Only a pretext for other forces [. . .] the will to power; *technology*" (G75 354). This is just a way of saying that, for moderns, activities that used to be conceived of as responses to an independent network of meaning are now simply expressions of interests.

These non-religious symptoms of modernity are mirrored in the religious situation of the age. In a world where nothing has normative force outside of human projects, there is clearly no longer any room for religion as a binding relationship between human beings and something transcendent. This characterization of the religious situation of modernity is presented in "The Age of the World-Picture" under the rubric of the "loss of the gods [*Entgötterung*]," a kind of Heideggerean counterpart to Weber's much discussed "disenchantment [*Entzauberung*]." Heidegger attempts to carefully articulate what he means by the "loss of the gods":

> This expression does not mean the mere elimination of the gods, crude atheism. The loss of the gods is a twofold process. On the one hand, the

16. For two good discussions of the theme of the "death of art" in Heidegger, see Dreyfus (2005) and Young (2001).

world-picture Christianizes itself inasmuch as the ground of the world is
posited as infinite and unconditioned, as the absolute. On the other hand,
Christendom [*Christentum*] interprets its Christianness [*Christlichkeit*] as a
world-view (the Christian world-view) and thus makes itself modern and up
to date. The loss of the gods is the condition of indecision about God and
the gods. Christendom is chiefly responsible for bringing it about. But loss
of the gods is far from excluding religiosity. Rather, it is on its account that
the relation to the gods is transformed into religious experience [*Erleben*].
When this happens, the gods have fled. The resulting void is filled by the
historical and psychological investigation of myth. (G5 76/58)

This passage presents Heidegger's understanding of the religious situation of the time as a symptom of what he calls "subjectivism." The "loss of
the gods" does not refer to the prevalence of atheists in the modern world.
Nor is Heidegger endorsing the "loss of the gods" as if it were a philosophical position. Indeed, Heidegger's discussions of the religious situation of the
time tell us little about his own personal views. As he puts it in his 1946 essay,
"Nietzsche's Word: God is Dead," "The attempt to experience the truth of
that statement of God's death without illusions is something different from a
confession of faith in Nietzsche's philosophy" (G5 254/190). Instead, the "loss
of the gods," and various cognate terms such as the "death of God," the "flight
of the gods," and the "absence [*Fehl*] of God," are all ways of trying to capture the prevailing religious situation of modernity. Here, in this passage from
"The Age of the World-Picture," Heidegger begins by attributing a major role
to German Idealism, the philosophy of subjectivism par excellence, within
the drama of "disenchantment." For Heidegger, German Idealism is best
viewed as an attempt to preserve meaning, value, and normativity in culture
without appealing to anything beyond the interests of reason. The interest of
reason itself, i.e., the goal of rational autonomy, is what, for the idealists, ultimately guarantees the norms that govern moral life, cultural activities like the
arts, and, at the most basic level, the coherence of experience itself.

Perhaps more significant, however, is the observation that Christianity
becomes a "world-view," i.e., merely a matter of personal conviction, in the
modern age. Heidegger had repudiated the understanding of Christianity as
a world-view already in WS 1920–1921. Reducing Christianity to a world-view
means interpreting it as one of many possible ways in which an individual
might find some security in his or her life projects. As a result, religion
becomes "religious experience," a kind of sentimental adornment to life
(cf. G65 123–124/86). Elsewhere, in an essay on Hölderlin's poem "Andenken,"
Heidegger describes this brand of religiosity as "Roman," meaning that the
human quest for security and self-satisfaction have replaced the normative
force of God (G4 114/136–137). In "The Age of the World-Picture," theistic
metaphysics, which tries to explain the meaning of religious life as fundamentally

responsive to an independent domain of value, is replaced by psychological explanation. Heidegger's thought is that this move strips away the final vestiges of normative force from religion. Taken as an expression of human psychology, the attitudes and activities that characterize religion are internally unintelligible. To take one popular psychological theory as an example: if God is a Jungian archetype, what could be the sense of *worshiping* Him?

The underlying idea is that, like everything else in the modern world, God has lost his putative "power to shape history" (G50 24). As he puts it in "Wozu Dichter?" (1946), the "absence [*Fehl*]" of God means that "a God no longer gathers men and things to himself visibly and unmistakably [*eindeutig*] and from this gathering ordains [*fügt*] world-history and man's sojourn [*Aufenthalt*] within it" (G5 269/200). One no longer has to take the "reality" of God seriously ahead of time in one's dealings with things (G5 255/190). There is no longer the possibility that, for Western culture as a whole, something transcending human interests could put a claim on it. There is no longer an independent measure that shapes and guides human activity ahead of time. This loss of any real possibility for transcendence is characterized as follows in "Das Wesen der Nihilismus," a text dating from 1946 to 1948:

> All transcendence, be it ontological or theological, is represented relative to the subject-object relation. Through the rebellion of subjectivity, even theological transcendence, and so the beingest of beings [*das Seiendste des Seienden*]—one says of it typically enough, "being"—moves into a kind of objectivity, namely, into that of the subjectivity of moral-practical faith. Whether man takes this transcendence seriously for his religious subjectivity as providence or merely as a pretext for the will of his own self-seeking subjectivity, nothing is altered about the essence of this basic metaphysical position of human nature. (G67 241)

According to Heidegger, then, the modern situation is one in which *theological* meaning, like all other meaning, is experienced as being grounded in human subjectivity. Human "culture" itself, as the sum of the projects undertaken in the name of securing human power, undergoes an idolatrous "deification [*Vergötzung*]" (G65 117/82). God no longer operates as a transcendent source of meaning and normativity in Western culture as a whole. Rather than shaping ahead of time the concrete practices of people, religion becomes a matter of subjective conviction, justified only by its capacity for "securing" projects undertaken not in the name of God, but of humanity itself.

The result is an ever-deepening loss of any active sensibility for the transcendent. As he puts it in notes from 1945 and 1946, "The basic experience: the whole horizon from out of which God could appear as God is wiped away—the holy" (G75 355). Borrowing a phrase from Hölderlin, Heidegger maintains that modernity is a "desolate" or "destitute" age (G5 269/200). The "radiance of divinity [*der Glanz der Gottheit*]," the sense of sacredness and transcendence so vividly experienced by people in other times and in non-Western cultures, "is extinguished in world-history" (G5 269/200).

For Heidegger, the modern age as a whole is in the grip of what Terry Pinkard has recently called "the Kantian paradox." To state the paradox in religious terms, for modern human beings God has a claim on us only because we make God have such a claim on us.[17] Neither God, nor anything else, has any normative claim on human action prior to the sheer willing of human agents. This, for Heidegger, is the clearest symptom of the deep framework that guides the modern age as such. This configuration, "subjectivism," determines in advance the way things show up as meaningful in human experience. The meaning that things have shows up as *deriving* from human beings themselves. So, if a religion is to have normative force for an individual, this is only because that individual has lent this religion its normative force. To say that the "radiance of divinity" is "extinguished" is simply to say that nothing is experienced as having independent normative force any longer.

Modernity and Theology

Macro-level cultural phenomena, such as the "death of art," and, more importantly for the present discussion, the "death of God," are viewed by Heidegger as expressions of the deep framework that governs the modern age as a whole. The same is true for the dominant modes of *intellectual discourse* in the modern age. As early as SS 1923, Heidegger proposes to investigate the intellectual discourse of the age in order to uncover the basic self-understanding of his own culture as expressed in this discourse. As his framework for the philosophical analysis of culture matures in the 1930s and 1940s, Heidegger holds fast to the basic intuition that intellectual discourse reveals the deeper assumptions of an age. Heidegger, of course, is most interested in the *philosophical* expressions of an age's deep framework. His often idiosyncratic readings of the history of philosophy from the Greeks to the Neo-Kantians have received extensive comment over the years. The primary concern of the present discussion is with Heidegger's more specific account of the way in which dominant trends in intellectual discourse reflect the deep framework of *modernity*. Just as macro-level cultural phenomena are, according to Heidegger, to be understood as disclosive of a deeper layer of meaning, so too is the intellectual discourse of an age.

---

17. Pinkard (2002): 59–60.

While Heidegger reserves most of his comments for philosophical discourse, he also has something to say about contemporary discourse in *theology*. He views the dominant strands of contemporary theology as articulations of subjectivism, and so as being complicit in the "death of God." This point is perhaps made most forcefully in a text composed in the late 1930s entitled "Überwindung der Metaphysik." One portion of the text, "The Age of the Theologians," includes the following strongly worded remarks:

> "Theologians" obtain the foremost rank and no longer have any need for a "God" or a decision about gods. These theologians are theologians both of "providence" and of "adventure," in that "technology" (planning, production, uncertainty within what is calculable) constitutes the truth of beings and hence characterizes metaphysics at its end. Theology becomes *diabology*, which is not of course limited to the harmlessness of the "devil" as a fallen angel, but rather first of all lets in and sets loose the unconditioned non-essence [*Unwesen*] of God into the truth of beings. The explicit development of the diabologians is imminent. (G67 154–155)

Heidegger's specific targets in this passage are unclear; it seems that he is denouncing contemporary theology *as a whole*. The problem, as he sees it here, is that "theologians" replace God as the focus of consideration. For Heidegger, this is a reflection of the deep framework in play in the modern world, which he identifies in this passage with "technology." In the age of technology, theologians no longer need "God." In other words, as is true of modernity in general, the ultimate grounds of normativity and meaning are the projects of human beings. In this sense, "theologians" matter more in the modern situation than does God. In the modern age, then, "theology" becomes "diabology." Theological discourse is no longer constrained in advance by God or by divine revelation; instead, the imperatives of various human projects set the agenda.

This critique of theological discourse, here expressed in terms of Heidegger's mature conceptual framework for interpreting culture, has its roots in the earliest stages of Heidegger's career. As Theodore Kisiel has shown, Heidegger enthusiastically received Franz Overbeck's scathing attacks on liberal Protestantism.[18] At roughly the same time, Heidegger was also busily appropriating Kierkegaard's attack on bourgeois "Christendom" and Luther's vitriolic assault on the theological and ecclesiastical systems of his day.[19] In SS 1920, Heidegger targets the contemporary conception of Christianity as a *Bildungsreligion* (G59 141). Indeed, this single term, *Bildungsreligion*, encapsulates Heidegger's whole objection to contemporary theological discourse. The liberal Protestantism of the late

---

18. See Kisiel (1988): 73–75.
19. See Crowe (2006).

nineteenth and early twentieth centuries assimilated Christianity to larger cultural projects of the post-Enlightenment, bourgeois world. Like his contemporaries Barth, Gogarten, and Bultmann, Heidegger viewed this tendency as a betrayal of the spirit of primal Christianity.[20] The dominant strands of theology had effectively compromised with the spirit of modernity, in which human beings and human cultural projects supplant God as the source of normativity and meaning.[21]

This is precisely the same worry that Heidegger expresses more dramatically in "Überwindung der Metaphysik." Rather than constituting an authentic challenge to the dominant conceptual paradigms of modernity, theological discourse compromises with them. Even worse, the churches, whose vocation is to preserve the authentic word of God, compromise with the political powers that mobilize the vast resources of technological modernity for the sake of a naked bid for power. Heidegger makes this point in "Geschichte des Seyns" (1938–1940):

> The wretchedness of Christianity is shown most clearly in the fact that it oscillates back and forth between unconditioned positions of power, and offers its services to one or the other according to its own need. Here, it can also be seen that the decision about the divinity of the gods can never fall within the purview of such a vacillating [hinschwingenden] Christianity. It cannot even have the slightest clue about it. (G69 80–81)

While the sense of passages such as these seems plain, it is also easy to mistake. Heidegger's passionate critiques of theology and of the churches need to be read against the background of his larger, positive, project. Both John D. Caputo and John Van Buren maintain that in his later (i.e., post-1930) writings, Heidegger turns his back entirely on his own Christian background and on his interest in developing a positive phenomenology of religious life.[22] This reading is, however, much too strong, for it fails to adequately contextualize Heidegger's criticisms of theology and religion within his philosophical project as a whole. The claim that he repudiates his earlier religious interests is in manifest conflict with many of his explicit statements on this issue during the later decades of his career. Moreover, this reading seems to rely on

---

20. See Bambach (1995), Barash (1988), Fehér (1995), and Van Buren (1994).

21. Heidegger does seem, during at least one stage of his career, to have viewed the recent emergence of "dialectical" theology and the accompanying "Luther Renaissance" as positive signs of a new direction in theology. In later years, however, he seems to have grown somewhat disillusioned with these developments (G66 415). Still, following World War II, Heidegger once again sought the company of theologians, with an eye on helping them to challenge the dominant assumptions of late modernity. On this general program of "ontological education," see Thomson (2005).

22. See Van Buren (1994): 367–376, 384–386; Caputo (1993a), (1993b), and (1994).

the assumption that vociferous criticisms of the particular historical situation of religion and theology in a particular age are incompatible with having any positive concern for developing a philosophical account of religion that articulates its essential elements. This is an assumption that is plainly at odds with Heidegger's famous motto, "Higher than actuality stands possibility." Applied to Husserlian phenomenology in *Being and Time*, Heidegger explains that the present state of phenomenology as a movement in philosophy should not be equated with its essence or, for that matter, with its original promise. Instead, the latter provides the real measure for any particular condition of the discipline. This is what Heidegger means when he elsewhere asserts that "critique of history is always critique of the present." To criticize the "today," the specific phenomena of the age, is in no way the same as rejecting the essential core of the phenomena as one understands them.

In a text composed in 1937 or 1938, Heidegger testifies to the continuing significance of religion in his attempts to work out his own views.

> But who could deny that a confrontation with Christianity discretely accompanied the whole preceding way?—A confrontation which was not and is not some "problem" that was latched onto, but rather at *once* the preservation [*Wahrung*] of the ownmost origin—of the parental house, the homeland, and youth—and the painful separation from it. Only someone thus rooted in a really vital Catholic world could have an inkling of the necessities that exerted an effect on the preceding way of my questioning like subterranean earthquakes. The Marburg period brought to this a still closer experience of a Protestant Christianity—all of which was already something overcome from the ground up, which, however, must not be destroyed. (G66 415)

There can be no doubt that Heidegger regarded the modern age as involving a profound *crisis* of religion. However, rather than providing warrant for a repudiation of the entire religious heritage of European culture, Heidegger viewed this crisis has having positive potential. After the revelatory remarks quoted above, he continues: "It is unseemly to speak of this most inward confrontation, which is not a question of dogmatics or articles of faith, but rather is only concerned with the One Question, whether God is in flight before us or not and whether we ourselves are still able to truly experience this, i.e., as something creative" (G66 415).

Caputo and Van Buren simply overlook Heidegger's indications in his later writings as to what this "creative" possibility consists in. Unlike Nietzsche, Heidegger does not view the "death of God" as an opportunity to jettison the tradition and create a new "table of values." Nietzsche, on Heidegger's reading, views the "death of God" as the beginning of a new, "higher history" (G67 180). According to both Caputo and Van Buren, Heidegger adopts a similar position, and sets out to create a new "myth" designed to legitimate

German nationalism. But, as Heidegger makes clear, Nietzsche's solution to the problem posed by the "death of God" fails to break out of the conceptual paradigms that created this problem in the first place.[23] Nietzsche is, according to Heidegger, unable to locate the proper "dimension for a God-seeking" (G67 193–194). He rhetorically asks, "Does Nietzsche think being itself such that he finds the dimension in which the divine can first emerge as the domain of the flight and arrival of the god?" (G67 199). The implied answer, of course, is "no."

In addition to misreading Heidegger's stance toward Nietzsche, both Van Buren and Caputo pass over Heidegger's attempts to clarify the nature of his critique of religion and theology.[24] One of the most important of these attempts can be found in "Nietzsche's Word: God is Dead," a text dating from the late 1940s in which Heidegger tries to summarize over a decade of Nietzsche research. Speaking on Nietzsche's behalf, as it were, Heidegger tries to clarify what it means to describe the modern situation in terms of the "death of God":

> Nor, therefore, does nihilism in Nietzsche's sense in any way coincide with the state (conceived in a purely negative way) of no longer being able to believe in the Christian God of the biblical revelation, since by "Christianity" Nietzsche does not mean the Christian life that existed once for a short time before the Gospels were set down in writing and before Paul disseminated his missionary propaganda. For Nietzsche, Christianity is the historical, secular-political phenomenon of the Church and its claim to power within the formation of Western humanity and its modern culture. Christianity in this sense and the Christian life of the New Testament faith are not the same. Even a non-Christian life can affirm Christianity and make use of it for the sake of power; conversely, a Christian life is not necessarily in need of Christianity. Therefore, a confrontation with Christianity is by no means an absolute battle against what is Christian, no more than a critique of theology is a critique of the faith for which theology is supposed to be the interpretation. (G5 219–220/164)

In this passage, Heidegger is making a distinction between what might be called "Christendom," as a cultural and political phenomenon, and "Christianity," as the teachings and practices of Jesus and the early church;

---

23. This point is also made in SS 1937, where Heidegger discusses Nietzsche's view that the "death of God" can only be overcome through the creativity of human nature (G87 49–50).

24. Caputo asserts that Heidegger's assertions about the religious import of his thought in the late 1940s are part of a "cover up" of his virulent atheism and anti-Semitism from the 1930s. See Caputo (1993a): 177–178. The attribution of such motives to Heidegger, however, (1) considerably exceeds what the textual evidence warrants, (2) misreads the nature of Heidegger's engagement with Nietzsche in the 1930s, and (3) ignores the evident enthusiasm with which Heidegger reconnected with religious thinkers and theologians after World War II.

and he attributes this distinction to Nietzsche. Whether Nietzsche in fact made such a distinction is less important here than the fact that Heidegger certainly *does* endorse this view. In a letter written to a colleague prior to the publication of the essay on Nietzsche (8 December 1945), Heidegger asserts: "Concerning 'Christianity [*Christentum*],' for me, indeed, just as for Kierkegaard, there is an essential distinction between 'Christianness [*Christlichkeit*]' (as the faithfulness of the individual) and 'Christendom [*Christentum*]' as a historical, cultural, and political epiphenomenon [*Erscheinung*] of Christianness" (G16 416).[25]

This distinction, between "Christianness" and "Christendom," shows up again in a preface written in 1970 for the essay "Phenomenology and Theology," in which Heidegger tries to work out in precise detail the relation between his own philosophical endeavors and those of his colleagues in theology. Indeed, he suggests that the whole purpose of the essay is "to occasion repeated reflection on the extent to which the Christianness of Christianity and its theology merit questioning" (G9 49/39). While Heidegger was not fully satisfied with this essay, as he relates to Blochmann in 1928 shortly after it was composed, he nevertheless published it many years later, indicating his own perceptions of its continued importance (see HB 25–26). Moreover, Heidegger makes reference to Franz Overbeck's *On the Christianness of Today's Theology* (1873) in the 1970 preface. As I have already pointed out, Heidegger was quite enthusiastic about Overbeck's immanent criticism of contemporary theology.

Heidegger's often scathing critiques of theology and the churches need to be read against the background of texts like "Nietzsche's Word: God is Dead" and "Phenomenology and Theology." Rather than rejecting the Christian heritage of European culture in the name a new mythology of "blood and soil," as Van Buren and Caputo allege, Heidegger viewed himself as a kind of provocateur, whose task was to challenge theologians to remain true to the original spirit of Christianity and to avoid all compromises with the spirit of the modern age. To his chagrin, Heidegger felt that theologians were all too willing to submit to the conceptual paradigms of the age, and were themselves shaped by its deep framework of subjectivism.[26]

---

25. Unlike English, German has only one standard term, *Christentum*, to refer to both "Christendom" *and* "Christianity," a fact that has undoubtedly led to much confusion in commentaries on Heidegger's thought.

26. The basic point that criticisms of Christianity can actually be compatible with profound reverence for its traditions seems to have been missed by commentators like Van Buren and Caputo. In his own recent study of Heidegger, Merold Westphal elaborates this point convincingly, arguing that Heidegger's critique of "ontotheology" is by no means an endorsement of atheism. See Westphal (2001). For a useful précis of the argument of this book, see Westphal (2005).

Philosophical Voices of Modernity: Neo-Kantianism and Nietzsche

Having looked at Heidegger's accounts of macro-level cultural phenomena as expressions of the guiding subjectivism of modernity, as well as the ways in which theology expresses this deep framework, Heidegger's discussions of the distinctively *philosophical* phenomena of the age have not yet been explored. Like the phenomena described above, the philosophical discourse of late modernity is viewed by Heidegger as expressing a deeper framework of fundamental concepts, which itself ultimately rests upon an understanding of being as such. During his long career, Heidegger lectured on and wrote about nearly every significant figure in the history of Western philosophy. His philosophical contemporaries and near contemporaries, however, were particularly important to his project, as they gave expression to the guiding cultural paradigms of his own age. Both the Neo-Kantians, at whose feet Heidegger had studied in the years before World War I, and Nietzsche, whose work had an explosive effect on both philosophy and German culture as a whole, represented for Heidegger *the* philosophical expressions of modernity.

Recent scholarship has begun rediscovering the importance of Neo-Kantianism for Heidegger's intellectual development.[27] Two important points, however, remain largely untreated by commentators: first, the role played by Neo-Kantian theories of religion in the development of Heidegger's own phenomenology of religion; and second, the evidence of a continuing engagement with Neo-Kantianism in his later works. Scholarship on Heidegger and Neo-Kantianism has focused exclusively on the earliest stage of his career, from his student days to the publication of *Being and Time*. I will correct the first deficiency in chapter 2; the second, I will address in the remainder of this section. My claim is that the continuity of Heidegger's philosophical interests will not be adequately understood unless (1) his later interest in Neo-Kantianism is taken into account, and (2) the nature of this later interest is sufficiently connected with his earlier engagements with this tradition.

Throughout the 1920s Heidegger lets it be known that, on his view, Neo-Kantianism is *the* philosophical expression of the present age. He is particularly interested in showing how the widespread concern with *culture*, with which religion is closely linked, reflects the place of Neo-Kantianism as the philosophical voice of modernity. On Heidegger's reading, in the late

---

27. The recent literature on the subject includes: Crowell (1994) and (2001); Dahlstrom (2001): 1–47; Heinz (2000); Kisiel (1993), (2000), and (2002); Kovacs (1994); Lyne (2000); Orth (1992); and Van Buren (1994).

nineteenth century, "culture" is synonymous with both the self-congratulatory historical consciousness of the age, and with the allied achievements of science and technology (G56–57 130/111). According to Heidegger, the whole concept of "culture" originates in the Enlightenment, and its self-authorizing distinction between benighted, barbarous ages and the "age of reason" (G56–57 132/112–113). Kant's "critical philosophy" can be seen as the most powerful attempt to ground such a normative view of culture. For Kant, culture consists in "the formation and perfection of mankind's rational determinations, rules, and aims" (G56–57 133/113). What Kant then bequeathed to subsequent philosophical reflection on modernity was "The displacement of the center of gravity of all philosophical problematics in consciousness, subjectivity, the I of transcendental apperception, of theoretical and practical reason and the power of judgment" (G56–57 134/114). In other words, the project of providing a philosophical foundation for the idea of "culture" becomes the project of locating the ultimate sources of normativity within the interests of reason as such. Hermann Lotze then carried this project to a further level by drawing a sharp distinction between the "validity [*Gültigkeit*]" of norms and the existence of states of affairs; this distinction passed over into Baden Neo-Kantianism unchanged. The Baden Neo-Kantians, then, took up the project of grounding "validity" on transcendental subjectivity. The result, according to Heidegger, is that "transcendental philosophy of value became the sole (serious) kind of philosophy of culture of the present" (G56–57 140–141/119).

As Heidegger points out, the Neo-Kantians explicitly took themselves as the champions of modern culture, and undertook the project of defending it against attacks by assorted historicists, relativists, and life-philosophers. Indeed, if anything can be said to definitively unite Neo-Kantianism as a movement, it is precisely this concern with consolidating the achievements of modern culture.[28] As *the* philosophy of modern culture, Baden Neo-Kantianism represents, according to Heidegger, a clear expression of the "today" (G63 40–43/32–34). The journal *Logos*, as Heidegger notes, served as the mouthpiece of this movement as a whole (G63 42/34). Kantian transcendental philosophy, with its sharp division between a priori normativity and empirical reality, was viewed by many—including Heidegger's teacher, Heinrich Rickert—as the key to defending modern culture against its critics.[29]

---

28. See especially Tenbruck (1994). A similar point is made by Ernst Wolfgang Orth in his contribution to the same volume, Orth (1994). Finally, in his essay, Harald Homann shows how the motives of the "philosophy of culture" crystallized around the journal *Logos*, founded in 1910, under the influence of prominent members of the "Baden" school. See Homann (1994).

29. See Rickert (1921) and (1999b).

As Heidegger notes at several points, the conceptual apparatus deployed by the Baden Neo-Kantians was grounded on the Kantian-Fichtean idea of the "spontaneity" of human reason, i.e., of the ability of human reason to constitute normativity in different cultural domains (see G59 137–139; 141). Indeed, Wilhelm Windelband, founder of the Baden school of Neo-Kantianism in which Heidegger was trained, describes the starting point of his philosophy of culture as the Kantian insight, "The world which we experience is our deed."[30]

From the very start of his critical engagement with this tradition, then, Heidegger maintained *both* that Baden Neo-Kantianism is the definitive philosophical expression of modern culture *and* that the heart of this movement is a commitment to transcendental idealism. As his thinking on these issues matured, Heidegger came later to identify these two aspects of Baden Neo-Kantianism much more closely. By the late 1930s, he had concluded that Neo-Kantianism, in virtue of the foundational role it ascribed to human subjectivity, was a significant philosophical expression of the deep framework of modernity. That is, the Neo-Kantian commitment to idealism reflected the larger subjectivistic paradigm of the age as a whole.

In "The Age of the World-Picture" (1938), one of Heidegger's first public presentations of his evolving theory of culture—as I have indicated above—he explicitly links Neo-Kantian value-theory, descended from the work of Hermann Lotze, with subjectivism (G5 101–102/77). The unpublished "Überwindung der Metaphysik" (1938–1939), from the same period, contains similar claims (G67 25). In particular, Heidegger emphasizes the Kantian idea that the "a priori," i.e., the normative concepts that shape experience and guide evaluations, is located within the "subjective" sphere as a crucial indication of the way in which Neo-Kantianism expresses the foundational perspective of the age (G67 87). Moreover, as he had as early as 1919, Heidegger associates Neo-Kantianism closely with the phenomenon of "world-view," going so far as to dub it the "scholasticism of world-view" (G67 120–121). In the WS 1938–1939 lecture course, he reiterates another point from 1919, viz., that the concept of "culture" itself, so important to the Neo-Kantian project, is rooted in modern subjectivism (G46 53).

In *Beiträge zur Philosophie*, composed during roughly this same period, Heidegger lists Baden Neo-Kantianism (though not by name) as one of the "symptoms" of modernity: "Getting stuck in thinking about and starting with 'values' and 'ideas'; in which the *structural form* [*Gefügeform*] of historical Dasein is viewed as something unchangeable, without any serious questions; thinking in 'world-views' corresponds to this" (G65 117/82).

---

30. Windelband (1911a): 260.

Here, Heidegger's point is that Baden Neo-Kantianism both expresses the dominant viewpoint of the age and attempts to consolidate it. As I have already pointed out, the Baden Neo-Kantians themselves, as well as other contributors to *Logos*, would most likely endorse this assessment. Heidegger, of course, puts a critical edge on it. For him, the "death of God" and the "death of art," the dominance of technical rationality, and the disenchantment of the world are all of piece with Neo-Kantian philosophy of culture. As he puts it in "The Age of the World-Picture," the "values" that figure so prominently in Baden Neo-Kantianism "are the powerless and threadbare mask of the objectification of beings, an objectification that has become flat and devoid of background" (G5 102/77). Indeed, later in the *Beiträge*, Heidegger repeats a charge first leveled in SS 1923, namely, that Neo-Kantianism is a species of Platonism which, while motivated by the distress of historical reality, is ultimately cut off from it (G65 218/152; G63 42/34). *Being and Time*, he argues, is best read as a direct confrontation with the Neo-Kantian movement (G65 234/165–166).

Baden Neo-Kantianism is still on Heidegger's mind in the 1940s, despite the fact that it had long since begun to fade away as a powerful intellectual movement. For example, in a lecture course from 1940, on Nietzsche, Heidegger presents his most lengthy treatment of the philosophy of value in over a decade (G48 25). He once again makes it clear that the basic categories of Neo-Kantianism, including "value" and "culture," are reflections of modern subjectivism:

> Since the rise of the concept of value, one has talked about the "cultural values" of the Middle Ages and the "spiritual values" of antiquity, and continues to talk this way, despite the fact that there was nothing like "culture" in the Middle Ages, nor was their "spirit" or "culture" in antiquity. Only since modernity began have there been spirit and culture as basic modes of human conduct that are desired and experienced, and "values," as the posited criteria for this conduct, have only been around since the most recent times. (G48 27)

Modernity, for Heidegger, is defined by the deep framework of subjectivism. Within this framework, things show up as worthwhile or valuable only in relation to human interests. The commitments implied by these interests provide the norms governing their success or failure. To say that the Middle Ages or antiquity lacked "culture" or "values" is not to say that these ages produced no great artworks or great ideas, or that they languished in unprincipled barbarism, but rather means that things showed up as mattering in a different way than they do for modern persons. According to Heidegger, the Greeks experienced their own cultural achievements not as products of human creativity, but as a response to the "nature" of things. Similarly, medieval persons, attuned as they were to the world as the creation of an all-powerful God, viewed their own activities in this light. As will be discussed in the next chapter, it is precisely this link between Baden Neo-Kantianism and the deep framework characteristic of modernity that, according to Heidegger, leads such accounts of religion astray. Concepts like "culture" and "value" are lifted from the Enlightenment project of establishing human autonomy, and then uncritically applied to religion, a sphere in which human autonomy is heavily qualified by a sense of dependence on the divine.

Besides Baden Neo-Kantianism, the other great philosophical expression of modernity for Heidegger is Nietzsche, and, more derivatively, neo-Nietzschean authors like Oswald Spengler and Ernst Jünger.[31] As with Baden Neo-Kantianism, Heidegger makes his assessment of Nietzsche's work unequivocally clear: "Nietzsche is the name for an age: the epoch of the unfolding and inception [*Einrichtung*] of the hegemony of man over the earth. Man as the subject of producing" (G50 84). Beginning in the second half of the 1930s, Heidegger consistently locates Nietzsche within the same stream of thought as Descartes and Kant, both of whom are paradigms of modern subjectivism (G48 309). He points to Nietzsche's well-known perspectivism as evidence for this sweeping claim, and suggests that, for Nietzsche, "The law of *esse* is 'representing' and the principle: reality is appearance" (G87 25). In his WS 1938–1939 seminar on "The Utility and Liability of History for Life," Heidegger maintains that the fundamental concepts of Nietzsche's position, e.g., "culture," are rooted in modern subjectivism (G46 114). Later, Heidegger again observes that Nietzsche "thinks in a modern way, i.e., *subjectively*" (G46 175).

Clearly, then, Heidegger takes Nietzsche's thought to be an important philosophical expression of the modern age. Beginning in the 1930s, Nietzsche seems to usurp the role previously played by Baden Neo-Kantianism in Heidegger's critique of the philosophy of culture. Nietzsche does not, however, completely eclipse the Neo-Kantians, as my discussion above has shown. Well into the 1940s, Heidegger still regards Baden Neo-Kantianism as a significant cultural force. Nietzsche does supplant the primacy of Baden Neo-Kantianism at least in terms of the quantity of writings devoted to the subject. It would be wrong, however, to view this as a substantial shift of Heidegger's interests. As I have just made clear, his concerns regarding both Baden Neo-Kantianism and Nietzsche are unified by his broader project

---

31. For an account of this aspect of Heidegger's study of Nietzsche, see Ibáñez-Noé (1995). Ibáñez-Noé contends that Jünger provides Heidegger with the "optic" through which he views the present age, and so also Nietzsche, as an expression of this age. At the same time, it is made clear that Heidegger's own framework for understanding history and culture is radically different from that of both Nietzsche and Jünger.

of cultural criticism. The conceptual apparatus that underwrites this criticism also lends continuity to Heidegger's apparently disparate discussions of the Neo-Kantians and Nietzsche. More significant, however, is a fact that has been passed over in silence by commentators on Heidegger's later work, namely, that he views Nietzsche's basic philosophical position as a species of Neo-Kantianism.[32] In this regard, Heidegger was somewhat ahead of recent trends in Nietzsche scholarship, which have attempted to locate his work more firmly within the nineteenth-century context.[33]

As early as 1937, Heidegger maintains the view that Nietzsche's position is best understood as a kind of naturalistic or biologistic Neo-Kantianism (G87 13, 18–19, 23). On Heidegger's account, Nietzsche belongs to an important strand of the Kantian tradition, which tended to read Kant's critical philosophy as an account of human psychology.[34] More "orthodox" Neo-Kantians, such as Herman Cohen and Wilhelm Windelband, rejected psychologistic or naturalistic readings of Kant in favor of a theory of logical forms or transcendental values.[35] Naturalistic Neo-Kantians, on the other hand, interpreted the structures of sensibility and understanding, described in the *Critique of Pure Reason,* as psychological faculties.

According to Heidegger, Nietzsche is one of the more important representatives of this particular strand of "heterodox" Kantianism. Heidegger outlines this reading in a 1937 seminar:

> Nietzsche's beginning [*Ansatz*]. Neo-Kantian positivism: 1. receptive material, 2. logic. Logic as that of the common intellect; mutual intelligibility requires that it be *fixed*, corresponding marks and signs, while in itself everything is "in flux." (This flux, then, as the struggle of the will to power.) This fixation is required for self-assertion and enhancement [*Steigerung*]. (G87 57)

For Heidegger, Nietzsche essentially takes over the Kantian schema of passive sensibility and active, synthetic understanding as a way of conceptualizing human cognition. The "flux" of irrational sense-data is synthesized or "fixated" by the intellect. Nietzsche, influenced by nineteenth-century Darwinism, held that this activity could ultimately be explained in terms of the struggle for power inherent in the natural order. In other words, in the

---

32. Julian Young comes close to articulating this aspect of Heidegger's reading of Nietzsche in Young (2005): 105.

33. Heidegger's "subjectivist" reading of Nietzsche has recently been defended by Ibáñez-Noé (2002). Ibáñez-Noé explicitly recognizes Heidegger as a pioneer of this way of interpreting Nietzsche.

34. For a discussion of this "naturalistic" stream of post-Kantian thought, see Koehnke (1991).

35. See Anderson (2005).

interests of power, human beings impose order and coherence on an other-wise meaningless stream of becoming. As Heidegger puts it, the "categories of reason," including the concepts of "value" and "meaning," are understood by Nietzsche as "perspectives of utility" established solely for the enhance-ment of power (G87 51). Nietzsche's theory thus mingles "biologism," i.e., nineteenth-century Darwinism, and "axiology" (G87 87). The resulting view is characterized in a sketchy note as follows: "Kant—critical idealism— Nietzsche—*biological*—perspectival *idealism*! Thinking as representing" (G87 148).

One of the consistent themes sounded in Heidegger's later discussions of Nietzsche is the latter's naturalizing or "biologizing" of the Kantian sub-ject, which still retains its place as the source of meaning and intelligibil-ity. *Ego vivo*, or "I live," replaces Descartes's *ego cogito*, or "I think," as the defining characteristic of human subjectivity (G87 87; G46 197). That is, in line with the broader tradition of naturalistic or "heterodox" Neo-Kantianism, Nietzsche rethinks the abstract concept of reason as such, trace-able from Descartes, through Kant, to Fichte, as the embodied subject of a life. Living, which ultimately means will to power, displaces thinking as the key to explaining human cognition and human action. "Life," rather than "reason," becomes the principle and the criterion for the positing of values (G5 266/169). While Neo-Kantian value theorists, such as Windelband and Rickert, strenuously resisted any view that placed biological drives at the center of an account of normativity, Nietzsche seems to have embraced this "biologistic" viewpoint.[36] According to Heidegger, Nietzsche conceives of the subject exclusively in terms of the "will to power" (G51 47/40). Will to power, of course, is the metaphysical principle that underlies nature as a whole in Nietzsche's thought. To redefine subjectivity as will to power, then, is to naturalize the subject in Nietzschean terms.

Given the enmity of "orthodox" Neo-Kantians from both the "Marburg" and "Baden" schools toward Nietzsche and his vitalistic epigones, Heidegger's reading appears to stretch credulity. However, Heidegger is cer-tainly to be commended for attempting to locate Nietzsche's thought within the broader trends of the age.[37] Moreover, his account is not predicated ulti-mately on philological correctness, but on the cogency of his overall analysis of modern culture. Assuming that modern culture as a whole is the macro-level expression of a deep framework, such that meaning and intelligibility

36. For Rickert's rejection of this attempt to "naturalize" normativity, see Rickert (1999b).

37. In this much, Heidegger anticipates recent Nietzsche scholarship, which has also tried to situation Nietzsche more firmly in his own historical context. Michael Steven Green, in his recent monograph, uncovers Nietzsche's connection with a particular strain of nineteenth-century Kantianism. See Green (2001). Other works that attempt to due justice to Nietzsche's historical situation include Poellner (1995) and Small (2001).

are derived from interests, the idea that the Neo-Kantians and Nietzsche are philosophical cousins begins to seem considerably more plausible. Indeed, both Nietzsche and the Neo-Kantians maintained that meaningful experience has its roots in the synthesizing activity of the human subject. The Baden Neo-Kantians, concerned as they were with consolidating the achievements of modern science and culture, took this basic claim in one direction in attempting to uncover a solid foundation for the normativity in play in all domains of cultural activity. Nietzsche, who was far more skeptical of the achievements of the age, went in a different direction, using the basic Kantian insight as a kind of corrosive agent designed to eat away at the pretensions of science, morality, and religion. The basic Kantian insight, however, figures importantly into both projects.

Anti-Realism and Religion

Up to this point, I have presented (1) Heidegger's general philosophy of culture, (2) his conception of "subjectivism" as the guiding "understanding of being" at work in the modern age, (3) the "symptoms" of this subjectivism, and (4) its dominant philosophical expressions. One final piece of the puzzle remains—one that is particularly important for grounding a fuller appreciation of Heidegger's phenomenology of religion. When viewed simply as expressions of subjectivism, the salient features of the religious situation of the age and its dominant philosophical articulations are likely to have at least some internal connection. After all, on Heidegger's account, philosophical positions are simply refined articulations of the same tacit "understanding of being" that grounds cultural phenomena, including *religious* phenomena. Yet, rather than leaving the matter thus, Heidegger defines more precisely the connection between philosophical *theories* of religion and the conceptual paradigms of the age. Here again, Baden Neo-Kantianism and Nietzsche occupy center-stage in Heidegger's reflections. A look at what Heidegger says about Neo-Kantian and Nietzschean theories of religion brings the ultimate targets of his phenomenology of religion into focus.

According to Heidegger, both the Neo-Kantians and Nietzsche adopt *anti-realism* in their theories of religion. Such theories tend to blend *metaphysical* claims, e.g., about the existence of God, with broadly *semantic* views about the meaning and structure of religion. In the case of late nineteenth-century and early twentieth-century anti-realism about religion, the broad post-Kantian consensus that traditional theistic metaphysics is no longer tenable often served to motivate the theories. Heidegger, however, in keeping with his sharp distinction between *ontic* discourse (i.e., discourse about what exists) and *ontological* discourse (i.e., discourse about structures of meaning or intelligibility), is largely uninterested in the metaphysical aspect of anti-realism. Indeed, one might point out—in support of Heidegger's more circumscribed concerns—that problems about how to make evaluative judgments, how to conduct one's life, and what to care about are all still important issues, regardless of one's metaphysical views. Thus, for Heidegger, what is important about Neo-Kantian and Nietzschean theories of religion is their account of the meaning, values, and norms that are distinctive to religion.

The Baden Neo-Kantians (and various fellow-travelers), while anti-realists, were considerably less hostile to religion than was Nietzsche. They tended to view themselves as continuing Kant's project of "making room for faith," though strictly within the limits set by critical idealism.[38] Heidegger, while mostly critical of Neo-Kantian theories of religion, does seem to have appreciated their efforts in this regard.[39] This, no doubt, explains part of the young Catholic Heidegger's attraction to Baden Neo-Kantianism, as evidenced in several letters to Heinrich Rickert from the 1910s (HR 15, 20, 37). Nietzsche, on the other hand, being the self-proclaimed "Anti-Christ" that he was, certainly had no time for reviving Kant's efforts in the philosophy of religion. Instead, he viewed the "death of God" as a positive historical event that cleared the way for a new cultural paradigm.

The earliest hint that Heidegger views the Neo-Kantians as anti-realists can be found in notes on medieval mysticism dating from 1918 and 1919. In a sketchy series of observations, Heidegger maintains that the Neo-Kantian attempt to ground religion in the domain of a priori normativity, by positing a kind of "atheoretical validity" that applies to religious ideas, ultimately goes astray because it belongs "in a space of a heterogeneous systematic (transcendentalism)" (G60 323–324). "Transcendentalism" is clearly meant to refer to Kantian "transcendental" or "critical" idealism. This brand of idealism is characterized by a picture of human cognitive activity according to which concepts are imposed on brute sense-data through the spontaneous activity of the mind. Such a position can be found, for example, in Rickert's *Der Gegenstand der Erkenntnis*, a work which Heidegger studied quite closely up until the 1920s.[40] On the Kantian picture, no intuitions are ever

---

38. See, for example, Rickert (1999a): 402.

39. In notes from 1918 and 1919, Heidegger approvingly quotes passages from Wilhelm Windelband's essay "Das Heilige" (G60 314–315). The same essay, along with Jonas Cohn's "Religion und Kulturwerte," are cited in SS 1919 (G56–57 145/123). Later, in *Being and Time*, Heidegger includes a generally favorable review of Ernst Cassirer's *Philosophie der symbolischen Formen* (SZ 51/490).

40. In a letter dated 27 January 1917, Heidegger relates his renewed study of this work directly to Rickert (HR 37). In a letter of 14 February 1928, Heidegger admits that the *Grenzen der naturwissenschaftlichen Begriffsbildung* has had a more lasting impact on his thought. Essentially the same Kantian or "critical" picture of human cognition can be discerned in this work, which applies it to historical science.

capable of anchoring "God" in empirical reality, the only domain in which assertions about existence or non-existence are appropriate. Instead, "God" plays the role of a regulative ideal, derived ultimately from the interests of reason.

A considerably more detailed account of Neo-Kantian anti-realism is offered in Heidegger's first lecture courses after World War I (KNS 1919, SS 1919). At the outset of the KNS 1919 course, Heidegger notes that the "holy," the defining category of religion, is a "value" for Neo-Kantians like Windelband (G56–57 9/8). A value is an "ideal ought as the principle of critical valuational judgment for everything that is" (G56–57 38–39/32). There is no sense that a "value" has any metaphysical status. Instead, it functions precisely like an "idea" in Kant's system; rather than serving to enlarge our knowledge of reality, an "idea" or "value" simply serves as a kind of rule for making judgments. In the following semester, SS 1919, Heidegger observes how the concept of "value" is rooted in the Neo-Kantians' shared interest in fulfilling the idealist project of consolidating modern culture. "Culture" in this case means "the formation and perfection of mankind's rational determinations, rules, and aims" (G56–57 133/113). Kant's critical idealism constitutes the framework for the "philosophy of culture" later inaugurated by Wilhelm Windelband (G56–57 140–141/119). The normativity that is in play in various domains of human culture is not, according to Windelband, to be grounded on some metaphysical reality like God or the Platonic Ideas. As Heidegger puts it, "The question is not about transcendent realities but about logical foundations. This question is not transcendent, but transcendental" (G56–57 142/120). The goal of the philosophical project is not to "copy the world," but to determine the norms or rules of rational activities, including *religion* (G56–57 144–145/122–123).

Neo-Kantian philosophy of culture, which included accounts of religion, was explicitly designed as a response to skeptical challenges against the normative authority of reason. Throughout the late nineteenth and early twentieth centuries, assorted historicists, relativists, and vitalists had all attacked the idea that there are universally valid norms governing activities as diverse as science, morality, and aesthetic judgment. The Neo-Kantian project was to undercut these attacks by showing how certain norms, grounded in ideal "values," were presupposed by all rational activity, including that of the skeptics.

However, what is distinctively Neo-Kantian is the claim that "values" do not exist; instead they are goals native to the interests of reason. For Windelband, Kant's achievement was to open up the possibility of deriving "every cultural value" from "the kingdom [*Reich*] of rational goals," as exemplified above all by the views developed in the *Critique of Practical Reason*, the *Critique of Judgment,* and *Religion Within the Limits of*

Reason Alone.[41] The philosophical approach that takes its cue from these exemplary treatments involves "uncovering the universally valid presuppositions of the activities of reason [*Vernunfttätigkeiten*] upon which everything that we call culture ultimately rests."[42] These "activities of reason" are goal-oriented behaviors that are responsive to evaluative judgments. Such judgments themselves, according to Windelband, are concerned with the "relation to a *purpose* [*Zweck*] or a *value* [*Wert*], which the subject ought to either acknowledge or recognize."[43] Like other "orthodox" Neo-Kantians, Windelband is convinced that naturalistic accounts of normativity, which tend to derive values from the biological and psychological needs of particular individuals (or of the species as a whole), cannot adequately address the "question of the justification or rationality of evaluations."[44] Thus, the "goals" or "values" that underwrite the rationality of various cultural activities must be those of abstract reason as such, which Windelband calls "normative consciousness [*Normalbewußtsein*]."[45]

This move, in turn, provides the basis for Windelband's account of religion. "God," according to Windelband, is just a way of depicting to ourselves the transcendence of values vis-à-vis local interests, as well as their unity as expressions of the interests of reason as such.[46] Despite his own explicit concerns about the distortions inherent in earlier rationalist theories of religion, Windelband ultimately holds that religion just is the "life of reason," that is, the way that individuals commit themselves to recognizing the validity of the values inherent in the interests of reason.[47]

This account of religion, and similar ones offered by Windelband's disciples Heinrich Rickert and Jonas Cohn, are clear examples of the kind of anti-realism that I am arguing is the primary target of Heidegger's phenomenology of religion. What is distinctive about the accounts offered by the Baden Neo-Kantians is not so much their position with respect to theistic metaphysics, but rather their view of the meaning of religion. Starting from the larger framework of transcendental idealism, Windelband and his students try to account for the hold that religion has on people by appealing to the interests of reason as such. The norms and values in play in religion, like those involved in all the domains of culture, are derived from these interests. However much such accounts are designed to "make room for faith," they

41. Windelband (1911a): 258–259.
42. Ibid., 262.
43. Windelband (1920): 245.
44. Ibid., 251–252.
45. Ibid., 255.
46. Windelband (1911b): 282; (1920): 256–257.
47. Windelband (1911b): 282.

clearly diverge from the understanding of religion as a response to an antecedent domain of value.

In SS 1920, Heidegger explores the nature and provenance of the sorts of theories offered by Windelband and his students. He begins with the observation that the Neo-Kantian project is to justify the normative force of judgments that are employed in various cultural domains. In this regard, Heidegger observes:

> For the most part, one is not clear about how religion fits into such cultural systems. Either one posits it as a further, unique domain of culture, or one sees it in simply the pious shaping [Gestaltung] and adoption [Aufnahme] of the three domains [science, art, morality] mentioned previously. Or, one doubts whether it should, in general, be viewed as a cultural creation; but then it is still uncertain as to which autonomous form of the self-development of spirit it ought to be reduced, and how the connection between religion and the domain of culture should be conceived. (G59 19)

Religion, on the Neo-Kantian view, is explicitly regarded as part of a larger totality called "culture," which is itself understood as the "self-development of spirit." The task for the philosophy of religion is to integrate religion, so understood, into the philosophy of culture as a whole. This means, in practice, either that religion needs to be assimilated to another domain, or that the norms unique to religion must receive their own anchoring in transcendental consciousness. Either way, religious meaning is derived from the interests of reason. Heidegger dubs this whole approach "cultural idealism," for it attempts to derive "the sense of all the vitality and actuality of life" by using the conceptual tools of "critical idealism" (G59 140). This designation is intended, no doubt, to bring home the anti-realist character of this school. Values and norms are "ideal"; they have no metaphysical reality, but are instead the goals that are postulated by the interests of reason. Religion is assimilated completely to "culture" as a human activity grounded in the spontaneity of human reason—religion becomes *Bildungsreligion* (G59 141). The appropriate concept of God is derived from this general idealist "idea of constitution" (G59 141).

In WS 1920–1921, Heidegger discusses in some detail the work of Ernst Troeltsch, the leading philosopher of religion at the time. He reads Troeltsch, if not as a card-carrying Neo-Kantian, at least as a "fellow traveler."[48] Troeltsch shares the Baden School's insistence that "There is a synthetic

---

48. This reading of Troeltsch is, of course, not entirely implausible. For example, in "Wesen der Religion und der Religionswissenschaft," Troeltsch aligns himself with the idealist camp. See Troeltsch (1922a): 457, 487–496. This is even more pronounced in Troeltsch (1922b).

a priori of religion like the logical, ethical, or aesthetic a priori" (G60 21). "God," on Troeltsch's view, becomes a name for the highest ideals that are immanent to human reason. "From the teleological nexus of (transcendental) consciousness one comes to the ultimate meaning [*Sinn*] that demands the existence of God" (G60 24). This same Neo-Kantian theory of value is discussed in Heidegger's works from the late 1930s as well. In "The Age of the World-Picture," which recapitulates the analysis given first in SS 1920, Heidegger argues that "values" are simply the "objectifications of needs as goals" set within the larger context of "culture" (G5 101/77). In the *Beiträge zur Philosophie*, Heidegger implicates Neo-Kantianism in the "idolization [*Vergötzung*]" of culture (G65 117/82). In "Überwindung der Metaphysik" (1938–1939), Heidegger mocks Kant's famous attempt to "make a place for 'faith'" (G67 92)—a project which, as I have already discussed, was taken up enthusiastically by some of the more important Neo-Kantians. The "holy," rather than being a transcendent source of meaning, is taken along with other values to "encompass the goals of 'culture'" (G67 118).

Throughout the decades following World War I, Heidegger maintains an ongoing interest in Neo-Kantian theories of religion as influential and robust instantiations of a specific kind of anti-realism. While his close engagement with Neo-Kantianism in the early 1920s has certainly been noted in the scholarly literature, his continued interest in this expression of modern sub-jectivism in the late 1930s has been universally overlooked. Heidegger consis-tently reads the Neo-Kantians, especially the members of the Baden School, as holding a theory of religion with the following features. First, religion belongs (however uncomfortably) within the larger pattern of norm-governed human activity called "culture." Second, as a phenomenon of culture, reli-gion must be explained within the framework provided by "critical" or "tran-scendental" idealism. Following Lotze, the Baden Neo-Kantians interpreted transcendental idealism as a systematic articulation of the a priori conditions of experience, and they understood these conditions as *rules* for judgments derived from universal values. This whole complex of a priori conditions belongs, however, to human reason, not to a transcendent domain of things-in-themselves. More specifically, the anchor for the explanation of culture is reason's interest in itself. Cultural activities like art, science, and moral life are made possible by a priori rules and values—and, so the Baden School reasoned, this must be true of religion as well. While Windelband, Rickert, and Troeltsch differed as to the details of their accounts, they all shared the common view that there must be a "religious a priori." Their views are char-acteristically semantic anti-realist views because they explicitly entail that the meaning of religion is derived from norms built into human reason.

That Nietzsche is an anti-realist about religion is certainly not an insight unique to Heidegger. However, when read against the background of his larger theory of modern culture, Nietzsche's anti-realism takes on a special significance. Rather than being an episode in the history of atheism, Nietzsche's anti-realism is an expression of the deep framework which, for Heidegger, unifies the "flight of the gods," the disenchantment of nature, and Neo-Kantian value theory. Hence, it comes as no surprise that Heidegger, in SS 1937, places the notion of "creating gods [*Götterschaffen*]" at the very center of his understanding of Nietzsche (G87 7). For Heidegger, this alleged "God-forming instinct" is closely connected with the paradigmatic status of art in Nietzsche's metaphysics—"art as *the* metaphysical activity of *life—creating*" (G87 7). Again, the core of Nietzsche's whole conception of religion is, for Heidegger, the idea that "man is here—whether strong or weak—in each case inventive and creative" (G87 194). That is, whether the "gods" created by human beings enhance life or diminish it, these "gods" remain human creations through and through.

"Creativity" is, as Heidegger points out in WS 1938–1939, "a basic capacity for *setting goals, limits, and measures as such*" (G46 174, emphasis added). Creativity plays a role in Nietzsche that corresponds closely to the role played by "normative consciousness" in Baden Neo-Kantianism. Creativity, on Heidegger's reading of Nietzsche, is the capacity to construct normative meaning. Like an artist who imposes her idea onto brute matter, a human being constructs the norms by which the reality of life is to be judged. For Heidegger, what is interesting about Nietzsche is not that he denies the metaphysics of theism, but rather his interpretation of religion within the framework of a broader philosophy of culture. After all, atheism is surely not a novel thesis with Nietzsche, so, Heidegger might have reasoned, it simply *cannot* be what is interesting about Nietzsche's views on religion. On Heidegger's reading, Nietzsche holds that religion was never *really* about metaphysics at all. Instead, it exemplifies a more general process whereby human beings *create* meaning for themselves. The import of the famous "God is dead" is not so much that a particular metaphysical theory is false, but rather that the values that have oriented a particular culture no longer hold sway. Thus, on Heidegger's reading, Nietzsche's view on religion is also anti-realist in the same way as that of the Baden Neo-Kantians. It is a view about the meaning of cultural activities like religion, according to which the norms and values that structure these activities are derived from human "creativity" rather than from the world as such.

In the 1940s, Nietzsche's anti-realism again figures prominently in Heidegger's accounts of his thought. For example, in SS 1944, while discussing the "death of God," Heidegger notes that, for Nietzsche, "The supersensible is not something that exists for itself, but rather is the *posit* of the *will to power*" (G87 259). In the following semester, interrupted by Heidegger's conscription into Hitler's *Volksturm*, Heidegger is even more emphatic about the significance of Nietzsche's anti-realism. "This is one of Nietzsche's essential thoughts, i.e., that the gods are 'created' by man. They are 'created' according to the particular [*jeweiligen*] 'religious talent' of peoples" (G50 107–108). More explicitly: "God and the gods are a 'product' of man" (G50 108). All of this rests, according to Heidegger, on Nietzsche's subjectivism and the conception of the subject as "one who creates [*Schaffenden*]" (G50 109). The Nietzschean conception of the subject, however, differs from that of the Neo-Kantians. For the Neo-Kantians, the values that guide judgments in various domains of culture are derived from *reason*. For Nietzsche—as Heidegger puts it in a 1946 essay—life, not reason, is the principle of the setting of goals (G5 226–227/169). Hence, "values are the conditions, posited by the will to power itself, of the will to power itself" (G5 232/173).

The two streams of philosophy that, for Heidegger, represent the dominant philosophical interpretations of modernity are, then, thoroughly anti-realist in their respective conceptions of religion. This is, of course, what is to be expected if the work of the Baden Neo-Kantians and of Nietzsche indeed express the "subjectivism" that shapes modern culture as a whole. With subjectivism as the reigning deep framework, things show up as being meaningful only relative to human projects, not in themselves. Rather than having to adapt to a pre-given normative order, human beings *impose* normative order on reality as suits their own particular goals. The anti-realist conceptions of religion espoused by the Baden Neo-Kantians and by Nietzsche, while different in many important respects, both reflect this general situation. The meaning of religious practices, for these theories, is not determined by a pre-given, divine domain of value and meaning. Instead, religion is understood as a cultural activity, the meaning of which is dependent entirely on human subjectivity. To Heidegger, theories such as these both reflect and entrench the religious crisis of the modern age. The aim of his phenomenology of religion is to challenge the assumptions that have precipitated this crisis, and to suggest a new, non-subjectivist, way of conceiving of religion.

TWO

Heidegger's Early Phenomenology of Religion

The most fecund, and so most thoroughly examined, period in Heidegger's work on the phenomenology of religion is the period that began in the final years of World War I and ended (roughly) with the appearance of *Being and Time*. During this period, Heidegger gave his only two lecture courses entirely devoted to this topic (1920–1921), gave a guest lecture on Luther (1924), and presented an address on the relationship between phenomenology and theology at Marburg (1927). Heidegger identified himself at this stage variously as a "Christian theo-*logian*," as a phenomenologist of religious life, and as a philosopher whose work was to prepare a new departure in theology. The aim of this chapter is to provide an exposition of some of the key elements of Heidegger's phenomenology of religion during this seminal period.

I begin by summarizing, in advance, some of the central themes in Heidegger's early work, themes that can be grouped together under the broader concept of "ontological realism." Next, I briefly examine three of the most important influences on the development of these key ideas: F. D. E. Schleiermacher, Edmund Husserl, and Adolf Reinach. Having thus laid the groundwork for understanding Heidegger's achievement in this period, I then examine his earliest efforts (1917–1919) in the phenomenology of religion.

Many of the ideas sketched out here recur throughout the remainder of Heidegger's long intellectual career. Next, I turn to the justly famous lecture course on Pauline Christianity (WS 1920–1921), showing how the ideas developed in the preceding years are more fully developed and articulated in this course. Finally, I examine the lecture course on Augustine's *Confessions* (SS 1921), Heidegger's last that was entirely devoted to a religious topic. Throughout my discussion, I show how Heidegger's ideas develop through a critical dialogue with Neo-Kantianism, and how the view that unifies all of this diverse material is a kind of "ontological realism" about religion.

Fundamental Themes

In his writings on religion composed between the end of World War I and the publication of *Being and Time*, Heidegger covers a significant amount of ground. In his attempts to work out a phenomenological account of religious life, he examines both classic sources, such as the New Testament, Augustine, and Luther, and the work of contemporary theorists like Rudolf Otto, Ernst Troeltsch, and Adolf Reinach. His oeuvre contains everything from fragmentary jottings to sustained, detailed expositions of key texts in the history of religion. The principal sources for Heidegger's emerging phenomenology of religion are: (1) notes for a planned course on medieval mysticism, dating from 1918 and 1919; (2) notes and student transcripts of the WS 1920–1921 lecture course on Paul's epistles; (3) notes and student transcripts of the SS 1921 lecture course on Augustine; and (4) the text of an address delivered at Marburg in 1927, entitled "Phenomenology and Theology." These are, however, by no means the only sources for Heidegger's views. Indeed, discussions of the phenomenology of religion and of religious and theological themes are scattered throughout his lectures, unpublished essays, and correspondence from this period.

In view of the breadth and volume of material relevant to the topic, the principal concepts and themes that anchor Heidegger's phenomenology of religion need to be clarified at the outset. This will serve to guide the reader through the often difficult territory of Heidegger's scattered musings on religion from this early period of his career. The themes enumerated below do not exhaust Heidegger's insights regarding religion, but they do capture the most characteristic and enduring elements of his unique position. Three core moments can be identified: (1) religion as being-in-the-world, (2) the "grace-character" of religious life, and (3) the problematic of the "givenness" or "objecthood [*Gegenständlichkeit*]" of God in religious experience. Taken together, these elements characterize Heidegger's considered position on the nature of religious life during this stage of his career.

For ease of exposition, this position as a whole can be designated *onto-logical realism*. Unlike the Neo-Kantian and Nietzschean theories considered in the preceding chapter, Heidegger's interpretation of the immanent sense of religious life is robustly *realist*. According to Heidegger, God, as the anchor of the meaning of religious life, cannot be viewed as merely a regulative idea (Neo-Kantianism) nor as a convenient fiction (Nietzsche). Rather, the meaning of religious practices like prayer, worship, social action, and theological reflection all depend upon a basic response to an independent realm of meaning. Religious life itself, the total complex of practices that are thus inherently referred to God, is experienced as a gracious gift. At the same time, while no less concretely given, God's objective reality is not like that of the objects of sense perception. Instead, God is given as the ultimate *horizon* or *background* of religious life. God is present to people in a largely tacit or pre-thematic way. The pre-theoretical understanding of being rooted in this awareness of God is "lived out" in religious life.

It is worth pausing here to ask, once again, what kind of a "realist" is Heidegger? In order to understand his position properly, several crucial distinctions need to be drawn. First of all, Heidegger's realism is *semantic* rather than *metaphysical*. One can liken his position on religion to his more famous discussion of the correspondence theory of truth in *Being and Time*. Heidegger's conception of truth as "disclosedness" is not offered as a *rival* to the correspondence theory, but rather as a completely different *sort* of theory, one that deals with the underlying patterns of human life that make assertions (which can be true or false) possible in the first place. For Heidegger, philosophy is a *hermeneutical* enterprise, the goal of which is to figure out the *meaning* of human life in the sense of the underlying patterns that render it intelligible. His realism about religion is a claim that is embedded within the framework of this larger project. His position is that a kind of realism (as to which kind, more below) is the best interpretation of the inherent structure of religious ways of life.

Heidegger is not, or at least not *primarily*, interested in the question of whether religious beliefs and practices successfully refer to a mind-independent reality. He would, of course, recognize that views about this latter question often motivate interpretations of religious life, but his interest is in the latter, viewed in relative isolation from any motivating metaphysical position. Thus, Heidegger's position is that realism best articulates the intelligible structure of religion as a way of life. Put in a different way, the *sense* of religious life embodies the fact that religious meaning is imparted or discovered, rather than created. Characteristically religious attitudes and activities are responsive to, rather than creative of, religious meaning and value. So, for example, Heidegger would maintain that the best interpretation of the Mass is *not* that people are depicting their values to themselves in some crude way, but rather that people are responding with gratitude to the divine gift of new life.

The second important distinction to make, for the purposes of clarification, concerns the motives for Heidegger's realism. His motives for adopting the position under discussion are *phenomenological* rather than *theological*. For some, the best argument for semantic realism about religion would be, quite simply, that the claims made by a particular religion are true. To continue with the previous example, one might maintain that the reason to think that the Eucharistic prayer aims at linking a community with God is because there is a God, and that God as instituted the sacrament as a special means of sharing Himself with the faithful. Or, similarly, one might reject anti-realist theories of religion, as does, for example, Alvin Plantinga, on the grounds that theism is true, and so there is no longer any obvious philosophical motivation for concocting anti-realist interpretations of religion.

While Heidegger may well have been sympathetic to such views, the motivations for his realism are different. They are *phenomenological*. This means, for one thing, that anti-realist interpretations of religion fail on *interpretive* grounds. They crucially and fatally misrepresent the immanent sense of religious life, largely due to a prior commitment to the explanatory framework bequeathed by modernist philosophy of culture. In this respect, Heidegger's critique of anti-realist accounts of religion is isomorphic with his more well-known critique of skepticism and of post-Cartesian epistemology in general in *Being and Time*. In §13 of that work, Heidegger argues that classical epistemological puzzles, notably the problem of the "external world," are rooted in allegedly "superficial" reinterpretations of the basic structure of human existence, i.e., being-in-the-world (SZ 59–60/86–87). The problem with skepticism, in this instance, is not its denial of some *metaphysics*, but rather its faulty premises.[1] In just the same way, Heidegger maintains that anti-realist accounts of religion are motivated by prior commitments to a particular explanatory scheme, rather than by careful reconstruction of the phenomena of religious life. Heidegger's own position is that a rigorous examination of concrete religious life shows that realism expresses its core meaning. What shapes religious life and motivates the commitments of religious people is the prior givenness—as an experienced reality—of religious meaning. A religion that proceeds by *creating* meaning willy-nilly is, on Heidegger's view, *not* a religion.

Heidegger's theory is also *phenomenological* in the sense that he grounds his case upon the careful exposition of the structures of certain characteristically religious attitudes and activities. This coheres with Heidegger's more general approach to doing phenomenology in other domains. His expositions begin with *exemplary* phenomena, which provide what he sometimes calls a

---

1. For a good discussion of this point, see Rudd (2003): 55–59.

"fore-having [*Vorhabe*]," an initial grip, on the subject matter under investigation. For example, in KNS 1919, he takes his own daily activities as a lecturer as an example upon which he bases an analysis of pre-reflective significance in the "surrounding world" (G56–57 70–73/59–61). In WS 1919–1920, he uses examples like his daily routine, attending a concert, and participating in a religious organization in order to explicate what he calls the "world-character of life" (G58 32–35). In this same lecture course, he follows Dilthey in holding that autobiographical and confessional literature provides a window onto the development of a person's practical identity or "self-world" (G58 56–60). Anticipating his famous use of a hammer in *Being and Time*, in SS 1923 he uses household items like a dining room table and an old pair of skis to illustrate the concept of everyday significance (G63 90/69–70). Other, similar examples abound, not only in his early writings, but also in the famous discussions of the jug and the highway interchange in essays from the 1950s. Yet another well-known example of this basic approach is the 1935 essay "On the Origin of the Work of Art," where Heidegger takes a Van Gogh painting, a poem about a Roman fountain, a Greek temple, and the cathedral in Bamberg as exemplifications of the deep structure characteristic of works of art.

The basic thought at work in all of these examples is that particular phenomena, in virtue of the inherent intelligibility they possess, provide the point of entry for a deeper analysis of the structures that constitute this intelligibility. The same methodology is clearly present in Heidegger's account of religion. As in the examples cited above, Heidegger is perfectly willing to admit that he is assuming the exemplary status of certain phenomena. But, he also urges us to consider that such assumptions are not merely inescapable, but are also indispensable. In the case of religion, as will become more clear throughout the remainder of my discussion, Heidegger takes phenomena like devotion, mysticism, and the "feeling of absolute dependence" to be exemplary expressions of the sort of meaning that constitutes religious life as a unique configuration of attitudes, activities, and artifacts. Philosophical theories of religion, according to Heidegger, stand or fall according to their ability to render the structures that constitute the inherent intelligibility of these exemplary phenomena.

The final distinction to get clear about here concerns what it is that Heidegger is a realist about. The relevant options are *ontological* and *ontic* realism respectively. An ontic realist maintains that a particular entity or class of entities has mind-independent existence. So, for example, a realist about events holds that, in addition to particulars and their relations, the world also contains events that cannot be reduced without remainder to particulars and their relations. Heidegger would certainly have to agree that, *for religion*, certain beings or classes of beings—gods, demons, saints—have mind-independent existence. But the belief in the existence of particular beings or classes of beings is not what he thinks is characteristic of religious life.

More generally, Heidegger's philosophical interest is not in the "furniture of the universe." While he no doubt held views about what sorts of things exist and in what ways (how could one not?), his explicit concern, articulated time and again, is *transcendental*. That is, his philosophical concern is with the a priori patterns of meaning that render human life intelligible in whatever specific form it takes. In a typically elliptical yet illuminating statement from the opening pages of *Being and Time*, Heidegger announces that "The being of beings is not itself a being" (SZ 6/26). What Heidegger takes to be distinctive about religious ways of life is not the "furniture of the universe" that a particular religion asserts, but rather the underlying pattern of meaning, the "world" of that religion. It is *this* that is the subject of Heidegger's realism. His surprising claim is that the religious world is not the product of human subjectivity, but rather the condition for its possibility. Any meaningful way of life depends for its meaning on the a priori patterns that constitute a world.

Thus, for example, the attitudes, behaviors, and artifacts that are characteristic of being a professional philosopher are intelligible or meaningful because of a complex network of relations to which things get assigned. It is certainly the case that, for example, my fountain pen, my well-worn copy of *Being and Time*, and my neglected desk calendar are all, in the first place and for the most part, intelligible to me because of the web of interests expressed by the phrase "being a professional philosopher." But, for Heidegger, this web of interests only makes sense against the background of a prior network of meaningful relations "to which [*woraufhin*]" I assign myself (or, have been assigned, as the case may be) (SZ 86/119). In other words, "Dasein, in so far as it *is*, has always submitted itself already to a 'world' which it encounters, and this *submission* belongs essentially to its being" (SZ 87/120–121). In his 1929 essay, "On the Essence of Ground," Heidegger puts the point this way:

> World as a totality "is" not a being, but that from out of which Dasein *gives itself the signification* of whatever beings it *is able* to comport itself toward in whatever way. [. . .] World has the fundamental character of the "for the sake of . . .," and indeed in the originary sense that it first provides the intrinsic possibility for every factically self-determining "for your sake," "for his sake," "for the sake that," etc. (G9 157/121–122)

Heidegger's realism cannot amount to the claim that a world "exists"; a Heideggerian world is not the sort of thing about which it makes sense to ask whether or not it exists. But, realism certainly captures Heidegger's insistence that meaning is not dependent upon interests. Rather, interests are meaningful possibilities only because there is a world that a person always already inhabits.

During the years following World War I (and, as will be seen in chapter 3, throughout the rest of his career), Heidegger's ontological realism about religion is expressed by three key ideas or thematic concentrations that recur in virtually every one of his sustained discussions of religion. These ideas do not, strictly speaking, *constitute* his ontological realism; rather, they give it a more specific and focused articulation. Ontological realism does not *reduce* to one's holding or entertaining the ideas sketched out below. At the same time, however, these three ideas—being-in-the-world, the "grace-character" of religious life, and the "givenness" of the divine—help to define what is at stake in ontological realism about religion, and they serve to explicate the characteristic commitments of a typical ontological realist.

Being-in-the-world

At the very heart of Heidegger's account is the claim that religious life is a mode of what he later calls "being-in-the-world [*In-der-Welt-sein*]." "Being-in-the-world" is Heidegger's famous formulation, from *Being and Time*, of the fundamental structure of human existence as such. Beginning in WS 1919–1920, Heidegger had begun to examine what he there calls the "world-character" of life. This refers to the fact that, at the deepest, most immediate level, human life is lived "within" various overlapping contexts of meaning. The "within" or "in" of human "being-*in*-the-world" does not mean spatial containment, but rather "intimate familiarity, being-involved-with [*Sein-bei*]" (G20 213/158). That is, human beings as such inhabit contexts of meaning in a more or less tacit or pre-theoretical way. "World," in "being-in-the-world," does not refer to the totality of things that exist, but rather to a "transcendental" context of meaning that makes it possible for things to show up within human experience as *meaningful* or *intelligible*. As Heidegger puts it in his SS 1925 lecture course, the totality of things

> [I]s first and only present in a particular *correlation of references*. This referential context is itself a *closed totality*. It is precisely out of this totality that, for example, the individual piece of furniture in a room appears. My encounter with the room is not such that I first take in one thing after another and put together a manifold of things in order then to see a room. Rather, I primarily see a referential totality as closed, from which the individual piece of furniture and what is in the room stand out. (G20 252–253/186–187)

A world, then, is an inconspicuous, but no less concretely given, set of "correlations of meaning" or "meaningful contexts" (G20 276/203). At a pre-theoretical or tacit level, human beings "understand" this set of overlapping contexts (G20 285–286/209). This whole unified complex of "understanding" and "world" is what Heidegger calls "a *perfect* tense *a priori*," a structure that is "always already" in place prior to any thematic dealings with particular things (SZ 85/117). This is an "a priori" that is *not* simply reducible to conditions of subjectivity, but instead can be explicated without reference to "consciousness" or "subjectivity" in any sense.[2] Moreover, in the order of explanation, this structure is *prior to* interests. And, the "a priori" of "world" is not something that is inferred or arrived at through transcendental deduction, but rather it is immediately given in concrete human life. The tacit understanding of "world" is "lived out" or "explicated" in the concrete practices that constitute the stuff of everyday human life. Paradigmatically, our "understanding" of world is "articulated" in pre-reflective practices such as using tools for certain purposes. At the same time, however, our social interactions and our theoretical or scientific activities also grow out of this tacit understanding.

All of this will be quite familiar to students of Heidegger's work, and it represents one of his most characteristic insights. Less attention, however, has been paid to the significance of this whole conceptual apparatus for his account of the immanent sense of religious life. And yet, Heidegger himself explicitly draws our attention to this "application" of the concept of "being-in-the-world" in two pieces from the late 1920s. The first, and clearest, mention of this point can be found in the 1929 contribution to the Festschrift for Husserl, "Vom Wesen des Grundes." This passage is explicitly referred to by Heidegger almost two decades later in his "Letter on Humanism" (1946), widely regarded as the most important post–World War II manifesto of his philosophy. This suggests that long after Heidegger had moved away from talk of "being-in-the-world," he still regarded this concept as his signal contribution to the understanding of religion. The 1929 passage runs:

> The ontological interpretation of Dasein as being-in-the-world decides neither positively nor negatively concerning a possible being toward God. Presumably, however, the elucidation of transcendence first achieves an adequate concept of Dasein, and with respect to this being it can then be asked how things stand ontologically concerning the relation of Dasein to God. (G9 159/123)

Heidegger's point here is that "being-in-the-world," or "transcendence," is not to be taken in a *literal* or *ontic* sense as a claim about the impossibility of human beings relating to something "otherworldly." To the contrary, he suggests that this very concept provides the key to working out the *ontology*— i.e., an account of the immanent sense—of religious life. In other words, the religious meaning of certain attitudes, activities, events, and objects derives from a specifically religious world. A similar passage from the SS 1928 lecture course on Leibniz makes what looks to be substantively the same point. Indeed, this lecture course contains material that shows up almost verbatim in the 1929 essay quoted above. In the following passage, Heidegger again

---

2. See Dahlstrom (2001): 98.

points to the significance of the concept of "being-in-the-world" or "transcendence" for understanding religious life:

> The problem of transcendence must be drawn back into the inquiry about temporality and freedom, and only from there can it be shown to what extent the understanding of being qua superior power [*Übermacht*], qua holiness, belongs to transcendence itself as essentially ontologically different. The point is not to prove the divine ontically, in its "existence," but to clarify the origin of this understanding of being by means of the transcendence of Dasein [. . .]. (G26 211/165)

The relevance of the concept of "being-in-the-world" to the phenomenology of religion is by no means an artifact only of Heidegger's work after *Being and Time*. Instead, in WS 1920–1921, Heidegger orients his entire analysis of Pauline Christianity via the concept of "factical life-experience," which is "the whole active and passive attitude [*Stellung*] of the human being toward the world" (G60 11). As in discussions of "being-in-the-world" from SS 1925 and *Being and Time*, Heidegger wants to emphasize how "world" is not an object, but a context of meaning that is inhabited at a pre-thematic level by human beings. "'World' is that in which one can *live* (one cannot live in an object)" (G60 11). As examples, Heidegger offers the "arts and sciences": "Insofar as it is possible that I am absorbed by the arts and sciences such that I live entirely in them, the arts and sciences are to be designated as *genuine life-worlds*" (G60 11).

There can be no doubt, then, that "being-in-the-world" plays a central role in Heidegger's phenomenology of religion. Religious life has the same structure as human life in general—its immanent sense is anchored in the fact that religious people "always already" inhabit a domain of specifically *religious* meaning. On Heidegger's account, the heart of religion is not assent to a doctrinal system, nor a particular pattern of behavior, but what might be called *religiosity*, a way of *being*, of inhabiting a determinate "space" or "nexus [*Zusammenhang*]" of meaningfulness. The life of a religious person is shaped ahead of time by what we might call "religious alreadiness [*Gewesenheit*]" or a specifically *religious* "perfect tense *a priori.*" This tacit or pre-thematic "understanding" of religious meaning is "lived out" in religious life, primarily in the concrete practices and attitudes that are characteristic of a religious community. At the same time, the more rarefied flowerings of religious life, such as theological reflection, are anchored in the same structure. Far from being an alien imposition, religious doctrines and the reflective process involved in their formation grow out of the articulated understanding of religious meaning that lies at the very ground of religious life.

What, then, is it for something to have religious meaning, to be intelligible in a specifically *religious* way? This is an issue that Heidegger seems only to have settled after 1929, as will be shown in more detail in chapter 3. Still, quite early on, there are many suggestions about the direction that this account will take. Recall that Heidegger bases his account on characteristic phenomena like devotion, conversion, and the "feeling of absolute dependence." Religious meaning is what Heidegger calls the "content-sense [*Gehaltsinn*]" of these attitudes. Borrowing in part from Augustine's distinction between *uti* or use and *frui* or enjoyment, Heidegger argues that the content-sense of characteristically religious attitudes is something of absolute, transcendent, and incommensurable value, which utterly resists any reconfiguration in terms of instrumentality. To have religious meaning, then, is to find a home in a network of relations ordered to such an absolute.

The "Grace-Character" of Religious Life

In a now famous letter to his friend Elisabeth Blochmann, Heidegger relates how, on his view, *all* of life is marked by a mysterious "grace-character" (HB 14). That is, at the deepest level, the meaningful totality that is human life rests upon inscrutable depths.[3] This is particularly true of what he calls moments of "life-intensification," moments when the quotidian course of life is interrupted or thrown into relief and the possibility of an authentic existence dawns for a person.[4] Religious life, however, is paradigmatically distinguished by this "grace-character." This is something that Heidegger highlights again and again as being absolutely central to the instances of religious life that he examines in the 1920s. In medieval mysticism, Schleiermacher's "taste for the infinite," Adolf Reinach's conversion narrative, and the early Pauline community, the new life that has been gained is always viewed as coming from beyond the individual, as ultimately flowing from God. Taking these (and other) examples to be paradigmatic of religious life as such, Heidegger concludes that the "understanding" constitutive of the immanent sense of religious life is not something that can be achieved by human reason, but something that must be *given*. For religious life to be possible, then, human existence must be fundamentally *receptive* or *open* to a mysterious process in which meaning is *given* or *discovered*, rather than *created* or *constructed*. This, on Heidegger's view, is something that anti-realist theories of religion, like those of the Neo-Kantians and Nietzsche, are simply unable to treat appropriately.[5] That is, paradigmatically

---

3. See Van Buren (1994).

4. The nature of these "graced moments," and their significance for Heidegger's practical ideal of authenticity, is explored in detail in Crowe (2006).

5. This emphasis on the "grace-character" of religious worlds no doubt explains Heidegger's early enthusiasm for the new "crisis" theology of Barth, Gogarten, and their followers. Against the liberal theologians of the nineteenth century, who seemed to transform Christianity into a cultural achievement on a par with art and science, these new firebrands tried to recover a robust understanding of *grace* and of *revelation* as transcendent interruptions of human existence. Jewish contemporaries like Franz Rosenzweig and (following his encounter with Rosenzweig) Martin Buber made comparable moves. In Protestant circles, this new theological position issued in a renaissance of Luther studies, to which Heidegger himself was a notable contributor.

religious phenomena like conversion become internally unintelligible on anti-realist accounts, which derive all meaning back to human interests.

The "Givenness" or "Objecthood" of God

Another theme, closely connected with both of the preceding, is that of the "givenness" or "objecthood" of God. Again and again, Heidegger asks about the sense in which God is present to human experience. To put it in the Husserlian terms that Heidegger deploys in his 1918–1919 notes, the question is about the possible "fulfillment" of the "intention" or "meaning" of "God." That there is such a "fulfilling intuition" is something that Heidegger seems never to have doubted. The difficulty comes in determining what, precisely, this "fulfilling intuition" is. Heidegger never seems to arrive at an answer that he regards as wholly satisfactory. On the one hand, he is at pains to account for the kind of concrete religious experiences characteristic of medieval mysticism and Schleiermacher's concept of the "intuition" of the "universe." At the same time, Heidegger is well aware that God is never "given" in the same way that sensory objects are. By SS 1921, Heidegger seems to have tentatively concluded that God is indeed present to religious life *as a whole*, rather than in isolated experiences. Religious life as a whole is enacted or "lived out" *before* God.

Influences

As is the case with many of his most important ideas, Heidegger developed the central thematic complexes of his phenomenology of religion while in dialogue with other thinkers. On the one hand, Heidegger works out his ideas against the background of a critical confrontation with Baden Neo-Kantianism and related streams of thought. More positively, however, he also takes up the insights of others, transforms them in subtle ways, and shapes them into his own conception of the subject matter. In what follows, I briefly explore three of the most important influences on the development of Heidegger's phenomenology of religion. Friedrich Schleiermacher (1768–1834), Edmund Husserl (1859–1936), and Adolf Reinach (1883–1917) are each acknowledged by Heidegger as decisive influences on the development of his phenomenology of religion. I will consider each of these thinkers individually.

Friedrich Schleiermacher: Realism and Phenomenological Method

In notes collected together for a planned course on medieval mysticism, Heidegger examines two of Schleiermacher's principle works, *Über Religion* of 1799 and the later *Glaubenslehre*. Heidegger identifies Schleiermacher with his own "phenomenological attitude toward the religious experience"

(G60 319). He admires Schleiermacher's account of the essence of religion as "sense and taste for the infinite," as well as his realist inclinations (G60 320–321). In letters to Elisabeth Blochmann, written just prior to the end of World War I, Heidegger offers extensive advice for her regarding her ongoing research on Schleiermacher, and the vocabulary he uses in these letters echoes Schleiermacher's early works such as *Über Religion* and the *Monologen* (1800). In a more public setting, Heidegger declares Schleiermacher's significance to his students in KNS 1919 (G56–57 18).[6]

As Heidegger's notes attest, he takes Schleiermacher to be an exemplar of a rigorous phenomenological approach to the subject of religion. For Heidegger, Schleiermacher shows (1) that religion should not be assimilated blithely to other spheres of culture, and (2) that uncritical assumptions about the nature of religion ought to be jettisoned ahead of time. As Heidegger puts this point in one note, "foreign teleologies"—i.e., the evaluative categories immanent to non-religious cultural spheres—should be eliminated from a properly phenomenological account (G60 321). Schleiermacher uses the vocabulary of religious devotion and of penitential self-control to express the proper attitude that one should take to the study of religion:

> It is, after all, the first requirement of those who only conjure common spirits that onlookers, who want to see their manifestations and be initiated into their secrets, prepare themselves through abstinence from earthly things and through holy silence; then, without distracting themselves by the sight of other objects, they look with undivided attention at the place where the vision is to show itself. How much will I be permitted to insist on a similar obedience, since I am to call forth a rare spirit that does not deign to appear in any oft-seen familiar guise, a spirit you will have to observe attentively a long time in order to recognize it and understand its significant features.[7]

Heidegger enthusiastically appropriates the notion that phenomenological analysis requires a kind of discipline analogous to the exertions required of novices to religious orders. In WS 1919–1920, Heidegger takes up the metaphor of religious devotion and applies it to his own phenomenological method, which he was slowly working out at the time. He styles this method one of "being purely devoted [*hingegeben*] *to a genuine situation of life*" (G58 137; cf. G58 168). For Heidegger, this means, above all else, suspending the inherited conceptual frameworks that have hitherto governed theories of

---

6. John Van Buren offers the most extensive examination of Heidegger's reception of Schleiermacher between 1917 and 1920. For the facts of this reception, see Van Buren (1994): 147–148. For a more detailed account of the impact of Schleiermacher's moral and political philosophy on Heidegger "around the years 1917 through 1920," see ibid., 345–350.

7. Schleiermacher (1996): 18.

religion. In Schleiermacher's time, this meant avoiding the reduction of religion either to primitive morality or to primitive metaphysics. For Heidegger, the main danger was to be found in Neo-Kantian accounts which assimilated religion into the larger sphere of "culture," interpreted as a totality of activities organized around "values."

Another significant aspect of Schleiermacher's writings on religion for Heidegger is the way in which Schleiermacher combines *normative* and *descriptive* elements in his analysis. Schleiermacher's stated goal in *Über Religion* is "to lead" his listeners "to the innermost depths from which religion first addresses the mind."[8] In other words, his aim is to uncover the essential structure of religion as such. He argues that criticisms of religion largely focus on extraneous or contingent features of its various historical manifestations, whereas a truly fair-minded and rigorous evaluation would occupy itself with the thing itself. Besides getting the "thing itself" of religion right, however, Schleiermacher also wants to uncover the essence of religion in order to provide an immanent standard for judging these manifestations of religion. That is, the essence of religion, which Schleiermacher hopes to uncover through a disciplined analysis, provides a *normative* point of reference for the criticism of religion itself. "Let us rather," he writes, "subject the whole concept to a new consideration and create it anew from the center of the matter."[9] An obvious application of this recommendation can be found in the Fourth Speech, "On the Social Element in Religion; or, On Church and Priesthood," where Schleiermacher outlines an "ideal" church on the basis of his previous analysis of the essence of religion. This double character, at once normative and descriptive, is, as I have pointed out in the introduction, taken up by Heidegger into his own phenomenology of religion. That is, in addition to merely getting the facts straight about the "immanent sense" of religion, Heidegger is keenly interested in reclaiming the core of "Christianness" in the hopes that it could serve as a point of reference for critical evaluation of contemporary manifestations of religion.

A final element of Schleiermacher's work that strongly influenced Heidegger is his *realism*. Breaking with the dominant Kantian-Fichtean account of religion, according to which the concept of God is devoid of empirical content and has, at best, the status of a regulative ideal, Schleiermacher insists that the heart of religion is the concrete "intuition" of the universe. Religion, he writes, "longs to be grasped and filled by the universe's immediate influences in childlike passivity."[10] The religious person directly intuits "the infinite nature of totality, the one and all."[11] Schleiermacher understands

---

8. Ibid., 10.
9. Ibid., 73.
10. Ibid., 22.
11. Ibid., 23.

"intuition" in robustly *realist* terms; he likens it to the perception of light, which must be traced to the efficacy of a reality external to the mind.[12] "In religion," he writes, "the universe is intuited; it is posited as originally acting on us."[13] Schleiermacher, like many of his Romantic contemporaries, reacted against Fichte's formulation of transcendental idealism, which seemed to reduce the world to a construction of the ego.[14] Religion, with its powerful "intuition of the infinite," clears the way for what he calls a "higher realism."[15] "Idealism," he urges, "will destroy the universe by appearing to fashion it; it will degrade it to a mere allegory, to an empty silhouette of our own limit-edness."[16] Heidegger enthusiastically received Schleiermacher's emphasis on the *passivity* or *receptivity* inherent to religious experience, and found his anti-Fichtean realism a vital counterweight to the neo-Fichtean idealism of the Baden Neo-Kantians.[17]

Edmund Husserl

The importance of Heidegger's early readings of Husserl, and of his close association with him in Freiburg during World War I and for several years afterwards, has long been recognized. A full exposition and documenta-tion of Heidegger's many-sided intellectual (and personal) relationship with Husserl is certainly beyond the scope of the present discussion. One of Husserl's ideas in particular, however, is relevant to Heidegger's phenome-nology of religion. This is the all-important notion of "categorial intuition," developed in the *Logical Investigations*. In SS 1925, Heidegger declares this to be one of the central achievements of phenomenology. Four decades later, toward the end of his long career, Heidegger reiterates the centrality of this concept in his own intellectual development (ZSD 86; G15 11). Husserl's concept of "categorial intuition" is designed to help us make sense of striking fact about our ordinary discourse. In making assertions, we utilize different kinds of terms to which nothing in sensory perception corresponds. Husserl's examples are (1) so-called "logical forms" like "all," "this," "some," "not," "or," "is," "a," or "the"; (2) terms of comparison; and (3) terms that designate

---

12. Ibid., 25.

13. Ibid., 53.

14. On Schleiermacher's "higher realism" in its Romantic context, see Pinkard (2002): 150–151; and Beiser (2003): 175–176, 133–134. On the influence of Schleiermacher's *Speeches* and his realism on Friedrich Schlegel's intellectual development toward "higher realism," see Beiser (2002): 456–461.

15. Schleiermacher (1996): 24.

16. Ibid., 24.

17. Heidegger recognized Fichte's influence on the Neo-Kantians quite early (G56–57 142–143/121). As Heidegger quite rightly points out, there is an "unbroken relation" between Neo-Kantian philosophy of culture and "Fichte and the tradition of the great world-views of German idealism" (G56–57 145/123). For a recent discussion of this issue, see Heinz (1997).

classes and universals (LU II/2 129, 137ff.). In an assertion like "The desk is brown," the "intention" that constitutes the meaning of the terms "desk" and "brown" is readily "fulfilled" by straightforward perceptual experience. The same cannot, however, be said for the "logical form" term "is." In order to address this situation, Husserl argues that the truth of assertions like "The desk is brown" requires that the "intention" of terms like "is" also be fulfilled, only not in perceptual experience. Instead, the meaning of these terms is fulfilled in "categorial intuition" (LU II/2 142–143).

As Daniel O. Dahlstrom has pointed out in his discussion of Heidegger's reception of the notion of "categorial intuition," this doctrine distinguishes the phenomenological position from both positivism or empiricism, on the one hand, and Neo-Kantianism, on the other.[18] Unlike the radical empiricists, Husserl and Heidegger are not committed to analyzing all meaning in terms either of sensory perceptions (such as the famous "I see red here now") or the stipulated truths of formal languages. Unlike the Neo-Kantians, Husserl and Heidegger are also not forced to account for the categories and other "logical forms" by deriving them from forms of judgment or from some other capacity of the subject. For Heidegger, moreover, the significance of Husserl's doctrine is that it allows us to appreciate the way in which ordinary perception is "saturated" by non-sensory meaning. That is, meaning is given *within* the ordinary perceptions, not imposed upon them. Dahlstrom summarizes the implications of this idea for Heidegger's philosophy thusly: "Being is prethematically given yet retrievable for Heidegger along lines structurally parallel to the way being is availed (identified, experienced) but not yet thematized in categorial intuitions that saturate every level of ordinary (quotidian, everyday) perception."[19]

With respect to the phenomenology of religion, the doctrine of "categorial intuition" has two more focused implications. First of all, it provides Heidegger with a way of talking about the "immanent sense" or meaningful structure of religious experience as *contained within the experience itself.* His project then becomes one of drawing out, explicating, or articulating this "immanent sense." Heidegger maintains that this can be accomplished without resorting to the conceptual frameworks of the philosophy of culture that played such an important role in contemporary theories of religion. Second, the doctrine of "categorial intuition" provides Heidegger with the germ of an insight into the structure of religious experience itself. God, after all, is not present in straightforward perceptions, as are elements of the created order. And yet, religious experience is animated by a pervasive sense of the presence of God, and mystics and other religious virtuosi claim that direct

18. Dahlstrom (2001): 77–78, 95.
19. Ibid., 96.

awareness of God is possible. God, like categorial form, is not an object of sense-perception, and yet God is "given" all the same. For Heidegger, as will be shown in detail below, the "givenness" of God is structurally parallel (to borrow Dahlstrom's apt phrase) with the "givenness" of categorial forms.

Adolf Reinach

The final figure to be considered here whose work decisively impacted Heidegger's efforts in the phenomenology of religion in the years immediately following World War I is Adolf Reinach. Reinach was an early student of Husserl's at Göttingen, and like others from this circle received Husserl's more realist *Logical Investigations* more enthusiastically than his later works, which are characterized by a kind of transcendental idealism. While Reinach is best known for his philosophy of law and his contributions to the development of speech-act theory, the final years of his life were also occupied with the development of a phenomenology of religion, spurred by a dramatic conversion experience during his military service in Flanders in World War I.

For Heidegger, the most important aspect of Reinach's work was the application of something very much like Husserl's doctrine of "categorial intuition" to the phenomenology of religion. According to Heidegger, Reinach's "valuable" distinction between "explicit knowledge and knowledge immanent in experience" clears the way for moving beyond Neo-Kantian, idealistic theories of religion. In his notes on Reinach, Heidegger observes: "Validity and cognitive meaning of religious experience *genuine*—and still today a problem—entirely new kind of sphere, where mere analogizing with the aesthetic realm of values or with the taking of values in general does not suffice, if it does not, from the beginning, take us in the wrong direction. Here alone is the cure: radical analysis" (G60 325).

Reinach's notes, many jotted down while in the trenches in Flanders in 1916, contain the seeds of a concept of tacit or "immanent" knowledge in religious experience. For example, on 27 April 1916, Reinach observes that "Schleiermacher was indeed correct: the idea of God is immanent in every real religious experience."[20] On 2 May 1916, Reinach makes the following observations:

> It is never the case that we become sure of [God's] existence through thinking about God. Rather, while the religious experience is streaming over us [uns entquillt], God is at the same time posited as existing in accord with the sense of the content of the experience. Knowledge is then able to grasp hold of this existence in artificial abstraction.[21]

---

20. Reinach (1989): 592.
21. Ibid., 595.

In longer notes on the "Structure of Experience," excerpted later by Heidegger, Reinach writes: "We separate explicit items of knowledge and those that are immanent to experience. Thus, the enjoyment of an artwork is not knowledge, but it forms the foundation for, and releases from itself the knowledge that the picture is beautiful."[22]

Reinach goes on to apply this same distinction to the experience of "being-sheltered [Geborgensein] in God." In neither aesthetic experience nor religious experience is an inference required such as "I experience myself as being sheltered in God, so God must exist." Instead, the experience itself contains a *tacit* awareness of God. It is only later that explicit reflection is able to separate this tacit awareness from the experience as a whole. In the midst of the experience, when it is "streaming over us," as Reinach puts it, there can be no question of theoretically secure knowledge. At the same time, the experience makes no sense apart from the supposition that God, in fact, is present. The experience is, to use the language Heidegger adopts from Husserl's account of "categorial intuition," "saturated" with God.

Reinach's influence on Heidegger can be detected in each of the three core ideas expressive of his ontological realism about religion. First, the notion of "immanent knowledge" closely anticipates Heidegger's conception of "being-in-the-world" as a tacit, pre-thematic way of inhabiting a context of meaning. Second, Reinach's personalized descriptions of a religious experience "streaming over" a person cohere with Heidegger's own insistence on the "grace-character" of religious life. Finally, Reinach's appreciative borrowings from Schleiermacher points toward a way of thematizing the givenness of the divine in religious life. Reinach's path-breaking work on the phenomenology of religion helped Heidegger see a way past the intellectualist a priorism of Neo-Kantianism.

Heidegger's Earliest Sketches of a Phenomenology of Religion

At some point toward the end of World War I, Heidegger began a study of medieval mysticism and related issues with a view toward developing a phenomenology of religion. Some of this material was supposed to have been incorporated into a lecture course planned for early 1919, called "Philosophical Foundations of Medieval Mysticism." Heidegger never completed his notes for this lecture course, and it was in fact never held. Nevertheless, these notes, along with others dating from 1918, are still extant, and they provide a valuable window onto the first stages in the development of Heidegger's phenomenology of religion. In what follows, I will examine

---

22. Ibid., 610.

this body of material with a view toward the three primary themes outlined in the first section of this chapter.

In keeping with his chosen topic, i.e., medieval mysticism, Heidegger clearly indicates his interest in the problem of the "givenness" or "object-hood" of God in concrete religious experience. Medieval mystics, from Bonaventure to Eckhart, struggled to articulate what they took to be direct experiential encounters with divine reality. The following note, jotted down sometime in August 1919, points quite clearly at this theme:

> Constitution of religious objecthood: is God constituted in prayer? Or is he already somehow *given ahead of time* religiously in *faith* ('love')? And is prayer a specific comportment toward him? To what extent is there a possible multiplicity of types of constitution? Is there an essential connection between them? (G60 307)

In this passage, Heidegger uses the Husserlian terminology of "constitution" to express this central theme. The question here is, how is God "given" in experience? To say that God is "constituted" in prayer or in faith is not to say that human beings create or "project" God through their own mental activities. Instead, this is simply a way of saying that God is "given" or "intuited" in different ways in different religious acts. This brief note expresses one of the central problems of Heidegger's phenomenology of religion, i.e., that of the givenness or objecthood of God. Already one can see here Heidegger's caution and reticence in treating this theme. No categorical answers are given to the series of questions posed in this note. Instead, Heidegger seems to suspend judgment about the ultimate results of the phenomenological analysis. He leaves open the possibility that God is "given" in multiple ways. While his intuition is clearly that these multiple modes of givenness are somehow or other unified, Heidegger is not even willing to assert as much, but only to raise the question. This is a question that recurs time and again in the notes from 1918 and 1919, and in his lecture courses from 1920 and 1921. In addition, this passage also provides some insight into Heidegger's methodology. Determining religious meaning requires the identification and analysis of characteristically religious activities (e.g., prayer) and attitudes (e.g., faith).

Later in this same series of notes from 1919, Heidegger alludes to Eckhart's mysticism as a source that might bear fruit in articulating the givenness of God in experience: "The constitution of the experience of God (birth of God)" (G60 309). A bit later, the notes seem to indicate Heidegger's interest in Eckhart's own exposition of the "objecthood" of God as freedom from all determinations (G60 315–318). He does not arrive at any clear conclusions. The idea, however, is to determine religious meaning or the "content-sense" of religious attitudes and activities by analyzing the structure of a characteristic religious phenomenon like mystical experience. What

Heidegger seems to have gathered from this example is that God, the divine reality toward which the web of relations constituting the world of religion is ordered, is radically distinct from anything that occupies the normal domain of human concerns.

The theme of the "givenness" of the divine emerges in notes on Adolf Reinach, whose own musings on the phenomenology of religion, cut off by his death in Flanders, had come into Husserl's hands and thence Heidegger's. Heidegger's note runs: "Our experiential comportment to God—which is primary, because it wells up graciously in us—gives direction for the specifically *religious* constitution of 'God' as a 'phenomenological object'" (G60 324). Again, the idea is to read off the structure of religious meaning from a paradigmatically religious phenomenon. In the case of Reinach, this is a profound conversion experience. Following his dramatic battlefield conversion, Reinach applied himself to the task of developing an explicit phenomenological account of this experience. His notes and jottings regarding this project provided, as discussed in the preceding section, a vital stimulus for Heidegger's own investigations.

Roughly during this same period, Husserl had sent Heidegger a copy of Rudolf Otto's *Das Heilige* in hopes that he would review it. Heidegger does not seem to have completed this project, either, though his notes in connection with Otto have been published along with the notes on medieval mysticism. Here is Heidegger's gloss on the central concept of Otto's work, "the holy": "[A]s correlate of the act-character of 'faith,' which itself is to be interpreted only from out of the fundamentally essential experiential context of historical consciousness. That does not mean the explanation of the 'holy' as a 'category of evaluation.' Rather, what is primary and essential to it is the constitution of an originary objecthood" (G60 333).

What interests Heidegger about Otto's work is precisely the same issue that interests him in the work of Reinach and Eckhart, namely, their analyses of the concrete experience of "God" or "the holy." Heidegger is considerably less enthusiastic about Otto's application of Neo-Kantian value theory to the results of his descriptive analysis of religious experience. Indeed, from Heidegger's point of view, this move distorts the whole issue. As Reinach, Eckhart, and Otto show, God or "religious objecthood" in general is not an abstract idea nor some ideal entity. Instead, it is something that is concretely given in lived experience. By starting here, and attempting to explicate the sense of this "objecthood," Heidegger is forced to abandon the sorts of antirealist views of religion characteristic of the Neo-Kantians. Neo-Kantian antirealism, as I have already discussed, is motivated by a prior commitment to the project of the "philosophy of culture." Heidegger, on the other hand, wants to jettison such inherited frameworks as much as possible, and to focus instead on the "thing itself" of religious experience. The question of how religion fits into a certain conception of culture need not even arise at this level of analysis. What does pose a problem, however, is precisely the fact that "God" or "the holy" *is* given in religious experience, despite God's being utterly different from a sensory object.

Anti-realist theories of religion, according to Heidegger anyway, render phenomena like mysticism, conversion, faith, and the sense of sacredness totally unintelligible. What is characteristic of these phenomena is that religious meaning is directly or concretely given in them. On the account offered by Neo-Kantians like Windelband, however, religious meaning is entirely a derivative of the interests of reason. Religious values are, by definition, "ideas," in the sense of concepts generated by the interests of reason that are never instantiated in experience. This type of account is forced to simply ignore the kinds of religious phenomena that anchor Heidegger's phenomenological account. Heidegger's argument—which, at this stage, is largely implicit—is that this fact proves fatal to anti-realist accounts of religion. A theory that cannot make sense of, nor even take seriously, paradigmatic activities and attitudes in a particular domain deserves deep suspicion. One might draw an analogy here to an argument that the Baden Neo-Kantians (such as Heinrich Rickert) often applied to naturalistic accounts of morality, namely, that these accounts fail because they cannot make sense of the normativity that is an inherent and defining feature of moral concepts and the judgments that employ them.

In these notes from 1918 and 1919, Heidegger also emphasizes the "passive" or "receptive" quality of religious experience vis-à-vis the "givenness" or "objecthood" of God. The Eckhartian phenomenon of the "birth of God" in the soul (discussed briefly above) is, on Heidegger's reading, preceded by the "a priori of natural depravity," which Heidegger further glosses as "incapacity." Despite its brevity, this note is making a clear point: human beings, by themselves, cannot produce or spontaneously engender an experience of God (G60 309). Similarly, the "experiential comportment to God" that Heidegger mentions in connection with Reinach's work is "graciously given" (G60 324). Hence, religious life is essentially *historical*, i.e., it has a definite beginning (G60 325). Religion, viewed from the standpoint of certain paradigmatically religious phenomena, positively insists upon the fact that religious meaning and value transcend human interests.

The "grace-character" of religious experience also figures prominently in Heidegger's series of notes on Schleiermacher's *Glaubenslehre*. The new element in these discussions is the idea that human existence must be inherently "receptive" or "open" in order for something like religious experience to be possible. This discussion is worth quoting at length:

> The "having-been-effected-from-somewhere" of consciousness is possible only on the basis of the essential *openness to values* and *primary love of*

meaning of the personally existing being. What can be affected is not a blank page, not an empty "I," not a point-like self, but rather only a personal being fulfilled and essentially longing for fulfillment, which has such a structure which makes possible for it being-fulfilled by certain goods of the life-world and, in being-fulfilled, makes possible further growth and becoming-felt. [. . .] The pure "I" is the primordial constituting element, *the* form of the possibility of being-effected and of being-fulfilled at all. It is not a value-free matter, but also not a good (an object to which value is attached). Primarily, it is the primordial form of openness for the valuable in general [. . .]. Being-able-to-posit-oneself and having-become-from-nowhere-else is in no way its essence. Its ownmost primordial ground is at once and authentically a perpetual vocation and calling as absolute constituent of spirit and life in general. It, too, is of another, namely *called* by another, whether become [so] or however, is entirely secondary (*anima naturaliter religiosa* [the soul is by nature religious]). (G60 350–351)

The general view expounded in this passage, viz., that human existence is fundamentally characterized by an *openness* or *receptivity* to value and meaning, appears also in contemporaneous letters to Elisabeth Blochmann. There, the "mystery" and "grace-character" of all human life is accentuated. The moments of intensification that make life particularly valuable and worthwhile cannot be simply willed, but occur on their own. In the same letter, Heidegger refers to his "preliminary work for a phenomenology of religious consciousness." The starting point of such a phenomenology is the concrete experience of, as he puts it, "having-been-effected-from-somewhere." Such an experience is only really intelligible if subjectivity is understood to be receptive or passive. The self must be structured as an *openness* to meaning, not as the spontaneous *source* of meaning as in Fichte and the Baden Neo-Kantians. Only on this picture of subjectivity is the experience of genuine *transcendence* intelligible. Again, by starting from the religious experience itself, Heidegger is able to dispense with the motives for anti-realist accounts. If, as modern theorists like the Neo-Kantians and Nietzsche suppose, the subject is the source of meaning, then religious meaning, too, must be *created* rather than *given* or *discovered*. But, if this prior commitment is suspended, and one looks simply at the phenomena themselves, then there seems to be no need to appeal to the creative powers of human psychology after all. To the contrary, the "fact" of religious experience suggests that the self is actually *receptive* to, rather than creative of, meaning.

This "grace-character" of religious experience also shows up in Heidegger's glosses on Bernard of Clairvaux. The "basic" or "fundamental experience" that makes "genuine religious experiences" possible is not something that can be acquired through some ecclesiastical manual. Instead, "The constitution of the noetic context of religious experience is something 'historical' (*qui bibit, ad hunc sitiat*). The basic experience is therefore not only temporally primary (perhaps it need not be), but also primarily *founding*" (G60 334). A later gloss continues in this vein: "receptivity as originary in the religious world" (G60 336). Here, Heidegger maintains that specific religious experiences are possible because of an a priori "noetic context" that allows things to show up as religiously meaningful. This "context" is, as Heidegger says, "historical" (G60 335), meaning that it *comes into being* at a definite time and then shapes life as it is lived in time. It is *given* in a "gracious" way, and is taken to be something that human beings cannot achieve by themselves. In all of the paradigmatic instances of religious experience that Heidegger studies, there is virtual unanimity on this point. Thinkers as diverse as Bernard, Eckhart, and Schleiermacher concur in their description of religious experience as in some sense *involuntary*, as welling up in the soul spontaneously, like a gift of grace.

The point is that the practices and attitudes that are expressive of a religious way of life are "founded" on an antecedent domain of meaning. These practices and attitudes, and the way of life of which they are constitutive elements, make no sense in the absence of what Heidegger is here calling their particular "noetic context." In *Being and Time* and elsewhere, Heidegger emphasizes again and again that things are meaningful and significant for us only because we have "always already" assigned ourselves (or been assigned) a position within an a priori network of relations, a network that is not our creation, but rather that which makes it possible for us to create a particular identity for ourselves and so to have a stake in our lives.

The concept of a "noetic context," found in Heidegger's brief notes on Bernard of Clairvaux, directs us to the third main theme in his early studies of religious life. Already in the August 1919 notes, quoted above, Heidegger expresses interest in the way in which religious life is structured or shaped in advance such that specific religious experiences, like those characteristic of mystics, then become possible. A religious life is one that is shaped by a pre-reflective or tacit understanding of religious meaning, an a priori "noetic context," that is "lived out" in religious practices.

In notes on Schleiermacher's *On Religion: Speeches to its Cultured Despisers*, Heidegger tries to articulate the immanent sense of religious life as a kind of *unity* that provides coherence and structure:

> The specifically religious intentional, feeling-like [*gefühlsartig*] relation of every content of experience to an infinite whole as basic sense is religion. *Devotion*: original, unreserved pouring in of a fullness that stimulates. The particular experience is *led back* into the inner unity of life. Religious life is the continual renewal of this process. *Acting*, then, is the echo of this feeling; only acting as a totality, not every individual act, should be so determined. (G60 321)

Here, Heidegger offers what looks like a definition of "religion"; it is the relation of specific experiences back to an "infinite whole." This formulation, of course, reflects Schleiermacher's conception of religion as a "taste for the infinite." Heidegger's emphasis, however, is subtly different from that of Schleiermacher. Schleiermacher, it will be recalled, is trying to express the structure of a certain kind of "intuition" or experience, which, on his view, is the ultimate source of religion. Heidegger, on the other hand, is after what he elsewhere calls the "immanent sense" of religious life. That is, he is trying to articulate the inherent structure that makes a person's life religious. Here, he suggests that this structure consists in a kind of "whole" to which particular experiences and activities are referred, and from which they receive their particular meaning. On this picture, religious life comes out as a kind of *habitus,* as a process of *repeatedly* integrating new experiences into the totality of the religious framework that is already in place. This is how Heidegger understands Schleiermacher's famous comment that, "Like a holy music, religion should accompany all the activity of life" (G60 321–322).

In a separate set of notes, this time on Schleiermacher's later *Glaubenslehre,* Heidegger emphasizes a strikingly similar set of ideas. His gloss runs: "The *constitutive form* of the somehow determined (immediate) self-consciousness circumscribes the sense of *personal existence* and integrates itself into the primordial constituting element of historical consciousness as such" (G60 330). Here again, Heidegger is interested in Schleiermacher's account of the way in which the "sense" of religious life is grounded in a cohesive "whole" that lies at the deepest level of "personal existence." This whole makes it possible for life to have religious significance, for things to show up as religiously meaningful.

In the series of notes on Adolf Reinach's phenomenology of religion, Heidegger yet again glosses Reinach's distinction between "explicit knowledge and knowledge immanent in experience" as "valuable" and "very significant" (G60 326–327). "Immanent knowledge" is Reinach's term for a kind of awareness that is largely unthematic and is rooted in our participation in an experience. In his example, a person might find herself in the experience of "absolute dependence" on God. Here, one "feels" oneself as participating in this relation, without the relation itself being objectified in reflection. At the same time, the experience of "absolute dependence" on God clearly involves some kind of awareness of the reality of God. But, this awareness is entirely unthematic. That is, the awareness of God involved in this experience is not based on an inference, such as the inference that awareness of "absolute dependence on God" clearly entails that there is a God on whom one is "absolutely dependent."

What Heidegger finds "valuable" and "significant" about Reinach's reflections is, no doubt, the claim that religious life is founded in a kind of tacit or unthematic knowledge of God. Rather than being grounded on an inferential process, religious life is grounded in an *experience* in which the reality of God is implicitly understood. This view anticipates some recent work in the epistemology of religion. According to "Reformed epistemology," the warrant for religious belief is to be found not in an inferential process but rather in "properly basic beliefs" that are grounded in certain sorts of experiences. For example, when contemplating a spectacular instance of natural beauty, such as the Grand Canyon, one might form the belief that "An infinitely wise being is responsible for all of this." One does not form this belief through an inference, such as (1) the Grand Canyon is strikingly beautiful and majestic, (2) it resembles great works of art in this respect, (3) great works of art are invariably the products of genius, and (4) so, an infinitely wise being is responsible for all of this. Instead, there is a kind of immediate "feeling" (to use Reinach's terminology) that immanently contains the "knowledge" of God's existence.[23]

On Heidegger's account, this kind of tacit, unthematic understanding lies at the very center of religious life. Heidegger is less interested in the project of uncovering the warrants for religious beliefs than he is in explicating the "immanent sense" of religiosity as a pattern of life. In his attempt to articulate the manner in which religious life is shaped in advance by a tacit understanding of religious meaning, Heidegger visits the writings of Bernard, Schleiermacher, and Reinach. The "noetic context" of religious meaning is, on Heidegger's view, rarely grasped explicitly. Instead, it is "inhabited" in a pre-reflective way. At the same time, the pre-reflective understanding of religious meaning that a person might have is "articulated" or "lived out" in concrete religious practices. For example, on the basis of certain special experiences, one might come to have a pre-reflective understanding of God's nature as suffering love. This understanding is "articulated" in devotional practices such as the Stations of the Cross. It might receive a further level of articulation in a prayer or a devotional manual. Yet another level of articulation is reached with explicit theological reflections on the nature of God and its implications for various theoretical problems. The unifying element that makes all of these activities intelligible remains the tacit understanding of religious meaning.

Winter Semester 1920–1921: Heidegger's Lectures on Pauline Christianity

For more than a year following the composition of his last notes regarding medieval mysticism, Heidegger was occupied with other matters. In lectures

---

23. Alvin Plantinga first articulated this position in its contemporary form in a series of papers. See Plantinga (1980) and (1981).

from 1919 to 1920, he attempts to reach some kind of reckoning with Neo-Kantianism (of both the "Baden" and "Marburg" schools), the dominant philosophical tendency of the time, and to work out his own characteristic position. The lectures from KNS 1919, SS 1919, WS 1919–1920, and SS 1920, while certainly not devoid of reference to religion, are more concentrated on the larger philosophical issues that occupied Heidegger at the time. During this period, his plans for developing a phenomenology of religion remain largely that, plans and programmatic sketches. Not until WS 1920–1921 does Heidegger finally return to a direct treatment of the phenomenology of religion. The planned course on medieval mysticism seems to have been completely abandoned, and Heidegger shifts his attention to what he calls, using the academic parlance of the time, "primitive Christianity [*Urchristentum*]." Familiar with the latest historical scholarship on the New Testament, Heidegger chooses Paul's epistles, the earliest documents of the New Testament, for his subject matter. The result is itself a remarkable text that documents the continuing development of Heidegger's phenomenology of religion.

While these lectures touch on a great deal that is of interest, my focus will be on the same broad, thematic concentrations as were located in Heidegger's notes from 1918 and 1919.[24] To recapitulate, these thematic concentrations are (1) the problematic of the "givenness" or "objecthood" of God, (2) the "grace-character" of religious life, and (3) the "alreadiness," "perfect tense *a priori*," or tacit "understanding" of religious life that shapes it in advance. The first of these thematic concentrations shows up throughout Heidegger's lecture notes. The first hint of this problematic appears in a note on Galatians 2:20, "I have been crucified with Christ. It is no longer I who live, but Christ who lives in me. And the life I now live in the flesh I live by faith in the Son of God, who loved me and gave himself for me." Heidegger's gloss on this famous passage is as follows: "Decisive for Pauline 'mysticism.' Reitzenstein points to the connection of the terminology with Hellenism. However, one should not interpret it in an exclusively philological way (hermetic writings)" (G60 70–71). What interests Heidegger is the sense in which Christ is "in" a person. The clue to determining this sense seems to be the second part of the verse, where "life" plays a central role. The suggestion seems to be that Christ is present "in" a life as a whole, in the actual enactment of a certain way of life. Rather than trying to trace out the historical influences on Paul's concepts, as in the "History of Religions

24. The classic treatment of this lecture course as a whole is Sheehan (1986). Theodore Kisiel has also explored this lecture course in two more recent studies. See Kisiel (1993) and (1994). For a critical assessment of the limitations of Heidegger's account of early Christianity, see Caputo (1994). For an analysis of the role of this lecture course in the development of Heidegger's concept of authenticity, see Crowe (2006).

School," Heidegger's explicit purpose is *phenomenological*. The question is, what is the *experience* that is expressed by this talk of being "in" Christ, of *living* "in" Christ? One finds Heidegger moving here toward a conception of religious life as a kind of being-*in*-the-world, as a way of pre-thematically inhabiting a domain of specifically religious meaning. At the same time, this reference to "Pauline mysticism" (a hot topic in the 1910s) suggests the continuing importance of the direct *givenness* of the divine as one of Heidegger's central concerns in working out a phenomenology of religion.

"Living *in* Christ" is also the sort of paradigmatic phenomenon that, on Heidegger's view, is rendered unintelligible by Neo-Kantian anti-realism. Recall that, for Windelband, religion is just the commitment to the ideal goals of abstract reason. To be sure, Windelband wants this to be taken as a model for how actual people are committed to actual religious traditions. But this commitment is *not* understood as a concrete encounter with the transcendent Lord of Creation, but rather as a free acknowledgment of the interests of abstract reason. Living *in* Christ is precisely what it sounds like, namely, a concrete, deeply personal mode of commitment.

The problematic of the "givenness" of the divine receives more discussion in the notes on the letters to the Thessalonians. Here again, Heidegger is interested in explicating the sense in which Christian life involves a real connection with God. That is, the question is that of how God is "given" in and through a certain way of life. Toward the beginning of his notes on 1 Thessalonians, Heidegger observes that the proper "reception" of Paul's proclamation "pushes the one who receives into an effective connection with God" (G60 94–95). The same point is made again a bit later: "*Paralambanein* [receiving] does not mean belonging, but rather receiving, along with the achievement of a living effective connection with God. God's being present has a basic relation to the transformation of life [*Lebenswandel*] (*peripatein* [literally, 'walking'; figuratively, 'living']). The reception itself is a living before God" (G60 95). Heidegger is quite explicit about the import of this discussion:

> For the explication, the task arises of determining the sense of the object-hood of God. It is a decline from an authentic understanding if God is primarily grasped as an object of speculation. That is only realized if one guides the explication through conceptual contexts. But this has never been sought, since Greek philosophy has been forced into Christianity. Only Luther has taken a preliminary step in this direction, and it is on this basis that his hatred of Aristotle can be clarified. (G60 97)

All of these notes represent Heidegger's gloss on 1 Thessalonians 1:9–10: "For the people of those regions report about us what kind of welcome we had among you, and how you turned to God from idols, to serve a living and true God, and to wait for his Son from heaven, whom he raised from the dead." Heidegger's point is that God is "given" not primarily to theoretical reason, but rather "in" a certain way of life. For the Thessalonians, this way of life is characterized as following after a dramatic conversion. The whole life of the post-conversion community is lived "before God." That is, it belongs to the "immanent sense" of Christian life that it is related to God, that God is present to it. God is the axis of this way of life, the point of orientation for the fundamental practices that are characteristic of Christian life. God, then, is the primary reality for Christian life: "Every primary context of enactment converges on God and is carried out before God. These sense of the being of God can first of all be determined from out of this context of enactment" (G60 117). That is, religious meaning, of the sort that defines and order the lives of the members of the Pauline church, is determined by a network of relations that converge on God. As to how God is to be understood, Heidegger is not particularly clear. What is clear is that religious meaning, and the world or network of relations that determine it, can only be more precisely articulated through the examination of the specific way of life that defines a particular community.

The "grace-character" of religious meaning, and of the way of life in which it is embedded, already prominent in the notes from 1918 and 1919, reappear in a pronounced way in the WS 1920–1921 lecture course. This theme can be detected first in a gloss on Galatians 4:9, "Now, however, that you have come to know God, or rather to be known by God, how can you turn back again to the weak and beggarly elemental spirits?" Heidegger's gloss runs: "*Gignōskein* [to know] in the sense of love (as in the first verse). The love of God toward human beings is what is fundamental, not theoretical knowledge" (G60 71). The "first verse," referred to parenthetically here, is most likely the first verse of the entire epistle, which reads "Paul an apostle — sent neither by human commission nor from human authorities, but through Jesus Christ and God the Father, who raised him from the dead." The sense that Heidegger is trying to draw out of both passages is none other than the now familiar claim that religious life is experienced as a gift of God. The real foundation of religious life is not "theoretical knowledge," or, as in Neo-Kantian theories, the demands of reason, but rather God himself. It is God who "knows" the Galatians and who therefore inaugurates their new way of life. It is God who authorizes Paul's mission.

Another way to say this is that the entire form of life (to adapt a Wittgensteinian phrase) that characterizes Paul's post-conversion existence, with its enacted understanding of religious meaning, shows up as being *received* rather than *constructed*. Conversion, of which Paul is such a famous and dramatic exemplar, is precisely the sort of phenomenon that, according to Heidegger, becomes unintelligible on anti-realist accounts of religion. Conversion overthrows pre-existing beliefs, attitudes, and interests.

From the inside, conversion (at least in the cases that Heidegger is describing, e.g., Paul and Adolf Reinach) seems sudden, radical, and unpredictable. For Heidegger, the idea that religious values derive from pre-existing rational interests makes conversion seem not only entirely too rational, but almost inevitable. It is worth noting that even Kant, to whom the Baden Neo-Kantians looked as establishing the basic nature of transcendental idealism, had to resort to mystery in order to explain how it could happen that one comes to replace sensible inclinations with pure moral motives.[25]

The new element in Heidegger's account of the "grace-character" of religious life is an emphasis on the role played by the "proclamation" of the gospel in engendering a new way of life. Here, the sudden, unexpected, and shocking announcement of the message of the "Crucified God" provides the catalyst for a fundamental reorientation of life.[26] Toward the end of his commentary on 2 Thessalonians, for example, Heidegger writes: "Christian factical life-experience is historically defined in that it originates with the proclamation that comes to a person in a moment and is constantly co-actual in the enactment of life" (G60 117). Here, Heidegger uses "historical" in precisely the same sense as in his 1918–1919 notes on medieval mysticism. To say that religious life is "historical" is to say both (1) that it originates at a certain point in time, with a certain identifiable event, and (2) that this originating point provides narrative structure and coherence to the life that flows out of it. Heidegger is no doubt playing off the double sense of the German word *Geschichte* in these passages. On the one hand, *Geschichte* means "history" in the sense of a series of occurrences, *Geschehnisse*, or in the allied sense of a scientific study of such a series. On the other hand, *Geschichte* can also designate a "story" or a "narrative." By describing religious life as "historical," Heidegger is trying to make the point that its inner coherence or narrative structure can be traced back to a definite starting point. As his other remarks indicate quite clearly, this starting point is to be regarded as an act of God. Hence, Heidegger can say that "Factical life emerged out of a genesis and became in a special way historical (enacted)" (G60 142).

Two passages, found at the conclusion of the WS 1920–1921 lecture course, make this point quite emphatically. The first of these reads:

> The Christian has the consciousness that this facticity *cannot be achieved through his own power, but rather stems from God* —phenomenon of the efficacy of grace [*Gnadenwirkung*]. An explication of this context is very important. This phenomenon is decisive for Augustine and Luther, cf. 2. Corinthians 4:7f., *tou theou kai mē ex hēmōn* [to God and not to us], then the opposite; *thlibomenoi, all' ouk* [afflicted, but not], etc. "We have

25. See Kant (1996): 90–92.
26. For a more detailed examination of this aspect of Heidegger's interpretation of the Pauline proclamation, see Crowe (2006).

the treasure (Christian facticity) in clay jars." What is merely available to us Christians is not sufficient for the task of realizing Christian facticity. (G60 121–122)

The passage that Heidegger refers to here, 2 Corinthians 4:7, reads, "But we have this treasure in jars of clay, to show that the surpassing power belongs to God and not to us." One would be hard-pressed to find a clearer endorsement of the essential nature of the "grace-character" of religious life. Heidegger calls upon the authority not only of Paul, but also of Augustine and that great Augustinian, Luther. Both Augustine and Luther, of course, are famous for their insistence that soteriological efficacy belongs solely to God. For Heidegger, the "treasure" (i.e., religious meaning) cannot be reduced to nor fully accounted for on the basis of "clay jars" (i.e., human interests). Heidegger's main concern is, of course, not the theological dispute between Augustine and Pelagius, nor that between Luther and the Ockhamists. Instead, he wants to base a phenomenological account of religion upon phenomena such as conversion. The idea is that the best way to make sense of the internal structure of such phenomena is to see how a network of relations constitutive of religious meaning—and not derived from prior interests— makes possible a new set of interests and a correspondingly new way of life.

At the very end of WS 1920–1921, Heidegger again reflects on this "grace-character" at some length. He writes:

> The enactment transcends the power of the human being. The human being cannot even conceive of it under his own power. Factical life cannot by itself provide the motives even to reach the *gignesthai* [having become]. By means of the over-stepping [*Übersteigerung*] of a significance [*Bedeutsamkeit*], life attempts to "gain a foothold [*Halt zu gewinnen*]." This concept of a "foothold" has meaning within a fully determinate structure of factical life-experience. One cannot apply it to Christian life-experience. The Christian does not find his "foothold" in God (cf. Jaspers). That is blasphemy! God is never a "foothold." [. . .] Thus, whoever has not "received (*dekhesthai*)" is excluded from enduring the facticity or appropriating the "knowledge" for himself. Cf. 1 Corinthians 3:21f., Philippians 2:12f. (G60 122)

The "enactment" or "carrying out [*Vollzug*]" of a Christian life is not something that a person can achieve under his or her own power. For Heidegger, this is absolutely central to the meaning of religious life as documented by the Pauline epistles. One cannot "will" oneself into having a connection with God of the requisite sort. Nor is God properly viewed as a human acquisition. God is experienced as giving himself to a person, not as lying at the end of a pathway of self-transcendence. God does not fulfill a psychological need, but enables a new way of life *ex nihilo*, as it were. It will be recalled that Heidegger finds this same emphasis in Augustine and in

Luther, as well as in Bernard of Clairvaux—all famous critics of the Pelagian view that human beings can attain, or even merit, salvation independently of God's grace.

Since his enterprise is *phenomenological* rather than *theological*, Heidegger is not compelled to assent to the truth of such claims. Again, his project is to call attention to the immanent sense of religious life. At the core of this immanent sense, as expressed in some of the most important texts in the history of Christianity, is the supposition that a religious life is a gift rather than an achievement. That is, *from the perspective of religious life*, which is precisely what Heidegger is trying to thematize, religious meaning is *given* or *discovered* rather than *created*. Religious life is experienced neither as the product of psychological need nor of the demands of theoretical reason, but as a mysterious event that interrupts and reorients the pattern of one's life.[27]

On Heidegger's view, the prevailing anti-realist theories of the time are incapable of really doing justice to this pervasive feature of religious life. For example, while Wilhelm Windelband bases his account of religion on the conflict between ideal normativity and psychological inclination, as experienced in the phenomenon of "conscience," his prior commitment to the framework of Neo-Kantian value-philosophy forces him to fall back on a subjectivist account of normativity.[28] For Heidegger, the phenomena of "grace, calling, and fate" cannot be adequately treated on the assumption that all normativity is internal to the structure of human subjectivity (G58 167). The actual experience of religious life, as documented by Paul, medieval mystics, and others, and which forms the starting point of Heidegger's own analyses, involves the experience of "being effected" by something that "transcends" the subjective sphere. It could only strike Heidegger's sources as odd to maintain that, despite the phenomenal character of this experience, the normative force of the content of religious experience is actually derived from human nature itself. On Heidegger's view, only a *prior commitment* to a modernist conceptual framework, such as Neo-Kantian philosophy of culture, could lead one to such a conclusion. When such commitments are suspended, then the "grace-character" of religious life can once again be taken seriously.

The third idea that appears in WS 1920–1921 is the most distinctively Heideggerian: the idea that the immanent sense of religious life ultimately rests on a tacit, pre-thematic "understanding" of religious meaning that is lived

---

27. For Heidegger, religious life is a paradigmatic instance of a more general structure that can be found in human life, whereby one's everyday existence can be radically interrupted or intruded upon in such a way that a decisive re-orientation and re-evaluation of life becomes possible for an individual. In *Being and Time*, Heidegger uses the term "conscience" as a catch-all for this type of experience. See Crowe (2005) and (2006).

28. For a brief but suggestive critique of Windelband's account by Heidegger, see G60 313.

out in the lives of the members of a specific religious community. Heidegger's brief glosses on Galatians introduce this idea to the lecture course for the first time. Commenting on Galatians 1:13–14, for example, Heidegger tries to draw his students' attention to importance of *conversion* in Paul's own life. This conversion plays itself out in the "conduct of life" or the "leading" of a certain kind of life [*Lebensführung*], in a whole "stance" toward life (G60 70). What results from a conversion such as Paul's is a new set of interests, which in turn generate new attitudes and behaviors. A bit later on, Heidegger observes how all theoretical "explication [*Explikation*]" of religious life, including the didactic and theological material in Paul's epistles, is based on "the sense of religious life itself." That is, explicit theoretical reflection has its roots in the tacit understanding of religious meaning that structures religious life as such. Finally, at the end of his discussion of Galatians, Heidegger presents his theory of "religious factical life-experience" *in nuce*. The aim of studying Paul, he writes, is ultimately to understand Paul's own "facticity" and its inner structure. The latter is succinctly articulated thus: "break in his existence—original historical understanding of his self and of his existence. From out of this, he performs his feat as apostle, as human being" (G60 74).

This remark begins by once again highlighting a feature of the "grace-character" of religious life, i.e., the fact that religious life begins with a radical interruption of a person's life as hitherto lived. What this "interruption" makes possible for Paul is an "original historical understanding." This is another way of formulating what Heidegger had earlier called the "noetic context" of religious life, in his notes on Bernard of Clairvaux written toward the end of World War I. That is, what Paul receives through this "break in his existence" is a tacit understanding of religious meaning that he then "lives out" in various, more specific, ways. As Heidegger puts it here, "From out of this"—i.e., on the basis of this tacit understanding of religious meaning—Paul "performs his feat as apostle." That is, his preaching, whereby he attempts to make explicit the basic commitments implied by a Christian way of life, is the articulation or "explication" of this tacit understanding.

This element of Heidegger's account of the immanent sense of religious life is even more pronounced in his discussions of 1 and 2 Thessalonians. At the beginning of his comments, Heidegger draws attention to Paul's frequent repetition of perfect tense verbs like "*genesthai* [to become]" and "*oidate* [you know, or literally, you have seen]" as "striking." This repetition is not, on Heidegger's view, accidental. Instead, it holds the key to Paul's profound understanding of the nature of Christian life. Theodore Kisiel, in one of his essays on this lecture course, presents the significance of this "repetition" for Heidegger's account quite clearly:

> Paul's recollection of this "event" [his own conversion, and that of the Thessalonians] in terms of the present perfect tense is itself middle-voiced,

> inasmuch as their facticity of having become is not wholly past and bygone, but at once constitutes their present being. This present perfect a priori (SZ 85) of their "genetic" becoming accompanied by its tacit knowledge, i.e., a pretheoretical understanding of the being of this becoming, thus places the entire diagram squarely on the level of the sense of actualization. Here, "knowing" (or understanding) and becoming (or actualization) are one to the point that becoming makes up the being of knowing, and knowing the very being of becoming.[29]

Here, Kisiel correctly links Heidegger's exposition of religious life in WS 1920–1921 with his later account of "being-in-the-world" in *Being and Time* (1927) and elsewhere. Paul's point in using the present perfect tense of the verbs is to articulate the manner in which what it means to be a Christian is bound up with having a tacit understanding of religious meaning that is "lived out" in concrete practices. The "break in existence" that both Paul and his Thessalonian converts have undergone is not simply an episode from the past that can be recalled with fondness. Instead, it is the inaugural event of a new, largely unthematic or tacit, understanding of reality that is oriented ahead of time by specifically religious meaning.

For Heidegger, the "knowing" or "understanding" that Paul is talking about cannot really be separated from the "becoming," from the process of living a Christian life. The latter, instead, gets its structure and meaning precisely from the ongoing efficacy of the former (G60 94). What Heidegger calls the "being already" or "having become [*Gewordensein*]" of the Christian life is not an event in the past that is over and done with, but something that always already defines in advance the "being now" of a Christian (G60 94). This "being already" shapes the "how" of a specific pattern or *Gestalt* of life. Heidegger continues: "It is a matter of an *absolute reversal* [*Umwendung*], or, more precisely, of a turning *toward* God and *away* from idols. The absolute turn toward God is explicated within the enactment sense of factical life in two directions: *douleuein* [serving] and *anamnein* [waiting], changing before God [*Wandeln vor Gott*] and waiting upon him [*Erharren*]" (G60 95).

The crucial term in this passage is "explicated." Heidegger's point is that a tacit understanding of religious meaning, here glossed as a "turning *toward* God," is "lived out" in certain determinate attitudes and practices. Put another way, the pre-theoretical understanding of religious meaning that is "received" through a "break in existence" is "enacted" or "actualized" in the course of one's life. This idea, first mentioned in notes from 1918 and 1919, constitutes the very core of Heidegger's distinctive phenomenology of religion. Moreover, Heidegger takes this material from 1 Thessalonians

---

29. Kisiel (1994): 182–183.

as providing a crucial clue about religious meaning or "objecthood [*Gegenständlichkeit*]." Idols are abandoned in favor of God. Idols are, at least for a Jew like Paul, expressions of human interests, including but not limited to the interests of power. Expressions of human interests are thus abandoned in favor of God, upon whom one "waits" and whom one is called to "serve." God, to whom the religious world of the early Christians is ordered, is something of surpassing value and majesty.

It is also clear from this passage that Heidegger places the accent on *practice* as the primary way in which this tacit understanding is "enacted" or "actualized." Again, this view anticipates some of the more famous parts of Heidegger's argument in *Being and Time*, where he maintains that our general, pre-thematic understanding of "world" is primarily articulated in first-order practices like tool-usage or everyday conversation. However, in *Being and Time*, Heidegger also wants to ground the possibility of higher-order practices, such as scientific experimentation and theoretical reasoning, on our tacit understanding of "world." This claim serves to anchor Heidegger's conception of the relation between philosophy, which explores this deep framework, and the sciences, which emerge from it without explicitly examining it. In WS 1920–1921, Heidegger makes a parallel claim with respect to the relationship between the tacit understanding of religious meaning always already present in religious life and the formation of doctrine through theological reflection. Against liberal theologians like Harnack, for whom dogmas are best understood as external accretions on the primal experience of religion, Heidegger maintains that theological reflection and its products are simply the higher-order articulations of the same tacit understanding of religious meaning that makes religious practices possible. He writes: "Knowing about one's own being already/having become [*Gewordensein*] is the starting point and origin of theology. The sense of theological concept-formation develops in the explication of this knowing and of its conceptual forms of expression" (G60 95). The same claim is made later on in a slightly different way: "Dogma, as abstract doctrinal content, set into relief in an objective-cognitive setting, can never become the leading element of Christian religiosity; rather, it ought to be the other way around—the genesis of dogma is only intelligible on the basis of the enactment of Christian life-experience" (G60 112).

At the end of the WS 1920–1921 lecture course, Heidegger returns to the thematic of this "knowing" or "understanding" that is immanent to Christian life as documented by Paul's letters. Here, he is first of all concerned with making sure that standard accounts of the nature of human cognition are not uncritically imported into the phenomenological explication of religious life (G60 123). While it might seem like a suitable concept, the notion of "practical knowledge" is also rejected by Heidegger as an accurate way to represent this "knowledge." Practical knowledge, or "know-how," such as that demonstrated by a skilled craftsman, might indeed be largely tacit or unthematic. A craftsman's facility at his work involves the internalization of traditional practices and skills, some of which may not have ever been explicitly formulated in rules or procedures. As tacit knowledge, this sort of practical "know-how" does bear a certain kinship with the "knowledge" that is characteristic of religious life. The latter, however, is better conceived of as a tacit knowledge of religious *meaning* rather than of certain skills and practices.

This suggests that Heidegger is working toward a distinction between instrumental meaning and religious meaning. In *Being and Time*, he famously provides a fully worked out account of instrumental meaning or "readiness-to-hand [*Zuhandenheit*]." At least in the texts currently available, there is nothing of similar scope or detail regarding religious meaning. However, the contrast with instrumental meaning is instructive. According to the account first articulated in KNS 1919, and fully developed in *Being and Time*, the intelligibility of an item of use, such as a hammer, derives from its role in a web of relations ordered to some practical interest or project, itself derived from a prior network of meaningful possibilities. Religious meaning, on the other hand, derives from a network of relations that is best conceived of as ordered to something that is not a practical interest. This is presumably what Heidegger intends by his rejection of the tendency to think of God as a tool that people need for getting a "foothold" in life. It is not some practical interest of mine that makes religious attitudes, activities, and artifacts intelligible as such; rather, it is something of intrinsic, absolute value that does so.

Another relevant difference is that, unlike a craftsman's practical knowledge, "the entire factical life-experience" of a religious person is "determined" by her special kind of "knowledge," such that "all *significances* in it must be determined radically on its basis" (G60 137). That is, the meaning of the person's whole life, and of the things that show up in her experience, is defined or shaped by this tacit understanding of religious meaning. All of the various "worlds" that the religious person inhabits—the "surrounding world" of things, the "with-world" of society, and the inner "self-world"—are each defined in advance by the larger religious "world." Religious faith, observes Heidegger, is determinative of life in an "arch-ontic" sense—"no juxtaposition in a series, but a motivational complex of factical life" (G60 144).

The central point that Heidegger is trying to make throughout his WS 1920–1921 phenomenological analyses of Pauline Christianity is that the "immanent sense" of Christian life is best characterized in terms of what he later comes to call "being-in-the-world." That is, Christian life is, at bottom, a way of inhabiting a pre-given domain of meaning. The largely tacit "understanding" or "knowledge" of this pre-given domain is what allows a religious person's experience to show up as intelligible, as *mattering*, in a religious way. This understanding anchors the "immanent sense" of a life *as* religious; that is, it constitutes a kind of unifying frame of reference in terms of which a person can make sense of his or her life as a whole. As a "noetic context" or "motivational complex," this tacit understanding of religious meaning shapes in advance a religious person's life as a whole. This is most evident, for Heidegger, in the way in which this tacit understanding is "lived out" in concrete practices such as prayer, communal life, or worship. The roots of explicit reflection on religious life also lie in this tacit understanding of religious meaning. To this general account of religious life, Heidegger adds the important proviso that the nexus or "world" of religious meaning is something in relation to which human beings are largely *passive* or *receptive*. On the phenomenal level, the whole complex of living out a tacit understanding of religious meaning shows up within religious experience itself as coming from beyond the individual and beyond the dominant culture, as being a gift of *grace*. Heidegger's analyses in WS 1920–1921, then, are best understood as a sustained phenomenological argument for a kind of *realism* about religious meaning, an *ontological* realism.

Summer Semester 1921: Heidegger's Lectures on Augustine

The basic insights that Heidegger arrived at between 1918 and the winter of 1921 constitute the relatively stable, but still-evolving matrix in which all of his subsequent analyses of religion are grounded. These insights are developed further in the SS 1921 lecture course, "Augustine and Neo-Platonism." In view of the fact that large portions of the WS 1920–1921 course are occupied by discussions of the state of philosophy at the time, philosophical methodology, the problems of historical consciousness, and other issues tangential to the phenomenology of religion in a strict sense, the SS 1921 course represents Heidegger's only full-scale lecture series devoted entirely to a religious subject. In this course, Heidegger develops and consolidates many of the core ideas that had been germinating in the preceding years. Concepts familiar from some of his more well-known writings, such as authenticity and "destruction [*Destruktion*]" also begin to take more definite shape in this lecture course. My primary concern in what follows, however, is with the development of two of the themes that have been identified in Heidegger's earlier writings on religion: the "objecthood [*Gegenständlichkeit*]" of God and the enacted understanding that constitutes the "immanent sense" of religious life.

The thematic of the "objecthood" of God plays a more prominent role in the lectures on Augustine than it did in WS 1920–1921, though it was not, as I have already discussed, entirely absent from the latter. Yet, in SS 1921, Heidegger brings this theme into prominence right at the beginning of his discussion of book 10 of Augustine's *Confessions*. Augustine famously begins his exercise in self-reflection by asking God, *Quid autem amo, cum te amo?*

"What do I love, when I love you?" Heidegger's gloss on this famous question reveals what it is that he hopes to learn from his close reading of this classic text: "Augustine attempts to find an answer to this question by investigating what there is that is worthy of love, and by asking whether there is something among these things that is God himself, or that gives a 'fulfilling intuition' if he lives in the love of God, what suffices for, or fulfills [*ausfüllt*], that which, in the love of God, he intends" (G60 178–179).

Heidegger is here paraphrasing Augustine's famous question in Husserlian language. Indeed, the question of what God is takes the same form as Husserl's question about the possibility of the "fulfillment" of ideal "intentions" or "meanings" in the *Logical Investigations*. In book 2, Husserl describes how a sentence like "The wall is white" contains a "surplus of intentions" that cannot all be fulfilled in sensory perception. The categorial "forms," intended in non-nominal words like "is," require some "fulfillment" if the whole intention is to be successful. As I have already discussed, Husserl answers this puzzle by postulating a kind of "categorial intuition" in which categorial forms are concretely given. For Heidegger, the intention "God" presents similar difficulties. God, of course, is not to be identified with any object of sensory perception, for God is wholly distinct from the created order. To ask of God, "What do I love, when I love you?" thus has a "surplus of intentions" that go beyond what can be fulfilled in a possible sensory experience. So, as with categorial forms, some kind of "saturated" intuition, one that contains different layers of meaning within it, is alone capable of fulfilling the intention expressed in Augustine's question.

After raising this issue, Heidegger recounts how Augustine investigates the whole created order, beginning with the "external" world of natural phenomena, in order to locate God. "He questions the earth, nature, the seas, and the abysses and whatever animals live in them, and the whole cosmos, the sun, the moon, the stars. And they respond: We are not what you are looking for" (G60 179). And so, Augustine turns inward, querying the soul as to whether God can be found within it. Here again, the results of Augustine's investigations turn out to be the discovery that "God is [. . .] nothing *psychic*" (G60 202). That is, while Augustine maintains that the most promising place to seek a "fulfilling intuition" of God is within his own soul, he does not identify God with the soul, with its faculties, or with mental processes. Nor is God to be thought of as a mental entity or an idea, for, says Heidegger in his paraphrase, God is "Lord of the soul" (G60 202–203). That is, the meaning of "God" transcends the created order of the mind as well as that of nature. These points serve, for Heidegger, to dramatize the fact that the "fulfilling intuition" corresponding to God is of a very distinctive sort. Neither crude nature-worship, nor sophisticated idealist accounts of religion, such as those of the Baden Neo-Kantians, adequately capture the phenomenon of the givenness or "objecthood" of God.

The surprising answer to the question of "where" God is to be found—and, therefore, the key to answering the larger question of the "objecthood" of God—is the *beata vita*, the "blessed life," the Christian life (G60 192). That is, the "fulfilling intuition" for the intention of God lies precisely in the enacted understanding which, as I have already shown, constitutes the "immanent sense" of religious life. Heidegger develops this idea most fully in remarks not on the *Confessions*, but on some of Augustine's more well-known sermons. He begins his discussion of this thematic complex with a gloss on Augustine's advice, *faciem cordis cogita*—"think of the face of the heart." Heidegger paraphrases this piece of advice with the note "God in the objecthood [*Gegenständlichkeit*] as it is appropriated by the heart in its authentic life" (G60 289). He continues:

> To interpret this as subjectivism is a misunderstanding. The issue is the conditions of access to God. God is not made, rather the self achieves the enactment conditions of the experience of God. In the effort regarding the life of the self, God is there. God as object in the sense of the *facies cordis* [face of the heart] exists [*wirkt*] in the authentic life of a human being. (G60 289)

To say that God is "objective" in the "face of the heart" is not, Heidegger emphasizes, to "subjectivize" God. That is, Augustine is clearly not trying to make God into a mental entity, an idea, or a concept. Rather, it is to say that God is somehow "there," somehow "intuited," to stick with the Husserlian language Heidegger had used earlier on in the lecture, in the enactment of a specific way of life. A relation to God is presupposed, as it were, as the very meaning of this way of life. Heidegger does not conclude from this, however, that God is a "regulative idea," a sort of necessary condition postulated by reason to account for the possibility of a religious life. This distorts the primary phenomenon that anchors the power and urgency of Augustine's theology, i.e., conversion. The way of life through which one comes into a relationship with God is not, as in Windelband's account, simply a way of representing to oneself one's commitments to the interests of reason. Instead, there is something beyond one's interests that motivates and organizes a new way of life. On Heidegger's account, as I have already discussed, a view such as Windelband's is motivated not by this phenomenal evidence but by a prior commitment to the explanatory framework of Kantian philosophy of culture. What the phenomenal evidence *does* seem to warrant, on Heidegger's view, is that the intention of God is "fulfilled" concretely in the living of a certain way of life. God is "intuited" as the normative *horizon* or ultimate *anchor* for this whole way of life: "all life-relations, the whole facticity permeated by you [God], enacted in such a way that all *enactment* is enacted *before* you" (G60 249).

In a long passage found toward the end of Heidegger's comments on Augustine's sermons, he reiterates this basic insight and attempts to develop it further:

> The idea of *mundare* [purifying] as condition of access is already present in Augustine's early philosophical writings—a Platonic idea, linked in Plotinus with the conception of asceticism. *Mundare* is carried out through *fides Christiana* [Christian faith] (not the demonic). *Fides* [faith] is an enactment context of trust and love, which must be an expectant attitude. Every cosmic-metaphysical reification of the concept of God, even as an irrational concept, must be denied. One must appropriate the *facies cordis* [face of the heart] (inwardness) oneself. God is present in the inner man if he has understood what width, length, height, and depth (*latitudo, longitudo, altitudo, profundum*) mean, and thereby understands the sense of the infinity of God for the thought of the heart. [. . .] Understand everything *in te* [in yourself]! *Latitudo* = richness, fullness in good works; *longitudo* = forbearance and persistence; *altitudo* = expectation of what lies above you (*sursum cor* [lift up your heart]); *profundum* = the grace of God. All of this is not to be understood as objective symbolism, but rather must be related back to the enactment sense of inner life. Symbolism of the cross: *latitudo:* where the hands are fixed; *longitudo:* the body that stands; *altitudo:* the expectation [illegible words] G.; *profundum:* hidden [. . .]. (G60 290)

In his sermon, Augustine uses the cross as a metaphor for Christian life. It is only, he suggests, in taking up such a life that one achieves a kind of intimacy with God. In Heidegger's gloss, God is "present in the inner man" when one "understands" the "dimensions" of such a life. That is, access to God is given in the enacted understanding that constitutes the core of the "immanent sense" of Christian life. This, then, is meant to be Heidegger's answer to the Augustinian question, paraphrased in Husserlian terms, of the possibility of a "fulfilling intuition" corresponding to God. God is "given" or "intuited" as a kind of horizon against which one's life comes to have religious meaning. Like the "categorial form" of a sentence like "The wall is white," God is not to be identified with any object of sensory perception. Instead, in understanding the nature of a Christian life, such a life is concretely intuited as being "saturated" with God. A Christian life is, after all, predicated on the reality of a relationship with God. As Heidegger puts it a bit later,

> [T]he experience of God in Augustine's sense does not lie in an isolated act or in a definite moment of such an act, but rather in an experiential nexus [*Erfahrungszusammenhang*] of the *historical* facticity of one's own life. This is something genuinely *primordial*, which can be detached from isolated modes of comportment that break loose from it and thereby lead to an empty conception of religiosity and theology. (G60 293–294)

The lingering issue, or course, concerns the "objecthood" or "sense of being" of God, that is, the religious meaning that is understood by a religious person and which shapes in advance her characteristic attitudes and activities. Scattered throughout his lecture notes for SS 1921, as well as in some remarks recorded in a student transcript, Heidegger gestures at a more substantive account of religious meaning. In keeping with his general phenomenological methodology, he tries to explicate the "content-sense" or meaning of a phenomenon by first of all examining its "relational-sense [*Bezugssinn*]." In other words, one can find clues about religious meaning by explicating the structure of typically religious attitudes. This approach is clearly at work, for example, in Heidegger's gloss on a passage from one of Augustine's sermons. The passage in question runs: *Nemo quiped vivit in quacumque vita, sine tribus istis animae affectionibus, credendi, sperandi, amandi* ["However, no one, in any walk of life, lives without his soul experiencing these three things—believing, hoping, loving"]. Heidegger's interpretation of this passage is framed by his attempt to understand Augustine's concept of love in the *Confessions*. His gloss explains *credendi* as "grasping trustingly [*vertrauend zugreifen*]" or "somehow establishing an end [*irgendwie ein Ende festmachen*]"; *sperandi* as "awaiting [*erwartend*]" or "holding oneself open for [*sich offenhalten für*]"; and *amandi* as "loving devotion [*liebende Hingabe*]" or "valuing [*für wert halten*]" (G60 204). The idea is that religious meaning—above all that of God (i.e., the way in which God is understood in a properly religious way)—is whatever is the appropriate object of these attitudes.

The contrasting attitudes can be located in Augustine's criticisms of magic and divination. Heidegger's gloss on a passage related to this issue runs: "God has to endure becoming a factor in human experiments. He has to respond to an inquisitive, pompous, and pseudo-prophetic curiosity, that is, a curious looking after oneself [*Sichumsehen*] in regard to Him, which does *not* submit [*fügt*] to his sense of objecthood [*Gegenstandssinn*], that is, which is non-sense [*Un-fug*]" (G60 224).

The attitudes contrasted here are "loving devotion" or "establishing an end," on the one hand, and inquisitive, self-regarding manipulation, on the other. To make something an end is to make *it*, whatever it is, into the final cause of one's attitudes and actions. The attitude characteristic of divination and magic, on the other hand, makes oneself into the final cause. God, rather than being an object of "loving devotion" or "submission," has the "sense of objecthood" of a tool. That is, the difference between the religious meaning of God and the way God is understood in magic is that, in the latter case, God has instrumental meaning vis-à-vis some interest. In the former case, God is an end in Himself. For Augustine, as Heidegger was well aware, God is the only thing that, properly speaking, is an end (G60 203; 357). That is, God is the proper object of enjoyment (*frui*) rather than of use (*uti*)

(G60 271), where enjoyment is synonymous with loving something for its own sake (G60 278).

These considerations help to express the nature of religious meaning by way of contrast with instrumental meaning. One might reconstruct Heidegger's account as follows. First, all meaning derives from a world, from an a priori network of relations. These relations are always ordered to something, be it a practical interest, or, in the case of religious meaning, something that is worthy of love independently of all practical interests. These relations are, in a broad sense, teleological. Religious attitudes, activities, and artifacts are all intelligible *as religious* because they embody or express some relationship to something that is intrinsically worthy of love. Admittedly, this account needs to be filled in considerably. It does not clearly provide for a distinction between, for example, aesthetic meaning and religious meaning, at least if one takes into account the typical attitude to works of art as being valuable in a non-instrumental way. Still, the structure of the account is obvious. Things have meaning in virtue of a complex web of relations that are more or less teleological in nature. What makes the world of religion distinctive must ultimately be the "telos" that anchors and orders these relations. However, at least in the early 1920s, Heidegger stops short of defining the nature of this "telos" more closely.

In the SS 1921 lectures on Augustine, Heidegger brings together two of the fundamental thematic complexes in his phenomenology of religion: the "objecthood" of God and the tacit understanding of religious meaning that grounds religious life. The former is to be located *within* the latter. That is, God is present not simply in reflection or in spectacular "religious experiences," but in the ongoing enactment of a tacit understanding of religious meaning. God forms the uttermost layer, as it were, of the pre-given nexus or "world" of religious meaning that shapes in advance the intelligibility of religious life.

In conclusion, the three texts examined in this chapter constitute a remarkable contribution to the phenomenology of religion. Despite their somewhat hasty and fragmentary character, they nevertheless express a definite position. This ontological realism shows up as the combination of these interlocking themes: (1) the "objecthood" or "givenness" of God in concrete experience, (2) the "grace-character" of religious life, and (3) the immanent sense of religious life as a mode of "being-in-the-world." Taken together, these themes suggest the view that religious meaning, anchored in a concrete experience of the divine, is *given* rather than *created*. This view stands out against anti-realist interpretations of religion like those offered by the Neo-Kantians and Nietzsche, which, according to Heidegger, are motivated not by a sober look at religious life but by an antecedent commitment to a particular philosophy of culture. As will be shown in the following chapter, this basic concern remains in place throughout Heidegger's career.

THREE

Heidegger's Later
Phenomenology of Religion

If the material surveyed in the preceding chapter (1918–1921) represented all that Heidegger wrote about the phenomenology of religion, this would be enough to earn him a place in the history of the philosophy of religion. His early works represent a clear alternative to the then prevailing Neo-Kantian accounts, and exemplify a distinctively *phenomenological* approach to the study of religion. Roughly, this approach is characterized by the insistence that philosophical theories are answerable to the phenomena. For Heidegger, these phenomena have an intelligible structure internal to them which is not the result of having imposed a conceptual framework upon inert material. A philosophical theory has to preserve this primal intelligibility. Yet, this is precisely what, according to Heidegger, anti-realist theories of religion fail to do. The primal intelligibility of characteristically religious attitudes and activities is best expressed by the sense that the value or meaning in play in these attitudes and activities is prior to human interests.

Heidegger's efforts in the phenomenology of religion by no means came to an end in the early 1920s. To the contrary, religion remained a central concern of the so-called "later" (i.e., post-1929) Heidegger as well. In 1951, he told participants in a seminar that he was still "inclined" to write a theology

(G15 436). Years later, he still credited his "theological origin [*Herkunft*]" with having a decisive influence on his subsequent career. In 1970, he saw fit to publish his 1927 essay "Phenomenology and Theology," for which he composed a new preface. It would therefore be quite surprising to find an *absence* of discussions of religion in Heidegger's later works.

The aim of this chapter is to examine the continuation of Heidegger's work in the phenomenology of religion following his return to Freiburg. Some readers might well view talk of "phenomenology of religion" in this period as being anachronistic, but I will show in what follows that a careful reading of Heidegger suggests otherwise. Despite various shifts of emphasis, new vocabularies, and even new concepts, there is substantial continuity between the ideas discussed in the preceding chapter and those developed by Heidegger after 1929. Heidegger after 1929 is still the committed antagonist of anti-realism, and is still a dedicated practitioner of phenomenology. His work in this period expands its scope beyond primitive Christianity to sketch outlines of a theory of religion as such, and to the articulation of a paradigm of religiosity explicitly designed to challenge the situation of the present age.

New Elements, Persisting Project

The works of the so-called "later" Heidegger (ca. 1929–1976) present a number of difficulties for any commentator.[1] First, the idiosyncrasies of Heidegger's style of philosophy, certainly present in his "early" period, become even more pronounced in these works. One faces the real danger of utterly misrepresenting Heidegger's project in an attempt to render it accessible to the uninitiated.[2] Second, there is the contentious issue of the "turn" in Heidegger's work during the 1930s. Was there, as Karl Löwith and William J. Richardson have argued, a deep shift in Heidegger's fundamental philosophical orientation following the alleged "failure" of the project of *Being and Time*?[3] Or, have Heideggerians been mistaken about the meaning of the term *Kehre* in Heidegger's works, as Thomas Sheehan has long maintained?[4] What light, if any, does the publication, in the last decade and a half, of Heidegger's earliest lecture courses at Freiburg shed on this "turn"?

---

1. The "periodization" of Heidegger's work is, in my view, always somewhat forced and artificial. Here, I am simply using "later" Heidegger as a marker for a group of texts written during a particular period.

2. For a recent attempt to address this issue of "accessibility," see Rush (2001). For an excellent examination of the "later" Heidegger's philosophical style, particularly in the paradigmatic work *Beiträge zur Philosophie*, see Thomson (2003).

3. For classic presentations of this view, see Löwith (1998) and Richardson (2003).

4. See Sheehan (2001a) and (2001b).

Was there, as some suggest, a "turn before the turn"? Was *Being and Time* really an aberration in an otherwise continuous project? All of these questions pertain, of course, to Heidegger's thought as a whole. They also bear upon the present issue, namely, his phenomenology of religion. There is, after all, no disputing the fact that the most sustained discussions of religion in Heidegger's corpus all date from the period prior to the publication of *Being and Time*.

At risk of appearing too cavalier, I will not take a position here on the issue of a "turn" in Heidegger's thought as a whole. Instead, I will address the most obvious differences between his early discussions of religion and his later talk of the "holy" and the "gods."[5] My contention is that these differences represent shifts of emphasis in a more or less stable, well-established project of critically addressing the religious situation of late modernity through a phenomenological methodology. The differences between the "early" and "later" Heidegger on religion are not sufficient to warrant the claim that his later work is a radical departure from the material discussed in the preceding chapter.

The first thing that a careful reader will notice about Heidegger's later writings is that none of them contain the kind of sustained, detailed phenomenological analysis of religious life of the sort found in the 1918 and 1919 notes, or in the lectures from 1920 and 1921. Instead, Heidegger's discussions of religious themes are scattered throughout his essays, lectures, and unpublished manuscripts composed roughly between 1929 and the end of his life. These scattered remarks are substantial enough, despite their often fragmentary nature, to deflate any claim that Heidegger simply *abandoned* the project of a phenomenology of religion. Instead, Heidegger shifts the emphasis of his analyses away from phenomenological *description* more toward outlining or "formally indicating" a *normative* concept of religiosity. The latter emphasis, of course, was already clearly present in his earlier studies of religion. Indeed, the distinctiveness of Heidegger's approach to the phenomenology of religion lies precisely in its combination of *descriptive* and *normative* dimensions. That is, getting the right theory about religiosity was never Heidegger's *ultimate* goal. With some exceptions, it becomes even less so in the years after 1929. Indeed, in 1935, when Heidegger authored his "On the Origin of the Work of Art" essay–which, as will be shown below, constitutes the principal statement of his later views of religion–his perception of cultural crisis had attained a new level of urgency. Paralleling his growing concern about the nature and consequences of technology and modernity, Heidegger

---

5. For an attempt at understanding the "turn" in relation to Heidegger's philosophy of religion, see Hemming (2002).

focused his attention on outlining a paradigm of religiosity capable of breaking out of the impasses of modern life.

The "later" Heidegger, perhaps even more so that the Heidegger of *Being and Time* and before, directed virtually all of his prodigious intellectual energy toward outlining and affecting a profound intellectual and cultural revolution in European life.[6] *Religion* occupies a crucial place in this revolutionary program. Indeed, Heidegger often used the combined Hölderlinian-Nietzschean formula of the "death of God" as a characterization of the overall situation of late modernity against which his revolutionary program was aimed. In the 1946 essay "Wozu Dichter?" Heidegger makes it clear that a reinvigoration and transformation of the religious heritage of Europe lies at the very heart of this program. Enlisting himself in the struggle against the "disenchanted" world of modernity, Heidegger writes:

> The turning of an age does not occur at just any time by the eruption of a new god or by the new eruption of an old god from an ambush. Where is he supposed to turn to, upon his return, if human beings have not already prepared for him his sojourn? How could there ever be for God a sojourn fit for God unless the radiance had already begun to appear in all that is? (G5 270/201)

In his well-known "Letter on Humanism," written also in 1946 but published the following year, Heidegger again draws his readers' attention to *religious* implications of his revolutionary program. Styling his project as one of replacing "homelessness" with "nearness," Heidegger asserts: "In such nearness, if at all, a decision may be made as to whether and how God and the gods withhold their presence and the night remains, whether and how the day of the holy dawns, whether and how in the upsurgence of the holy an epiphany of God and the gods can begin anew" (G9 338/258).

Yet another text from 1946, "Nietzsche's Word: God is Dead," echoes the "Letter on Humanism." At the close of the latter, Heidegger likens his activities to a farmer's laying "inconspicuous" furrows in a field (G9 364/276). The sense is that Heidegger understands his work as *preparatory* rather than as a finished system. Just as a farmer breaks up the soil in preparation for planting, so, too, Heidegger understands his own contribution as running ahead of possible systematic developments and shifts in culture. To use his parlance from the 1920s, Heidegger is trying to effect a cultural revolution through critical questioning and through "formal indication" of an alternative to

---

6. This claim forms the centerpiece of Young (2002).

the situation of late modernity. This is precisely the point that he makes in "Nietzsche's Word":

> This essential thinking, essential and therefore everywhere and in every respect only *preparatory*, proceeds in inconspicuousness. [...] To share in thinking is the unobtrusive sowing of sowers: the sowing is not made good by acknowledgement or profit, and the sowers may never see blade nor fruit and not know a harvest. They serve the sowing, and even more willingly they serve the preparation for sowing. Before sowing comes plowing. It is essential to reclaim the field that had to remain in obscurity while the land of metaphysics was inescapably dominant. (G5 211/158, emphasis added)

In his later writings, then, Heidegger is above all concerned to "sow" seeds for a future revolution in European life. That this revolution is meant to have religious implications is beyond doubt. Indeed, several years after these three pieces were written, Heidegger began to connect with a new generation of theologians in hopes of stimulating a movement beyond the conceptual paradigms of modernity. In his 1970 preface to "Phenomenology and Theology," Heidegger still hopes that his own sketch of a paradigmatic "Christianness" will challenge and stimulate those whose business it is to interpret and articulate faith (G9 45/39). And so, the relative dearth of sustained phenomenological analysis of religion in Heidegger's later writings suggests not an abandonment of his earlier project, but rather the strengthening of one aspect of that project over another.

Perhaps the more pronounced difference between Heidegger's early and later discussions of religion is the prominent role played by the Greeks and by Hölderlin in the latter. Between 1918 and 1921, when Heidegger's work on the phenomenology of religion was at its most intensive, his stated theme was what he, following many other scholars of the time, called "primitive Christianity [*Urchristentum*]." For Heidegger, this referred first and foremost to the religious life of the New Testament. But Heidegger also used this designation to describe various religious renaissances that occurred over the subsequent millennia. The most important examples, to him, were Augustine, the medieval and early modern mystics, Luther, Schleiermacher, and Kierkegaard.

However, after the 1927 essay "Phenomenology and Theology," which he delivered before a group of theologians in Marburg, Heidegger did not devote himself to a specifically *Christian* theme or audience again until 1953, when he attended a meeting at the Protestant Academy at Hofgeismar. Instead, he chose as the theme of his lectures Hölderlin (WS 1934–1935, WS 1941–1942, SS 1942) and the pre-Socratic Greeks (WS 1942–1943, SS 1943). During the 1930s and 1940s, his brief addresses and essays are almost all devoted to Hölderlin, and none of them is concerned with "primitive Christianity."

In some cases, commentators have viewed this as an *abandonment* of Christianity on Heidegger's part.[7] This claim is, of course, of more biographical than philosophical significance. More importantly, it has often been made in an exaggerated fashion. Both Caputo and Van Buren, for example, maintain that during the 1930s and beyond, Heidegger took on the old Romantic and Nietzschean project of a "new mythology."[8] In this case, this "mythology" was meant to legitimate German nationalism, and to replace the moribund God of Christianity with the vital, passionate pantheon of ancient Greece.[9]

This reading drastically misrepresents Heidegger's work. That he rejected the hellenophilic nostalgia of his Nietzschean contemporaries is made abundantly clear in "Wozu Dichter?" (1946), where he labels the "flight to the Greek gods" a "self-deception" (G5 294–295/221). Moreover, in remarks appended to the text of the WS 1942–1943 lecture course on Parmenides, Heidegger writes:

> Our discussions about "the Roman" are being interpreted as stemming from an anti-Christian hostility. Let us leave it for theology to decide whether the meditation on the essence of truth we have attempted here could not, taken in context, be more fruitful for the preservation of Christianity than the aberrant desire to construct new "scientifically" founded proofs for the existence of God and for the freedom of the will on the basis of modern atomic physics. (G54 248/166)

Heidegger's suggestion, made here in his typically elusive manner, is that his focus on and enthusiasm for the conceptual world of ancient Greece might provide just the sort of new paradigm that could help Christianity to reassert itself in the modern age. He certainly has no interest in the "impossible" task of resurrecting the lost grandeur of Greece (G54 248/166). Moreover, Heidegger elsewhere makes it quite clear that he has no intention of carrying out Nietzsche's call for a new "table of values" or a new "god" to fill the vacuum left by the "death of God." As I have already discussed (see chapter 1), as early as SS 1937, Heidegger criticizes Nietzsche's concept of the "God-forming instinct" (G87 7), which of course lies at the very center of Nietzsche's neo-Romantic program. In WS 1944–1945, he once more questions Nietzsche's view that the "gods" are simply projections of the "religious talent" of peoples (G50 107–108). In "Wesen der Nihilismus," through a series of rhetorical questions, Heidegger indicates his doubts about whether the famed Nietzschean "God-seeker" is even capable of entering into the domain in which what he seeks can be found (G67 193–194, 199).

---

7. See, for example, Caputo (1993a) and (1993b).

8. For a good recent account of this stream of German intellectual history, see Williamson (2005). The classic account is Frank (1982).

9. Caputo (1993a): 174–175, 181; and Van Buren (1994): 376–377, 384–386.

What, then, to make of Heidegger's obvious enthusiasm for ancient Greece and for that lover of all things Hellenic, Hölderlin? Heidegger answers this question for us quite clearly. Both Hölderlin and the Greeks are viewed by Heidegger as *possibilities*, in the sense in which he uses this term in §§74–75 of *Being and Time*. In these sections of the text, Heidegger explains how people adopt patterns of life from their tradition, subtly transforming them by taking them up in their own temporally unique situation. Making reference to Nietzsche's early conception of "critical history," he goes on to outline a kind of "authentic historicality" in which possibilities from the past are taken up as patterns for the future in such a way that critical light is thrown on the present (SZ 396–397/448–449). This is, by his own frequent admission, precisely what Heidegger aims to do with Hölderlin and the Greeks.

In WS 1941–1942, with Hölderlin in mind, Heidegger calls great poets "history-founding [*geschichtsstiftende*]" individuals, the "richness" of whose works possesses hidden "spaces of resonance [*Schwingungsräume*]," untapped potentialities capable of being taken up as models for the future (G52 15). Hölderlin's poetry is, for Heidegger, "like a lonely peak in the growing need, which first opens around itself another space of truth" (G52 38). In 1944 notes on Hölderlin's *Empedocles*, Heidegger makes it clear that he is interested in the "future" of Hölderlin's poetry (G75 332). That is, in keeping with his earlier motto that "higher than actuality stands possibility" (SZ 38/63), Hölderlin's poetry is less a matter of historical interest for Heidegger than it is of interest as an existential and *revolutionary* possibility. Hölderlin "poetically grounds the other beginning of our history" (G75 336). Quite conscious of the idiosyncrasies of his readings of the poet, Heidegger makes it clear that his interpretation "does not want to be 'the' interpretation of this poetry; it belongs completely and singly to the preparation of another beginning, and claims no correctness or validity of the sort that belongs to the 'science of literature'" (G75 336). In notes written during 1945 and 1946, Heidegger argues that Hölderlin offers a glimpse of a new cultural paradigm, a "destiny," a "stroke of fate that is sent far beyond both us today and the coming generation" (G75 350). Hölderlin's poetry is a "future that comes towards us [*Zu-kunft*]" (G75 350). In "Wozu Dichter?" (1946), Heidegger summarizes nearly over a decade's worth of wrestling with Hölderlin by asserting unequivocally that the poet is a paradigm, one that allows us to critically confront the modern age, the "desolate time" (G5 272/202). Hölderlin's importance lies in his ability to "risk language," i.e., to stretch the boundaries of our dominant conceptual frameworks (G5 310/233).

One of the ways in which Hölderlin is exemplary for Heidegger is in the poet's own dialogue with Greek culture. Hölderlin, like Heidegger, has no interest in resurrecting ancient Greece, but rather in finding his own "essential space" or "fate" (G52 89–90). In this much, Hölderlin's hymnic poetry marks a transition from "Greece to the future" (G52 94). Hölderlin "listens" to the past so that it might give a measure for human freedom, "in which the human being can himself be historical for a while at the particular time [*jeweils*]" (G52 161). Heidegger models his own confrontation with the heritage of ancient Greece on Hölderlin. In "The Age of the World-Picture," he contrasts the Greek understanding of being with that of modern subjectivism by way of critically exposing the deficiencies of the latter (G5 90–91/69). In his travel notebook from 1962, Heidegger physically re-enacts a Hölderlinian confrontation with ancient Greece. He searches for a "clue" for a "new domain," one that "lies behind us, not before us" (G75 215–216). "The Greek," he asserts, "is still something awaited, something intimated from the poetry of the ancients, brought near through Hölderlin's elegies and hymns, thought on my own long path of thinking" (G75 224). He characterizes his whole project thus: "Neither hopelessness, nor the detached comparison of today with what once was, moves these thoughts. The only question posed the sense of whether a homely sojourn might still be vouchsafed to human beings as it formerly was to the Greeks, in a more original, greater, richer, and more measured way" (G75 235).

The crucial groundwork for Heidegger's approach to Hölderlin and to Greek antiquity is laid in §§74–75 of *Being and Time*. In this part of the text, he articulates his conception of historical consciousness that he had been developing for a decade or more in lectures and occasional writings. On his account, history is neither simply a series of events nor the "objective" study of this series of events; instead, as he puts it in numerous places in the 1920s, we "are" history. "Historicality [*Geschichtlichkeit*]," the ongoing process of the transmission, realization, and redefinition of a cultural inheritance, constitutes the fundamental datum of Heidegger's account. For Heidegger, individuals can participate in this process either "inauthentically" or "authentically." The latter option involves a critical re-appropriation of elements of one's cultural inheritance as *possibilities* or *models* for the future. Heidegger makes it clear that slavish imitation is out of the question. Thus, his conception of historical consciousness is meant to steer a path between militant modernism, on the one hand, with its concomitant rejection of the "past," and reactionary conservatism, on the other hand.[10] This is precisely the case also in his later work, where Heidegger is occupied with coming to terms with the Greek world and with Hölderlin's poetry. For Heidegger, both represent not some lost "golden age," but rather missed opportunities or possibilities that can be taken up and modeled in the future. Most importantly,

---

10. For a detailed account of the nature and development of Heidegger's conception of "historicality," see Crowe (2006). See also Sluga (2001) and Bambach (1995).

the paradigms offered by Hölderlin and the Greeks provide a standpoint from which to critically examine the broad cultural situation of late modernity.

The Concept of "The Holy"

In addition to his shift of focus away from "primitive Christianity" and toward Hölderlin and the Greeks, there is also a more substantive difference between Heidegger's early and later phenomenology of religion. While certainly not absent from his work in the years immediately following World War I, the concept of "the holy" or "the sacred [*das Heilige*]" occupies a particularly prominent place in his later (post–*Being and Time*) writings.[11] As Heidegger makes clear, the concept of the holy is a vital element of his overall account of religion. This claim is prominent in the 1946 "Letter on Humanism," where Heidegger introduces "the holy" as "the essential sphere of divinity" (G9 338/258), asserting that "only from the essence of the holy is the essence of divinity to be thought" (G9 351/267). While Heidegger offers little clarification of what these claims amount to, it is clear that he wants to locate the concept of the holy at the very center of his phenomenology of religion. "Holiness" is another word for what I have been calling "religious meaning"; "the holy" is, therefore, that which ultimately enables things to show up as having religious meaning. As has been discussed above, Heidegger's discussions of religion in the early 1920s, while they certainly provide an outline of the basic contours of a theory of religious meaning, do not contain a completely developed account. But, one can see what such an account would have to look like. For Heidegger, meaning derives from a world, in the sense of a network of relations of a broadly teleological nature. Whatever it is that anchors and orders this network of relations is what stamps the character of a world. In the case of a religious world, the network of relations is anchored in a distinctive "telos." "The holy" is Heidegger's name for this "telos" in his writings after 1929.

The "Letter on Humanism," Heidegger's most well-known postwar "manifesto" of his basic philosophical position, provides a crucial clue for understanding that this is in fact what is at issue in Heidegger's account of "the holy." The stronger formulation of the claim about the pivotal status of the "the holy" is framed by Heidegger's attempts to address common criticisms and misunderstandings of his thought that had surfaced over the years, most

---

11. In 1918, Husserl asked Heidegger to review Rudolf Otto's recently published work, *Das Heilige*. While Heidegger never completed this project, it is clear that he was quite familiar with Otto's work, and, like Husserl, heralded it as a contribution to the nascent phenomenology of religion. Also, in SS 1919, Heidegger cites Wilhelm Windelband's essay by the same name. He seems to have read this essay for the first time a year or so prior to giving this lecture course.

recently in Sartre's "Existentialism is a Humanism." Sartre famously enlisted Heidegger into the ranks of the "atheist" existentialists, alongside himself and Nietzsche. Heidegger, however, is clearly at pains to separate himself from this attribution. According to Heidegger, Sartre's claim rests on a misreading of the central concept of "being-in-the-world." As I have already argued at length, all indications are that this concept is the bedrock of Heidegger's phenomenological interpretation of religiosity. "World," Heidegger makes clear, does not "imply earthly as opposed to heavenly being, nor the 'worldly' as opposed to the 'spiritual'" (G9 350/266). That is, to say that the fundamental feature of human existence as such is being-in-the-world is not to make a *metaphysical* claim about the position of humanity within the cosmic order. While Heidegger acknowledges his debts to the early Christian (particularly Johannine) understanding of "world," he also makes it clear that he is using this term in his own distinctive way (G9 143–144/112). He explicates his conception of "world" in "Letter on Humanism" thusly: "'World' is the clearing of being into which the human being stands out on the basis of his thrown essence" (G9 350/266). The "world," then, is not the domain of sensible, finite, temporal things, but rather the nexus of meaning that human beings always already inhabit and which allows them to discover entities as having various sorts of significance.

Thus, strictly speaking, the concept of being-in-the-world implies nothing about the cosmological position of human beings, nor about the existence or non-existence of God. And yet, as Heidegger is quick to point out, while "being-in-the-world" does not *entail* any metaphysical or theological commitments, it does hold promise as a crucial element in a worked-out phenomenology of religion (G9 350–351/266–267). In "Letter on Humanism," Heidegger merely alludes to the connection between the "holy," as a necessary condition for understanding the meaning of "God," and his own characteristic conception of "being-in-the-world." However, by looking at some other texts, this connection can be elucidated in some detail.

In his lecture course for SS 1928, Heidegger first draws a link between the concept of the "holy" and "being-in-the-world." His remarks run as follows:

> The problem of transcendence must be drawn back into the inquiry about temporality and freedom, and only from there can it be shown to what extent the understanding of being qua overpowering [*Übermacht*], qua holiness, belongs to transcendence itself as essentially ontologically different. The point is not to prove the divine ontically, in its "existence," but *to clarify the origin of this understanding of being by means of the transcendence of Dasein, i.e., to clarify how this idea of being belongs to understanding of being as such.* (G26 211/165, emphasis added)

Admittedly, this remark remains largely programmatic in character, as does that from "Letter on Humanism," despite the intervening gap of almost twenty years. However, the passage from SS 1928 clarifies the nature of Heidegger's program more thoroughly than do his later remarks. "Transcendence," it will be recalled, is a term Heidegger uses in 1928 and 1929 for what he elsewhere calls "being-in-the-world." That is, "transcendence" is a designation for the basic structure of human existence, such that human beings pre-reflectively "inhabit" a nexus or domain of meaning that allows them to make sense of things. Another way that Heidegger puts this claim is to say that human beings always already have a tacit "understanding of being." It is in terms of this concept of an "understanding of being" that, Heidegger says, the basic structure of human religiosity can be explicated. Again, Heidegger is careful to say that the concepts of "being-in-the-world" and its cognates do not, by themselves, commit one to any particular metaphysical or theological view. Instead, these concepts can potentially illuminate the basic structure of religiosity. By now, this should be a familiar idea. In the preceding chapter, I argued that the concept of "being-in-the-world" provides the fundamental conceptual apparatus in terms of which Heidegger tries to work out a phenomenology of religion in the early 1920s. His understanding of the basic contours of this project remains virtually unchanged between 1921 and 1928, and between 1928 and 1946.

In the passage from SS 1928 quoted above, Heidegger describes "the holy" as the *content* of a particular "understanding of being." This point makes possible an instructive analogy to a more familiar element of Heidegger's thought. In *Being and Time*, Heidegger describes "understanding" as a crucial element in the totality of being-in-the-world. Understanding, in the sense that it is used here, is not an explicit conceptual grasp of something. Instead, it is the assignment of oneself to a particular project, such as a particular practical interest (e.g., being a carpenter). This assignment opens up a network of relationships ordered to this project, a network that enables things (e.g., the tools in a carpenter's workshop) to make sense to us. Religion is similarly characterized by a pre-reflective understanding of something that orders a complex network of relations in such a way that things show up as mattering in a specifically religious way.

Heidegger's use of "the holy" and "superior power" interchangeably testifies to the influence of Ernst Cassirer's influential account of "mythical thought" in the second volume of his *Philosophie der Symbolischen Formen*.[12] Indeed, the influence of Cassirer's work is easy to detect in Heidegger's shift away

---

12. See Cassirer (1955).

from the phenomenology of a particular religious tradition, i.e., Christianity, toward the more general account that is found in his writings from the 1930s and later. Cassirer's Neo-Kantian analysis of "mythic consciousness" came to Heidegger's attention during the mid-1920s. Heidegger's earliest reference to it is in *Being and Time* (SZ 51, note xi). Shortly after this treatise appeared, Heidegger authored a critical review of Cassirer's *Das mythische Denken*, which was appended to the 1929 book *Kant and the Problem of Metaphysics*. This review offers substantial clarification regarding the concept of the "holy" and its role in Heidegger's mature account of religion. This review is a watershed moment in the development of Heidegger's phenomenology of religion. Cassirer's work induced him to undertake a more comprehensive account of religion *as such*. He had already embarked upon an abortive attempt at such an account between 1917 and 1919, particularly in connection with Rudolf Otto's *Idea of the Holy* and under Husserl's encouragement. However, beyond a few suggestive notes, Heidegger never made much progress in this early attempt at a *general* phenomenology of religion. In the mid-1920s, Cassirer had, so to speak, beaten Heidegger to the punch. As his reference to Cassirer in *Being and Time* shows, Heidegger hoped to take up his earlier project again, outfitted with the more developed conceptual framework that had been worked out in the intervening years.

Commenting on part 2 of Cassirer's book, Heidegger finds occasion to expand upon the basic understanding of being characteristic of what he calls "mythical Dasein." The fundamental feature of "mythical Dasein" is the understanding of "presence" as "overpoweringness [*Übermachtigkeit*]." This comprises the "horizon" within which the ordinary or "common" can show up as such (G3 257/181–182). In other words, the "sacred [*Heiligem*]" constitutes the background or horizon that allows ordinary "reality" to show up precisely *as* ordinary or profane. Heidegger elaborates:

> This character of being of the mythical "world" and of mythical Dasein itself is the sense of the *concept of mana* [*Mana-Vorstellung*], which has come to the fore in the study of myth during the most recent decades as one, or rather, *the* fundamental category of mythic "thought." Mana does not designate a definite sphere of objects, and it can also not be attributed on the basis of certain "spiritual" forces. Mana is the most general character of being, the "how" in which reality comes over [*überfällt*] all human Dasein. The expressions "mana," "wakanda," "orenda," and "manitu" are interjections in the immediate being overcome by surging beings. (G3 257–258/182)

This fundamental understanding of being as *mana*, as "sacred" or "holy," is "articulated" or "lived out" in the most basic practices of what Heidegger calls "mythical Dasein" (G3 258/182). Thus, Heidegger's claim is that "mythical Dasein" is a particular configuration of "being-in-the-world," of pre-reflectively inhabiting a tacit understanding of meaning which is then expressed in thought and practice. As in his lectures on religion in WS 1920–1921, Heidegger wants to stress the primacy of *practice* as an articulation or expression of religious "being-in-the-world." "Cult" and "ritual" are, in this case, the basic articulations of the understanding of being characteristic of "mythical Dasein" (G3 263/185). Heidegger suggests, on two separate occasions, that his own conceptual apparatus of a "radical ontology of Dasein" holds the key to clarifying the structure of myth, and he takes Cassirer to task for his Neo-Kantian assumptions (G3 265, 267/187, 188). He goes on to apply the concept of "thrownness" or *Geworfenheit*, familiar from *Being and Time*, to the task of explicating the structure of "mythical Dasein":

> In "thrownness" lies a being delivered over of Dasein to the world such that a being-in-the-world is overwhelmed by that to which it is delivered over. Overpoweringness is only able to manifest itself as such *for* a being-delivered-over-to. [. . .] In such dependence [*Angewiesenheit*] on the overpowering, Dasein is struck dumb [*benommen*] *by* this and is therefore only able to experience itself as belonging to and associated with this reality. In thrownness, therefore, every being that is somehow uncovered [*enthüllte*] has the character of being of overpoweringness (mana). (G3 267/188)

In this passage, Heidegger uses the concept of "thrownness" to express one of the fundamental themes of his phenomenology of religion. As early as 1919, in glosses on Schleiermacher's writings, Heidegger had stressed the *receptive* or *passive* structure of religious life. Religion is predicated on the capacity of human beings to be "open to" "worlds" of meaning. In WS 1920–1921, Heidegger highlights the way in which specifically Christian religiosity is structured by the *reception* of the proclamation. This basic structure forms a central piece in his case for ontological realism in the philosophy of religion. His claim, it will be recalled, is that once the antecedent commitment to the explanatory apparatus of Neo-Kantianism is suspended, and one allows religious phenomena to "speak for themselves," as it were, it becomes clear that religious meaning is experienced as *transcending* the subjective sphere. This basic point reappears here in the 1929 review of Cassirer's work on mythology. While he questions Cassirer's application of Kantian explanatory schemes to primitive religious phenomena, he finds Cassirer's emphasis on the basic category of *mana* to be suggestive of a more accurate understanding of these same phenomena. More specifically, the concept of the "overpowering," of *mana* or the "holy" fits quite well into Heidegger's own interpretation of religiosity as a mode of "being-in-the-world."

For Heidegger, the "holy" is *the* crucial term in the "understanding of being" that lies at the very core of human religiosity. The idea that religion rests upon or is constituted by an "understanding of being" is something that Heidegger had consistently maintained for more than a decade leading up to his 1929 review of Cassirer. In response to Cassirer's work, however, Heidegger expands the scope of this fundamental commitment. That is, the "understanding of being" as "holy" or "overpowering" is located at a level deeper than the more specific "worlds" constitutive of particular religious traditions. The "holy" now becomes something like the enabling condition of religiosity as such.[13] In other words, religion, as a specific mode of "being-in-the-world," is made possible by a deeper tacit understanding of being as "overpowering," as an autonomous, mysterious source of meaning. While the germs of this view are clearly present in Heidegger's earlier studies of religion, he seems to have arrived at a new appreciation for the centrality of the "holy" in religion in the late 1920s.

Between the 1929 Cassirer review and the 1946 "Letter on Humanism," Heidegger repeatedly revisits the concept of the "holy." His basic understanding of this concept remains more or less stable throughout this period. However, rather than looking to Cassirer's *Philosophy of Symbolic Forms* or to ethnographical studies of Polynesian religion (from which the concept of *mana* was originally derived), he turns to Hölderlin's poetry, particularly his *hymnic* poetry, for refinements and alternative articulations of the basic contours of the idea. As I have already pointed out, Heidegger's interest in Hölderlin in general is motivated by his conviction that Hölderlin had already intimated a possible alternative to the prevailing "deep framework" of modernity. By looking to Hölderlin for an understanding of the "holy," Heidegger therefore signals that the concept of the "holy" is meant to do more than simply express a fact about human religiosity. Rather, it is also meant to play a central role in his attempts to articulate a way out of the perceived crisis of late modernity. The understanding of being as "holy" is meant to constitute an alternative to modern subjectivism, for which meaning is a "product" of human subjectivity.

In a 1943 essay on Hölderlin's poem "Homecoming/To Kindred Ones," Heidegger picks up on the poem's theme of "gaiety." On Heidegger's reading, "gaiety" is interchangeable with what Hölderlin elsewhere calls the "holy." Importantly, this brings out another side of the fundamental "object [*Gegenstand*]" that anchors religious meaning. In the 1929 Cassirer review, Heidegger focuses mostly on the overwhelming absoluteness of the religious object. Here, however, the designation "gaiety" expresses the fact that the object of religion is also something that is attractive and valuable, something

---

13. In this respect, Heidegger's position in 1929 comes close to that of Rudolf Otto in *Das Heilige* (1917). Otto, famously, argues that the "concept of the holy" constitutes the fundamental bedrock of *all* explicit forms of religiosity. Like Cassirer, he relies on ethnographical data, as well as his own extensive knowledge of the Judeo-Christian tradition, to support this claim. While Heidegger was familiar with Otto's work as early as 1918, he seems not to have developed his own conception of the "holy" until the late 1920s.

that brings joy and a sense of liberation from quotidian concerns. This combination of absoluteness and attractive value had figured into Heidegger's account of religion as early as 1918, when he sketched some notes for a review of Rudolf Otto's *Das Heilige*. It reappears in his explication of 1 Thessalonians in WS 1920–21, where Heidegger characterizes the life of the early church as a dynamic combination of "anxious worry" or awe before the judgment seat of God and unshakeable joy even in the midst of tribulation. Or again, in his discussion of Augustine from SS 1921, Heidegger emphasizes that God is both an object of love and of "chaste fear [*timor castus*]."

Here, in the 1943 essay, Heidegger first of all observes that "gaiety" is a name for a background or horizon of meaning that, while not reducible to particular things, allows the latter to show up as meaningful within the field of human experience. He writes: "But nearer still and becoming ever nearer, though less apparent than birches and mountains and therefore mostly overlooked and passed by, is the gaiety itself in which people and things appear" (G4 16/35).

In this passage Heidegger attributes a fundamental characteristic of his concept of "world" to Hölderlin's "gaiety." In the opening section of *Being and Time*, Heidegger argues that behind the facile self-evidence of the concept of "being" lies a deeper truth, viz., that "being" itself is an "enigma [*Rätsel*]" (SZ 4/23). That is, while it is the horizon against which things become intelligible to human experience, "being" itself remains largely invisible to everyday practice and even to metaphysics. Neither theoretical transparency nor explicit awareness is a necessary feature of having an understanding of "world" (SZ 86/119). "World," the horizon against which things show up as meaningful, remains largely invisible. Attention is focused on the things and people that are encountered within the space of meaning opened up by a world. This is precisely the point Heidegger is making about "gaiety" in the passage quoted above. "Gaiety" is Hölderlin's name for the *horizon* within which his poetic experience of the landscape makes sense.

A bit later on in "Homecoming/To the Kindred Ones," Heidegger explicitly links Hölderlin's conception of "gaiety" with the "holy":

> This pure opening which first "imparts," that is, grants, the open to every "space" and to every "temporal space [*Zeitraum*]," we call gaiety [*die Heitere*] according to an old word of our mother tongue. At one and the same time, it is the clarity (*claritas*) in whose brightness everything clear rests, the grandeur (*serenitas*) in whose strength everything high stands, and the merriment (*hilaritas*) in whose play everything, liberated, sways. [. . .] It is the holy, "the highest" and the "holy" are the same for the poet: gaiety. (G4 18/37)[14]

---

14. Heidegger briefly revisits this exposition of the "holy" in terms of "brightness [*Heitere*]" in the 1945–1946 text, "Hölderlins Dichtung ein Geschick" (G75 364).

As in the 1929 Cassirer review, Heidegger takes the "holy" to be the horizon or background against which things can show up as being meaningful in a certain way for human beings. Heidegger unpacks the sense of "holy" for Hölderlin by playing off the roots of the word *heiter*, meaning "gay" or "cheerful." In its original usage, this word and its cognates referred to the sky or the "heavens." More specifically, it referred to a bright or clear sky, and it shares the same root as the Latin *caelum*.[15] The "holy," then, is analogous to the bright sky that allows things to show up clearly to human beings. At the same time, like the "heavens above," it possesses a kind of awesomeness or majesty that is particularly reflected in certain things. Like *mana*, it is "overpowering," and it is concentrated or expressed most unmistakably by particularly sacred things, locales, or persons. Moreover, like the sky, it is beyond human control. One and the same sky can be bright and cheerful one day and ominous and threatening the next. All of these features form central aspects of the "understanding of being" as "holy." But the "holy" is also something that is celebrated, something that brings joy by connecting people with something that transcends the world of everyday concern, in which everything is characterized as meaningful in an instrumental way. Along with possessing awesome transcendence, the holy is something of surpassing value. Rather than a *particular thing* or any collection of things, the "holy" is a kind of horizon or background.

In an essay on "Wie wenn am Feiertage . . .," composed prior to "Homecoming/To Kindred Ones" but published later, Heidegger links the "holy" with Hölderlin's conception of "nature." In Hölderlin's work, the concept of "nature" grows out of his critique of Fichtean idealism. Like many in the early Romantic generation, Hölderlin was captivated by the figure of the "holy, rejected Spinoza," as Schleiermacher called him, or the "God-intoxicated man," as Novalis put it.[16] In Hölderlin's rendition, Spinozist "nature" becomes a primal unity that exists prior to the separation of subject and object, and which can be intimated in rare moments of religious-aesthetic rapture. In his novel *Hyperion*, the action is driven by the protagonist's periodic intuitions of this primal unity, his loss of it, and his subsequent quest to rediscover it.[17] Heidegger, as critics have pointed out, is less interested in the details of Hölderlin's anti-Fichtean metaphysics than in the features of his discourse of the "holy" he finds useful for articulating his own phenomenology

---

15. See Kluge (2002): 404.

16. Schleiermacher (1996): 24; von Hardenberg (1960): 651.

17. For a good account of Hölderlin's position in the Romantic reaction to Fichte, see Pinkard (2002): 139–144. Another excellent overview of Hölderlin's thought is Larmore (2000). The classic account of Hölderlin's philosophy is Henrich (1992).

of religion.[18] However, it is also worth noting that Hölderlin's reaction to Fichte's idealism bears some striking resemblances to Heidegger's critique of Neo-Kantianism, which, on Heidegger's reading, shares a good deal with Fichte's *Wissenschaftslehre*. In any event, the accuracy of Heidegger's readings of Hölderlin is not at issue here. Instead, my focus is on the way in which his reading of Hölderlin enables Heidegger to refine and develop the concept of the "holy" first expressed in the 1929 Cassirer review.

One of the important features of Hölderlin's "nature" that Heidegger picks up on in "Wie wenn am Feiertage . . ." is, once again, its a priori structure. "Nature," he observes, "is prior to all actuality [*Wirklichen*] and action [*Wirken*], even prior to the gods" (G4 59/81). He quickly goes on to try to clarify this somewhat enigmatic statement:

> Nature is not by any means "above [*über*]" the gods in an isolated domain of reality that is "higher than [*oberhalb*]" them. Nature is higher than "the" gods. She, "the powerful," is still capable of something other than the gods as the clearing [*Lichtung*] in which everything can first be present. Hölderlin calls nature the holy because she is "older than the ages and above the gods." Thus, "holiness" is in no way a property borrowed from a determinate god. The holy is not holy because it is divine; rather the divine is divine because in its way it is "holy" [. . .]. The holy is the essence of nature. (G4 59/81–82)

The "holy" or "nature" is not a particular being that occupies a place in a hierarchy of beings. One might contrast it with Plato's "idea of the Good" or Plotinus's ineffable "One," both of which are substantially real and which are located at the top of such a hierarchy. The relation between Hölderlinian nature and particular beings, including natural things and the gods, is thus not one of ontical dependence. The "holy" or "nature" is not the *cause* of the gods. Despite superficial similarities, this conception of "nature" is to be kept separate from any association with the cosmogonic and theogonic myths of many ancient and tribal peoples that have the gods (and everything else) being generated, in a quite literal way, by a vaguely defined and religiously insignificant primal deity. Instead, as Heidegger makes clear, Hölderlinian "nature" is the "clearing [*Lichtung*]," the "world" or "space of meaning" that makes it possible for particular things, *including the gods*, to show up as meaningful within the field of human experience. This passage looks ahead to the schema that Heidegger presents in the 1946 "Letter on Humanism,"

---

18. Heidegger's readings of Hölderlin have drawn critical comment from literary historians and philosophers alike almost since his first publications on the subject. Perhaps the most thoroughly argued of these critiques is Henrich (1997).

and adds substantial clarification to the latter. Heidegger does not subordinate God or the gods to the "holy," as if the latter were some "super-deity." Instead, the "holy" is a domain of meaning that is tacitly understood in such a way that concrete human encounters with "divine" beings first become possible. That is, the "holy" is what anchors the network of relations in which the gods have religious meaning. This thought recalls the contrast, highlighted by Heidegger, that Augustine draws between magic and properly religious attitudes. For a magician, God no longer has properly religious meaning, but is rather only meaningful in an instrumental way.

"Nature" or the "holy" is also not to be confused with the "natural" world, the planet Earth, or some idolized rural landscape. To call "nature" the "holy" is not to deify the natural world at all. Instead, in Heidegger's hands, the "holy" is transformed into an a priori structure that makes it possible for things to show up as meaningful in a certain way. He tries to express the matter thusly: "It [nature] is the primordial [Anfängliche], and it remains in itself unbroken and 'whole [heil].' This originary [ursprünglich] 'wholeness [Heile]' gives a gift to everything real by virtue of its omnipresence: it confers the grace of its own abiding presence [Verweilung]" (G4 63/85).

In a contemporaneous text, Über den Anfang, Heidegger makes it clear that this talk of "beginning" and the "primordial [Anfängliche]" does not connote temporal priority or causation, but rather to what Being and Time called the "perfect tense a priori" (G70 54–56). That is, as a "beginning," "nature" or the "holy" is the "world" or nexus of meaning that is always already in play, such that human beings can then experience things as being intelligible or meaningful. This is essentially in line with what Heidegger had to say in the 1929 Cassirer review, where he explained the "holy" as part of an "understanding of being."

A bit later on in "Wie wenn am Feiertage . . . ," Heidegger returns to one of the central themes of the conception of the "holy" first worked out in the 1929 Cassirer review. He observes that, in Hölderlin's poetry, "The holy confronts all experience with something to which it is unaccustomed, and so deprives it of its ground. Deranging [Ent-setzend] in this way, the holy is the awesome [Entsetzliche] itself" (G4 63/85). Recall that, for "mythical Dasein," things show up against a horizon of "overpoweringness [Übermächtigkeit]" or awesomeness. This remains a salient feature of the "understanding of being" that enables religiosity throughout Heidegger's later discussions. As will be shown in more detail below, the awesome "otherness" of the "holy" constitutes the horizon within which divine beings can show up as divine. For Heidegger, the "divinity [Gottheit]" of the "gods," i.e., that which constitutes their being as gods, consists precisely in such awesome otherness. It is only within an understanding of being as fundamentally mysterious and transcendent (vis-à-vis human interests) that such beings can even show up as such.

The works discussed in the preceding paragraphs by no means exhaust Heidegger's examinations of the concept of the "holy."[19] However, these works do include Heidegger's most *sustained* and *detailed* discussions of the "holy," as well as discussions that directly bear on the theme of this study, namely the phenomenology of religion. The importance of "the holy" to Heidegger's phenomenology of religion is most clearly expressed in the 1946 "Letter on Humanism." There, Heidegger maintains that the *intelligibility* of the divine, and, by extension, of the practices directed toward the divine, rests upon a more fundamental layer of meaning which he calls "the holy." The "holy" is not a principle from which concepts of particular deities are derived. The "holy" is not a concept of a property that all deities or objects of religious significance share. Nor is the "holy" itself a being, a "super-deity" that engenders the more recognizable deities of the world's religious systems and mythologies. The "holy" is Heidegger's term for the objective side of an *understanding of being* that anchors the intelligibility of religious concepts and practices. As I have discussed previously (see chapter 1), Heidegger's view is that, in the modern world, religious concepts and practices have lost the meaning that they once had. More specifically, they have lost their compelling *normative* valence. The modern period is characterized by a lack of appreciation for the possibility of radical transcendence, of something genuinely "wholly Other," to borrow Rudolf Otto's famous characterization of the "holy." For Heidegger, a tacit understanding that such transcendence *is* possible is the *sine qua non* for a vital religiosity. The "flight of the gods" is a reflection of the loss of understanding reality as *holy* at its deepest level. Only when there is room for something genuinely mysterious, inexplicable, and transcendent can concepts of the divine and their associated religious practices carry the kind of weight and significance that they have traditionally borne.

Heidegger initially came to this view through his encounters with other philosophers who attempted to understand the nature of myth and of myth-informed cultures. Otto and Cassirer, in particular, provided Heidegger with catalysts for his own views. The distinctive aspect of his attempt to work out the concept of the "holy" lies in his turn to Hölderlin's poetry. Heidegger appreciated Hölderlin as someone who had maintained a sense for the "holy" even in the midst of the growing domination of the "deep framework" of modern subjectivism. Even in the "darkness" of increasingly disenchanted modernity, Hölderlin holds out an alternative understanding of reality as fundamentally mysterious. For Heidegger, reawakening a sense for the "holy" is a necessary part of moving beyond the cultural impasses of modernity.

---

19. For a comprehensive survey of Heidegger's discussions of the "holy," see Helting (1999).

Phenomenology of Greek Religion

While Heidegger's efforts to develop a phenomenology that focused exclusively on *Christian* religiosity came to an end in the 1920s, he by no means abandoned his interest in developing a *general* phenomenology of religion. Indeed, beginning in the 1930s, and continuing into the 1960s, he works out, in outline, a phenomenology of *ancient Greek religion.* Unlike his earlier efforts, Heidegger's later discussions are not concentrated in any one text. This means that a considerable amount of reconstruction is required in order to determine the basic contours of Heidegger's position on Greek religion. Fortunately, the basic elements of his early views of religion remain more or less intact throughout the rest of his career. This aids the task of reconstruction considerably. More specifically, Heidegger maintains his commitment to the view that religion is a mode of "being-in-the-world," and to the ontological realism that accompanied this commitment in his early work, right through till the end of his career. His emphasis on the concrete "givenness" of religious meaning, on the "horizon" or "background" nature of religious meaning, and on religious practices as articulations of a tacit understanding of religious meaning are all present in his later discussions. Moreover, Heidegger still follows his characteristic method of starting with paradigmatically religious phenomena (the Greek temple, religious festivals, etc.) and then proceeding to explicate the structures that render these intelligible precisely *as* religious phenomena.

The theme of the concrete givenness of the divine in religious experience had occupied Heidegger right from the beginning of his interest in the phenomenology of religion. In 1918–1919, he investigated this theme in Schleiermacher and in medieval mysticism. In WS 1920–1921, he examined the role of the early Christian proclamation as a vehicle for the givenness of God. In SS 1921, he picks up on the sense of the "objecthood" of God in Augustine's *Confessions* and other writings. In all of these instances, Heidegger is trying to account for something that the anti-realist views of religion current at the time had difficulty accounting for. Religious experience scarcely figures into the typical Neo-Kantian theories. This is not surprising, since the Neo-Kantians trace all religious meaning back to a priori values which, by their very nature, are never "given" in experience. Similarly, in Nietzsche's biologistic version of Neo-Kantianism, the gods worshiped by a particular group of people are considered products of their "religious talent" rather than concrete realities given directly in experience. Heidegger's emphasis on this concrete givenness represents a clear sign of his opposition to these sorts of anti-realist accounts.

This emphasis is by no means only an artifact of Heidegger's earliest writings on the phenomenology of religion. In fact, in lectures from the 1940s and essays from the 1950s, Heidegger points to just this aspect of Greek religion. Greek religion, with its festivals, sacrificial cults, and ecstatic practices is indeed characterized by the *closeness* of gods and human beings at certain times and places which are sanctified by divine epiphanies.[20] Heidegger draws explicit attention to this central element of Greek religion in the WS 1942–1943 lecture course on Parmenides. The "uncanny ones," the Greek *daimones*, are encountered as the *extraordinary* breaking into the "ordinary" (G54 151/102). He captures the concreteness of Greek religion by observing that "*Hoi theoi*, the so-called gods, the ones who look into the ordinary and who everywhere look into the ordinary, are *hoi daimones*, the ones who point and give signs" (G54 154/104). A god is a being that "presents himself." The Greek words for the divine, on Heidegger's account, all indicate "the *self-emergent* looking one and being as entering into beings" (G54 165/111, emphasis added). Heidegger's addition of the feature of being "self-emergent" is worth taking note of here. The divine was experienced by the Greeks as an autonomous, transcendent force that made itself present in often sudden and terrifying ways within the normal course of human experience. Heidegger recapitulates this crucial feature of the Greek idea of divinity in his 1954 essay "Aletheia (Heraclitus, Fragment B 16)," where he calls the gods "the shining ones who cast a glance [*Hereinblickenden*]" (G7 281, 284). Once again, he offers this as an explanation of the Greek words for divine beings, *daimones* and *theaontes* (G7 285). Commenting in this essay on Homer and Pindar, Heidegger emphasizes the *concreteness* of the Greek experience of the divine:

> But we notice that in the Greek language, above all in the saying of Homer and Pindar, words like *zatheos, zamenes, zapuros* are used. Linguistics explains that *za*-signifies an intensification; *zatheos* therefore means "very divine," "very holy"; *zamenes*, "very forceful"; *zapuros*, "very fiery." But this "intensification" means neither a mechanical nor a dynamical increase. Pindar calls locales and mountains, meadows and riverbanks *zatheos* precisely when he wants to say that the gods, the shining ones who cast a glance, often really allow themselves to be glimpsed here, to come to presence in appearance. These locales are particularly holy, because they arise purely to allow the appearing of the shining one. (G7 281)

The theme of the *concreteness* of Greek divinity, first noted in the early 1940s, remains a more or less constant feature of Heidegger's later accounts of Greek religion. In "Aufenthalte," Heidegger's travel journal from his 1962

---

20. See, for example, Otto (1965). Heidegger, it is worth noting, was quite familiar with Otto's work, which was widely read and discussed in the 1930s and 1940s. See G39 108. Another good discussion of this central aspect of Greek religion is Burkert (1997).

visit to Greece, he recalls precisely this central feature of Greek religious experience. While visiting Olympia, Heidegger mentions the "nearness of the gods" that played such a crucial role in the periodic festivals held at the site (G75 222). Reflecting on his impressions of Delos, one of the most important religious sites of classical Greece, Heidegger describes the epiphanies of Apollo and Artemis, deities who were both closely linked to the island (G75 231). Heidegger also notes how cultic sites, such as the famous temple of Athena on Athens's Acropolis, serve to localize and concentrate the concrete presence of the divine. "The temple of Athene Parthenos," he observes, "the child born from the head of Zeus, testifies [*bezeugt*] to the presence of the god whose 'Lightning steers all things' (Heraclitus, Fr. 64)" (G75 236).[21] Another temple in Attica likewise hints at the "invisible nearness of the divinities" (G75 238). Just as, in his writings from 1918 to 1921, Heidegger stressed the *concrete givenness* of the divine in human experience as a central aspect of Christian religiosity, so in his later studies of the Greek "world" he picks this out as an important characteristic of Greek religious life.

In SS 1921, commenting on some of Augustine's sermons, Heidegger maintained that God is intuited concretely in religious life as the normative *horizon* that defines in advance the meaning of a Christian way of life. He does not, however, share the Neo-Kantian view that the idea of God is merely *regulative*, merely a necessary condition posited to account for the structure of a particular way of life. Instead, the "objecthood [*Gegenständlichkeit*]" of God, God *as* this normative horizon, is concretely given in religious experience. In his later accounts of Greek religious life, Heidegger similarly maintains that the gods are "given" as a normative background or horizon that structures in advance the patterns of Greek life. This point is made most clearly in the WS 1942–1943 lecture course on Parmenides. Here, Heidegger says of the Greek *daimones* that "they define in advance what is ordinary [*im voraus das Geheure bestimmenden*], without deriving from the ordinary itself. They indicate the ordinary and point to it" (G54 151/102). A fuller characterization is offered a bit later on in the text of this lecture:

> The *daimones* are more essential than any being. They not only dispose [*stimmen*] the "demonic" "demons" into the disposition [*Stimmung*] of the horrible and frightful, but they determine every essential affective disposition [*Gestimmtheit*] from reverence, to joy, to mourning and terror.

---

21. This account of the role of the temple in concretizing the Greek experience of the divine first appears in the 1935 piece "On the Origin of the Work of Art." There, Heidegger observes how "The building encloses the figure of a god within this concealment, allows it to stand forth through the columned hall within the holy precinct. Through the temple, the god is present in the temple. This presence of the god is, in itself, the extension and delimitation of the precinct as something holy" (G5 27/20).

> Here, to be sure, these "affective dispositions" are not to be understood
> in the modern subjective sense as "psychic states" but are to be thought
> more originally as the attunements to which the silent voice of the word
> attunes the essence of the human beings in his relation to being. (G54
> 157/106)

In this passage, Heidegger picks up on the fact that the epiphanies of
the divine in ancient Greece were often more *auditory* than *visual*. One
hears the "voice [*Stimme*]" of the gods, for example, while in battle or in a
lonely spot. Playing on the resonance of the German word *stimmen* and its
cognates, Heidegger tries to specify the nature of the Greek deities. The deities define in advance the way things show up as meaningful, as mattering to
people. Their presence gives a kind of affective coloring to things, and elicits
corresponding responses from human beings. The gods, then, are present in
Greek religious life as a kind of horizon or background against which things
show up as meaningful, and to which human beings respond with religious
practices such as cultic worship. The crucial point is that this horizon is not
an abstraction or a theoretical construction, but a reality that is quite literally
given in experience through moods.

This view of the gods as constituting a normative horizon for Greek life
coheres with Heidegger's general understanding of religion as a mode of
"being-in-the-world." "Being-in-the-world" is his term for the basic structure of
human existence, which can best be understood as pre-reflectively "inhabiting"
a domain of meaning that grounds the intelligibility of things and of human
practices. This conception of religion as "being-in-the-world" forms the heart
of Heidegger's distinctive phenomenology of religion from the beginning of his
career. His investigations of medieval mysticism, of Pauline Christianity, and
of Augustine's *Confessions* are all explicitly aimed at uncovering this embedded structure of religious life. This element of Heidegger's phenomenology of
religion is also clearly present in his discussions of the Greek "world" from the
1940s and later. Perhaps one of the best examples of this comes from the lecture course for SS 1942 on Hölderlin and Sophocles. Heidegger picks up on
the crucial concept of the *polis*, using Sophoclean tragedy as a kind of window onto the inner structure of this idea. On his view, the *polis* is not simply a
geographical location or a political organization, but instead is the "stead [*die
Statt*]" or the "site [*die Stätte*] of the human historical sojourn in the midst of
beings" (G53 101/82). In other words, *polis* is Greek "being-in-the-world." He
elaborates this interpretation in a longer passage as follows:

> To the *polis* there belongs the gods and the temples, the festivals and
> games, the governors and councils of elders, the people's assembly and the
> armed forces, the ships and the field marshals, the poets and the thinkers.
> Yet we are never to conceive of all this according to the civil state of the
> nineteenth century. None of these are merely pieces of embellishment

> for some state ordinance that puts value on producing "cultural achieve-
> ments." Rather, from out of the relation to the gods, out of the kind of
> festivals and the possibility of celebration, out of the relationship between
> master and slave, out of a relation to sacrifice and battle, out of a relation-
> ship to honor and glory, out of the relationship between these relation-
> ships and from out of the grounds of their unity, there prevails what is
> called *polis*. (G53 101/82)

Polis, on Heidegger's reading, is the Greek equivalent of what he calls
"being-in-the-world" in *Being and Time*. It consists of the constitutive relations between human beings and various axes of meaning—religious, political, economic—which anchor the intelligibility of things and practices. For
the Greeks, the religious axis of meaning, the "gods and the temples, the festivals and games," is determinative for their way of life as a whole. Heidegger
makes precisely this point by contrasting the Greek "world" with modern
"culture." The latter, on his view, is simply a collection of so-called "embel-
lishments" to the otherwise meaningless monotony of industrial modernity
and bureaucratic society. This reduction of religion to "culture," to an adornment affixed to an intrinsically unsatisfying way of life, is a central aspect of
what Heidegger calls the "flight of the gods." What we have in this passage
is a clear instance of Heidegger's combination of normative and descriptive elements in his phenomenology of religion. On the one hand, he is at
pains to articulate the deep structure of Greek life without recourse to categories derived from modern "philosophy of culture." At the same time, he
clearly aims to contrast the richness and meaningfulness of Greek life with
the culturally impoverished, "disenchanted" character of modernity. For the
Greeks, religion is not just one more addition to the "culture business" that
offers temporary respite from the "daily grind." Instead, the entire *meaning* of
Greek life is pervaded by religion.

This view of Greek life as pervaded by religious meaning goes back at
least as far as the 1935 essay "On the Origin of the Work of Art." It is certainly continuous with Heidegger's account of primitive Christianity in WS
1920–1921, where he points out how all the concrete "relations" constitutive
of the Christian way of life are refracted through the filter of a tacit understanding of religious meaning. Both the Greek paradigm and the Christian
paradigm contrast notably with the impoverished, washed-out character of
modernity that Heidegger calls "decrepitude [*Verwahrlosung*]" in the late
1940s. In the 1935 essay on art, Heidegger makes this point by reflecting on
the nature and function of a temple in the Greek "world." His basic position
is captured clearly in the following passage:

> It is the temple work that first structures and simultaneously gathers
> around itself the unity of those paths and relations in which birth and
> death, disaster and blessing, victory and disgrace, endurance and decline

acquire for the human being the shape of its destiny. The all-governing expanse of these open relations is the world of this historical people. (G5 27–28/21)

The temple, in which the god is palpably "present," brings home the fact that the entire "world" of the Greeks is shaped in advance by this specifically *religious* axis of meaning. The temple, Heidegger observes, "first gives to things their look, and to human beings their outlook on themselves" (G5 29/21). It concretely and visibly anchors the entire "world" of the ancient Greeks, much as the "proclamation" did for the early Christians. Heidegger explains his concept of "world" thusly:

> World is never an object that stands before us and can be looked at. World is that ever non-objective [something] to which we are subject as long as the paths of birth and death, blessing and curse, keep us transported into being. [. . .] By the opening of a world, all things gain their lingering and hastening, their distance and proximity, their breadth and their limits. (G5 30/23)

A "world," in other words, is a normative horizon or "background" that enables things to show up as meaningful to human experience. A world grounds the *meaning* of human life itself. The practices characteristic of a particular culture are ways of articulating the tacit understanding of "world" that pervades and unifies a culture. For the Greeks, their world "glows" in the "reflected glory" of the gods (G5 30/22). The modern situation, on the other hand, is one in which the "radiance of divinity" is largely extinguished. For the Greeks, religious meaning occupied the center of their way of life, rather than the periphery, as, on Heidegger's view, it does in modern life.

The conception of Greek religious life first developed in "On the Origin of the Work of Art" resurfaces again in Heidegger's 1962 travel journal, "Aufenthalte." Heidegger reflects on the centrality of religious meaning in Greek culture at Olympia, "the place where," as he puts it, "once the whole of Greece united during the hottest days of the summer for the peaceful celebration of competitions, and where they celebrated their highest gods" (G75 221). The Greek "world" as a whole was pervaded by the religious meaning expressed in the festivals at Olympia, as exemplified by the practice of dating time in "Olympiads" (G75 221). The historical "sojourn [*Aufenthalt*]" of the Greeks, i.e., their "being-in-the-world," was enacted always "in the face of and in the service of the gods" (G75 233). Similarly, a temple of Poseidon on the coast of Attica hints at "the invisible nearness of the divinities" that "consecrates all growth and every human work" (G75 238).[22] Commenting

---

22. This emphasis on the cultural role of *temples* is reiterated in his discussion of the temple of Aphaia on Aegina (G75 240). This was, of course, one of the central themes in "On the Origin of the Work of Art."

on the cult of Aphaia on Aegina, Heidegger observes that "the relation to the goddess equally defined the world-relation of the Greeks, without allowing this to be blurred into an indeterminate pantheism" (G75 241).

A stable aspect of Heidegger's phenomenology of Greek religious life, which is present from the 1930s to the 1960s, is this explication of its deep structure as a mode of "being-in-the-world." For the Greeks, reality was pervaded by religious meaning. An understanding of this pervasive meaning surfaces in everything from the poetry of the classical dramatists to the everyday labors of the populace as a whole. The Greek "world," the normative horizon that grounded the intelligibility of things and of the practices designed to deal with those things, was inescapably religious. Just as he had done in the early 1920s with Christianity, Heidegger applies his basic concept of "being-in-the-world" to the task of explicating the deep structures of Greek religiosity. The result of this explication is a picture of way of life that contrasts profoundly with the washed-out uniformity of technological modernity.

The "Gods"

Besides his lectures and essays on ancient Greece, many of Heidegger's other well-known writings from the later period of his career contain discussions of religious themes. In a WS 1955–1956 lecture course at Freiburg, Heidegger offers a reading of texts by Angelus Silesius, a late-seventeenth-century mystic. In another essay from the 1950s, Heidegger draws a famous contrast between the "God" of "ontotheology" and the God worthy of religious devotion. Perhaps most famously, in a 1966 interview with *Der Spiegel*, published after his death, Heidegger announces that "only a God can save us." His concerns with the religious situation of modernity, with the historical intertwining of philosophical and theological thought, and with other religious themes are as strong as they were during the 1920s, when he was identifying himself as a "Christian theo-*logian*." The same holds for his attempts to work out a phenomenology of religion. In essays from the late 1940s and 1950s, Heidegger offers an account of "the gods" as well as an outline of nature of religiosity as a mode of "being-in-the-world" which parallels to a significant degree his earliest work on these topics.

The "gods," "divinities," or "godly ones [*die Göttlichen*]," despite their conspicuous presence in some of Heidegger's best known later writings, remain one of the least understood aspects of his thought. Indeed, disagreement regarding the precise nature and status of these obscure figures continues. On the one hand, there are commentators like Julian Young and James C. Edwards who maintain that Heidegger's talk of the "gods" is not meant to be taken in any literal religious sense, but instead is a rhetorical or quasi-poetic "trope" meant to capture ideas that could, in principle, be adequately expressed without this confusing veneer of religious significance. On the other hand, Mark A. Wrathall views Heidegger's later discussions of the "gods" as having straightforward religious significance. Both views have their attractive features, but, as I will argue below, one is in the end forced to adopt something approximating Wrathall's position.[23]

James C. Edwards's interpretation aims at clarifying the difficult concept of the "fourfold [*Geviert*]" in Heidegger's essays from the 1950s. According to Edwards, the four elements of the "fourfold"—earth, sky, godly ones, mortals—represent the "conditions" that make a particular way of life possible.[24] He reads the "godly ones [*die Göttlichen*]," or the "divinities" in his translation, as follows: "They are presences from another world, annunciators of a place of haleness and wholeness. The divinities are the reality both of human need for such weal and of our hope that it will someday be vouchsafed to us."[25]

Despite the mention of "another world," Edwards's reading is clearly an attempt to "de-mythologize" Heidegger's talk of "the godly ones." On Edwards's account, the latter symbolize or embody aspects of human experience. Indeed, he explicitly asserts: "In spite of using the trope of theological language, it is clear that Heidegger is not identifying the divinities with the personified natural presences of religious belief."[26] In calling Heidegger's usage a "trope," Edwards intends that we are not meant to understand "the godly ones" in a literal sense as objects of religious devotion or the like. Indeed, Edwards's examples of "divinities" include "poems, paintings, [and] works of philosophy," none of which have much in common with "gods" as traditionally understood.

Julian Young, in what is undoubtedly the best recent commentary on Heidegger's later work, offers an account of Heidegger's "gods" that parallels Edwards's reading, in that Young also seems committed to understanding the "gods" as being metaphors for something that is not particularly or exclusively religious. Young's reading differs from Edwards's in the details, though not in spirit. The crucial step in Young's interpretation comes in the following passage:

> For Heidegger the gods are always closely associated with what he variously call[s] the divine "destinings" (QCT p. 34), "laws" (HE p. 312) or "edicts" (I p. 116). He says, for example, that Greek tragedy "brought the presence of the gods, [i.e.,] brought the dialogue of divine and human destinings to radiance" (QCT p. 34). In some sense, the gods *are* the "divine destinings."[27]

---

23. Wrathall (2003).
24. Edwards (1997): 167.
25. Ibid., 172.
26. Ibid., 172.
27. Young (2002): 95.

The precise sense in which the gods "are" these "laws," which Young takes to be constitutive of the "fundamental *ethos*" of a historical people, is spelled out a bit later. The gods "announce" these laws "by being embodiments, incarnations or *exemplars* of the laws."[28] As such, the "gods" play the same role in Heidegger's later thought that "heroes" (allegedly) do in *Being and Time*. In other words, the "gods," like the earlier "heroes," are charismatic exemplars of "existence possibilities" that are embedded in the traditions of a particular culture. While in some religious traditions, including Christianity, it is certainly true that the "gods" are to be imitated or emulated, it also seems true that, if this is all there is to the "gods," then much of what has been traditionally taken to be characteristic of "divinity" has been wiped away by Young's Heidegger.

Edwards and Young are on solid ground when it comes to their general understanding of the "fourfold," the conceptual framework within which Heidegger's later discussions of the "gods" occur most frequently. The "fourfold," as both Edwards and Young observe, is the later Heidegger's version of what he had called "world" in *Being and Time*. That is, the "fourfold" is a nexus of meaningful relations, or "conditions" of meaning, that grounds the intelligibility of human practices and of the things with which human practices are engaged. A quick reading of the text in which Heidegger first introduces the "fourfold," the 1949 version of "Das Ding," bears this out, for Heidegger explicitly uses the concept of "world" to help articulate his basic point (G79 12). The "godly ones," as elements of the "fourfold," play a central role in this nexus of meaning that comprises the "horizon" or "background" against which human experience in all its dimensions makes sense. In this much, I am in agreement with both Edwards and Young. Mortal dwelling "in" the "fourfold" is another way of describing what Heidegger calls "being-in-the-world" in *Being and Time*.

Indeed, no one would deny the "godly ones" a central place in the "fourfold." Heidegger's most detailed discussions of this idea all incorporate these figures (G79 17; G7 152). The question, however, is whether or not Edwards and Young are correct in understanding these figures as metaphors for a non-religious idea or group of ideas. Unfortunately, the otherwise careful and illuminating accounts offered by Edwards and Young of the substance and import of Heidegger's later philosophy break down on this score. First of all, in his lecture course for the summer of 1942, Heidegger criticizes contemporary views of "myth," according to which it consists of poetic tropes that conceal a literal meaning (G53 139/111). On this venerable view, the philosopher is in the business of "liberating the mythological poem from

---

28. Ibid., 96.

the mythical" and "recasting its remaining content into the rigid grid and detritus of empty concepts" (G53 139/111). As he puts it in a later essay on Parmenides, such a view fails to appreciate the nature of mythos as a way of disclosing reality (G7 253). Heidegger would, therefore, most likely resist attempts to read his talk of "the gods" as a poetic or mythological "trope," as a metaphor for something that can be explained away without any reference to "religion."

That Heidegger does not want to evacuate "the gods" or "the godly ones" of religious meaning is shown more clearly still by the concrete examples that he gives. As I have already pointed out on numerous occasions, a central feature of Heidegger's phenomenological methodology is to start with para-digmatic phenomena (in this case, religious phenomena), and then to expli-cate the structure that makes them religious. As early as in his loose notes from 1918 and 1919, Heidegger offers noteworthy examples to anchor his more abstract analysis. The situation is much the same with his discussions of the gods in the 1940s and 1950s. These examples are all carefully chosen because they are paradigmatically religious. To read them as poetic or rhe-torical tropes is to strip them of their characteristic significance.

Recall that, for Edwards, the examples of "the divinities" are "poems, paintings, works of philosophy" and the like. When we turn to what Heidegger actually says about what the "godly ones" might be, things appear quite differently. When Heidegger issued a revised version of the essay "Das Ding," he attached a letter that he had written to an inquiring student named Buchner. He evidently did so because he was of the opinion that this exchange clarified the difficult ideas presented in the essay. Most signif-icant for my discussion are the three examples of "the godly [Göttlichen]" that Heidegger gives: "the godly in Greek culture [Griechentum], in pro-phetic Judaism [Prophetisch-Jüdischen], in the preaching of Jesus" (G7 185). These are just the sorts of paradigmatic phenomena that one would expect to find if Heidegger is interested in building a phenomenological account of religion as such. That is, these are the sorts of phenomena that belong unmistakably to a religious world. Certainly, poems, paintings, and, indeed, just about anything else could have religious significance. But the examples Heidegger gives here are clearly intended as paradigms of religious phenom-ena, the sorts of things that provide a "fore-having" or initial purchase on a domain of phenomena. The structures characteristic of these paradigmatic phenomena are supposed to form the core of a wider account of religion as such. Prophetic Judaism (e.g., the oracles of Jeremiah and Isaiah, and the story of Jonah) involves a robust, vivid sense of divine transcendence. This is rendered completely unintelligible if it is assumed that poems, paintings, and philosophy books are on a par with God. The former can certainly be (and no doubt were) meaningful in religious terms; but they only have this meaning because they are seen in relation to something that utterly transcends them in value and in power. Similarly, Jesus of Nazareth would doubtless have been surprised to hear that the Kingdom of God is just a metaphor for a cultural artifact. And the Greeks, with their distinction between *nomos* (custom, human societal norms) and *phusis* (nature, the objective order of value), would have certainly allowed that particular things can have religious significance, but they would hardly have found it true that the gods are on a par with such things. Thus, all of Heidegger's examples have features that make them importantly distinct from the products of human cultural activity. Eliding this distinction, in the way that Edwards and Young do, runs counter to the entire thrust of Heidegger's phenomenology, which insists upon fitting the philosophical account to the intrinsic intelligibility of the "things themselves."

Heidegger's actual examples of "the godly," then, seem to contradict the understanding of "the godly" presented by Edwards and Young. Edwards, in fact, ignores this passage altogether. Young, on the other hand, quotes it in full, though he overlooks the problems it poses for his "de-mythologized" reading of Heidegger's "gods."[29] In the 1949 version of "Das Ding," where Heidegger first introduces the concept of the "fourfold," his famous description of the earthenware jug also presents problems for the sort of reading favored by Edwards and Young. When describing how the jug "gathers" the "godly ones," Heidegger clearly has in mind the way in which the jug can play a role in religious practices. He writes:

> The gift of the poured stream [*Gusses*] is the drink [*Trunk*] for mortals. It quenches their thirst. It enlivens their leisure time. It brings joy to their sociality. But the gift of the jug will also, from time to time, be dedicated for consecration [*zur Weihe*]. [. . .] The poured stream is the oblation [*Trank*] offered to the immortal gods. (G79 11)

The jug, in this instance, "gathers" the fourfold in that it features in a practice the meaning of which crucially depends on "the godly ones." "Consecration [*Weihe*]," a word also used by Heidegger in "The Origin of the Work of Art" in connection with the dedication of a temple in ancient Greece, and used in ordinary German to refer to the crucial moment in the Mass, can hardly be understood *except* as a religious practice. Similarly, offering an "oblation" from the jug to the "immortal gods," a common theme in Greek poetry, is a practice that makes sense only as part of the overall sacrificial religious system of the Greeks. Heidegger's example of how a thing

---

29. See Young (2002): 97. On Young's view, this passage is primarily about the fact that the "existence possibilities" or our culture no longer have the requisite kind of charismatic authority to motivate human action.

"gathers" the "fourfold" from the later essay, "Bauen Wohnen Denken," has a similar religious valence. In this case, it is not a jug, but a bridge, that serves as Heidegger's example of a "thing." The bridge "gathers" the "fourfold" in "the figure of the saint of the bridge" (G7 155). The point of these examples is that things have religious meaning when they express or embody a network of relations ordered to divine reality. The act of consecration is a religious act because its structure and meaning are dependent upon a whole web of religious concepts, attitudes, and practices. Of course, consecration could be, for some reason, stripped of these relations, so that it is viewed simply as an objective fact, or becomes an empty, formulaic activity. In either case, however, it has really ceased to be the specific activity that it is; we might still choose to call it by the same name, but it no longer means the same thing. Heidegger's phenomenological approach, however, demands that he avoid stripping off the relations that constitute the native intelligibility of a phenomenon.

Also in "Bauen Wohnen Denken," when Heidegger discusses the relationship between "mortals," i.e., human beings, and these "godly ones," the most natural interpretation is that Heidegger is talking about a kind of authentic religiosity. The passage runs:

> Mortals dwell in that they await the godly ones *as godly ones*. In hope they hold up to the godly ones what is unhoped for. They wait for the hints of their arrival and do not overlook the signs of their absence. They do not make gods for themselves and do not worship idols. In the very depth of misfortune they wait for the weal that has been withdrawn. (G7 152, emphasis added)

Note how, in the first line of this passage, Heidegger adds the seemingly superfluous repetition "as godly ones." This repetition is, however, far from insignificant. Heidegger is trying to make it clear that "mortals" relate to "the godly ones" precisely *as* "godly ones," not as metaphors for the human experience or as social constructions. The latter interpretations of "gods" and "godly ones" are precisely those which, as I have shown in the previous section, Heidegger was at great pains to refute.

On Young's account of this passage, Heidegger is advocating a "conservation" of existence possibilities already present in one's cultural inheritance.[30] Heidegger is, no doubt, advocating the maintenance of traditional practices that challenge the dominance of technical rationality in the modern world. But *which* practices are these? They are *religious* practices, which are not merely ways of honoring one's tradition, but of honoring the godly ones precisely *as* godly ones. On Edwards's view, what Heidegger is trying to

---

30. Young (2002): 113–114.

say in this passage is that people ought to recognize their inherent finitude, their need for wholeness or completion, and their inability to achieve this on their own.[31] There is no doubt that one of Heidegger's primary charges against modernity was the lack of humility and reverence, and the pervasive, almost Promethean, attempt to overcome human finitude through the titanic efforts of modern technology. Again, however, this cannot be *all* that Heidegger is trying to say in this passage. Indeed, he makes exactly this point in many places throughout his writings without making any mention of "the godly ones" and the dangers of "idolatry." Heidegger's comments here are targeted specifically at the *religious* situation of modernity. This is a situation in which "religion" is reduced to a private "world-view" for the edification the individual, where theologians eclipse God as the center of religious life, and where religious institutions compromise all too readily with dominant power-brokers.[32]

The "godly ones," who figure so importantly into the "fourfold" as a way of conceiving of the "world" or nexus of meaning that grounds human activities, are clearly understood by Heidegger as having religious significance. As his carefully chosen examples make clear, he is not using "godly ones" or "gods" as poetic or rhetorical tropes, or as metaphors for something that can be said equally well in another way. While there are, no doubt, many attractions to "de-mythologizing" Heidegger's "gods," doing so would do violence to what he actually says. Heidegger is, by his own account, trying to capture the central role played by "the godly ones" and the religious practices that they figure into within a way of life that he is trying to advocate. This way of life is, for him, particularly embodied in the culture of the ancient Greeks. Rather than being an adornment added onto an otherwise complete life, religion played a crucial role in shaping Greek culture as a whole.

Given, then, that the "gods" or "godly ones" are not simply "tropes" designed to say something that could be said equally well in another way, who (or what) *are* these "gods"? Three passages, all taken from well-known pieces from the late 1940s and early 1950s, give a remarkably uniform picture of Heidegger's view of the "gods." I will present each of these passages below. The first comes from the 1949 version of "Das Ding," the second from the 1950 version of this essay, and the third from the 1951 essay "Bauen Wohnen Denken."

---

31. Edwards (1997): 172.

32. This passage from "Bauen Wohnen Denken," it is worth noting, parallels some of Heidegger's glosses on Augustine's criticisms of idolatry and magic, which both ascribe merely instrumental meaning to the divine. Heidegger's view of authentic religiosity rests upon the same distinction that is at work in Augustine, i.e., that between instrumental meaning and genuinely religious meaning.

The godly ones are the beckoning messengers of divinity [*Gottheit*]. From its hidden holding sway, the God appears in his essence that removes him from any comparison with what is present. (G79 17)

The godly ones are the beckoning messengers of divinity. From its hidden holding sway, the God appears in his essence that removes him from every comparison with what is present. (G7 180)

The godly ones are the beckoning messengers of divinity. Out of the holy sway of divinity, the God appears in his presence or withdraws into his concealment. (G7 351)

These statements, coming from three distinct works, are notably uniform in their formulation. This suggests strongly that Heidegger viewed the basic idea presented first in the 1949 version of "Das Ding" as his settled view of the nature of "the godly ones." In all three passages, these figures are defined as "beckoning messengers," as pointing to "divinity [*Gottheit*]." While some translators, including Edwards, read *Gottheit* as "Godhead," the more natural reading is "God-hood," or "divinity." On the former reading, Heidegger comes out as saying that the "godly ones" are "messengers" of some *particular being*, namely, the "Godhead." However, a glance at "Moira (Parmenides VIII, 34–41)," shows that Heidegger uses this term in the sense of "divinity." Critiquing what he regards as the usual superficial approach to Greek religion, Heidegger writes:

> One makes the conversation with Parmenides' path of thought too easy for oneself if one misses the mythical experience in the word of the thinker and objects that, in comparison to the unambiguously stamped "divine persons," Hera, Athene, Demeter, Persephone, the goddess *Aletheia* is quite undefined and is an empty construction of thought. In making his reservation one talks as if one were in possession of a long-since secured knowledge of what the *divinity* [*Gottheit*] of the Greek gods is, such that it makes sense to talk about "persons" here, as of the essence of truth were decided so that, in case it appears as a goddess, this could only be an abstract personification of a concept. (G7 253, emphasis added)

In this passage, Heidegger uses the term *Gottheit* to refer to "divinity" or "God-hood," rather than to a being called "the Godhead." "Divinity" is that in virtue of which gods *are* gods. To say, then, that the "godly ones" are "beckoning messengers of divinity" cannot mean that the "godly ones" are *beings* that perform some service for another *being*. The best way to understand what Heidegger is saying in the three passages quoted above is to begin by recalling his lifelong interest in the *givenness* or "objecthood" of the divine. One of the hallmarks of Heidegger's account of religion, which distinguishes it sharply from Neo-Kantian accounts, is his contention that the divine can concretely appear within the field of human experience. Given this concern, the most natural reading of the quoted passages from "Das Ding" (1949 and 1950) and "Bauen Wohnen Denken" (1951) is that the "godly ones" are *manifestations* of what it is to be divine. As to what it is to be divine, Heidegger's remarks elsewhere suggest that it is quality of *otherness*. This can be gathered from another 1951 essay, ". . . dichterisch wohnet der Mensch . . .":

> And what is this [that is intimate to human beings]? Everything in heaven, under heaven, and on the earth that radiates and blooms, resounds and puts forth scent, rises and comes forth, but also goes away and falls, that which cries and keeps silent, and also that which grows pale and darkens. Into what is thus intimate to human beings, but foreign to God, the *unfamiliar* sends itself in order to remain sheltered in it *as unfamiliar*. (G7 204, emphasis added)

The suggestion in this passage is that to be a "god," to participate in "divinity," is to be somehow permanently *strange* or *inexplicable*. "Divinity" is characterized via a contrast with "intimacy" or "intimate familiarity." The latter describes the familiar items of daily life, the inconspicuous but palpable realities of human existence. To be "divine" is to somehow escape from the domain of what is "normal," what can be "dealt with" or "explained" through standard coping practices. This is why, in "Letter on Humanism," Heidegger argues that "only from the essence of the holy is the essence of divinity to be thought" (G9 351/267). The "holy," it will be recalled, is Heidegger's term for what anchors the network of relations constitutive of religious meaning. "Divinity" is a mode of religious meaning of a preeminent sort.

This conception of the divine as "wholly other" is, of course, not new with Heidegger. Many of his own intellectual heroes, particularly Luther and Kierkegaard, as well as some of his contemporaries, such as Karl Barth, drew a sharp ontological boundary between the created and uncreated orders, the latter being occupied solely by God. As a consequence, they tended to be suspicious of the claims of so-called "natural theology." Barth's *Der Römerbrief*, with its uncompromising insistence on the inadequacy of human reason vis-à-vis God, reintroduced this theme into the intellectual consciousness of the Weimar era and gave birth to the "dialectical theology" movement. Heidegger was quite familiar with both the traditional and contemporary formulations of this view of God. Indeed, many of his own more famous discussions of God, such as his repudiation of the attempt to fit God into a theory of value, his sharp attacks on "onto-theology," and his commitment to the well-established distinction between the "God of the philosophers" and that of vital religiosity, resonate powerfully with this line of thought. It is important to recognize, however, that Heidegger's views are *not* derived from prior metaphysical commitments or from other theological premises. Instead,

Heidegger bases his somewhat elusive view of "divinity [*Gottheit*]," as that which constitutes a deity *as* a deity, on *phenomenological* premises. That is, he maintains the thesis of the "otherness" of the divine on the basis of experiential encounters between human beings and divine beings as preserved in the historical traditions of Western culture.

Heidegger's phenomenological approach dictates that the nature of "divinity" be read off from the concrete experiential content of religiosity. As he stresses time and again, the theory of religion must follow upon the *experience* of religion, rather than the other way around. In practice, this means that Heidegger starts from the historical records of human religiosity, such as Paul's epistles, Pindar's odes, or Hölderlin's hymns, and then tries to elucidate the objective structure of religiosity. The result is an exceptionally spare account of what it means to be a "god." The common theme in Heidegger's sources is of an *interruption* and *derangement* of the normal course of human experience. For Heidegger, the meaning of divinity is to be gleaned from such experiences of interruption or derangement. The result is an account of the "divinity [*Gottheit*]" of divine beings as "otherness."

Religion and "Being-in-the-World" in Heidegger's Later Works

As has been argued throughout this study, the heart of Heidegger's phenomenology of religion is the concept of "being-in-the-world." In his accounts of so-called "primitive" Christianity in the early 1920s, as well as in his brief analyses of Greek religion in the 1940s, 1950s, and 1960s, this concept forms the pivot around which Heidegger's theory turns. "Being-in-the-world" is, of course, an idea most closely associated with *Being and Time* (1927), the fruits of Heidegger's lectures and unpublished essays from the years following World War I. The idea, however, is by no means abandoned in his later work. Instead, it is expressed in a new vocabulary which Heidegger seems to have regarded as more adequate to capturing his basic view.

Beginning with the lecture "Das Ding" (1949), Heidegger replaces "world" with "fourfold [*Geviert*]" and "being-in" with "dwelling." In both this lecture and in the 1950 essay that later grew out of it, Heidegger identifies the "fourfold" of earth, heaven, godly ones, and mortals with "world" (G79 19; G7 181). The "fourfold" is a sphere of meaning that is prior to everything "present," i.e., to the particular things that human beings encounter in their lives as well as the practices designed to deal with them (G79 12). As Heidegger makes clear in the third Bremen lecture, "Die Gefahr," the "fourfold" as "world" is the "preserve" of the "being" of things, i.e., the domain of meaning that grounds their intelligibility (G79 48). Heidegger later states that he is indebted to Hölderlin for this more colorful depiction of "world" (G4 170/194).

Returning to some ideas first presented in *Being and Time*, Heidegger describes the relation of human beings to this sphere of meaning as "dwelling." As in *Being and Time*, he emphasizes how this relation is so "habitual," so immediate and pre-reflective, that it is scarcely noticed (G7 149). "Human being," he asserts, simply "consists in dwelling and, indeed, dwelling in the sense of the sojourn of mortals on the earth" (G7 151). Or, more fully: "The simple oneness [*Einfalt*] of [earth, sky, godly ones, mortals] we call the *fourfold* [*Geviert*]. Mortals *are* in the fourfold, in which they *dwell*. But the fundamental characteristic of dwelling is sparing. The mortals dwell in the manner that they spare the fourfold in its essence. Accordingly, the sparing that dwells is fourfold" (G7 152).

Human existence is pictured here as a matter of pre-reflectively "inhabiting" four interconnected axes of meaning. These axes of meaning—earth, sky, godly ones, and mortals—comprise a system of relations within which things show up as meaningful. What is particularly significant about this notion of mortal dwelling in the "fourfold" is that Heidegger incorporates a specifically *religious* dimension of meaning into what appears to be a generic account of the structure of human existence as such. First of all, the incorporation of the "godly ones" within the "fourfold" testifies to Heidegger's ongoing commitment to the position that I have been labeling "ontological realism." The "godly ones" are not *particular beings* but are instead a particular dimension of the general nexus of meaning that human beings pre-reflectively inhabit. The meaning that things (jugs, bridges, etc.) and human practices (prayer, communal celebration, etc.) have is grounded in just this dimension. As such, the "godly ones" *transcend* both human practices and the ontic "furniture" of reality. They form a crucial part of a normative background or horizon that is irreducible to either things or practices.

At the same time, there is no suggestion that the "godly ones" are Neo-Kantian "values" or regulative ideas that are presupposed in norm-governed activities. While not properly thought of as particular things, the "godly ones" are certainly not "projections" or anything of that sort. If we follow up on Heidegger's suggestion that his conception of the "fourfold" owes a good deal to his reading of Hölderlin, then we can look to a passage from the 1936 essay "Hölderlin and the Essence of Poetry" for clarification of Heidegger's position:

> But the gods can come to expression [in poetry] only if they themselves address us and place us under their claim. A word that names the gods is always an answer to such a claim. Its answer always springs from the responsibility of a destiny. Only because the gods bring our Dasein to language do we enter the realm of the decision concerning whether we are to promise [*zusagen*] ourselves to the gods or whether we are to deny [*versagen*] ourselves to them. (G4 40/58)

The gods or "godly ones" are, as Heidegger later puts it in "Hölderlins Erde und Himmel," one of the "voices of destiny" (G4 169/194). That is, they belong to an a priori dimension of meaning that grounds the possibility of human actions. Our responses, our practices, and their assumed conditions, do not generate the gods. Rather, our practices only make sense because the divine has always already put some kind of normative claim on us. All of this is just another way of asserting ontological realism, i.e., of saying that religious meaning is anterior to interests. Human attitudes and activities, such as, for example, atheism and religious faith, are properly viewed as responses to possibilities grounded in an antecedent network of relations with a specific character.

Second, by including the "godly ones" in his account of mortal "dwelling" in the "fourfold," Heidegger is quite clearly challenging the dominant cultural situation of late modernity. This situation has two important *religious* features. First, it is characterized by the subjectivization and privatization of religion as a kind of optional adornment affixed to an otherwise unsatisfying life. Second, the only meaning things can have in the modern age is the meaning that they have within the human projects of "culture" and technological domination of the earth. They are denuded of *intrinsic* meaning, and so no longer place a normative claim on human practices. By including the "godly ones" within his account of "being-in-the-world" in the late 1940s and 1950s, Heidegger is outlining an alternative to both of these features of modern life.

Here, it is useful to recall Heidegger's approach to history in general and to the phenomenology of religion in particular. With regard to historical realities such as Greek culture, Heidegger's approach is to view them as repeatable possibilities of existence, as paradigms that, when appropriated as possibilities for the future, cast a critical light onto the present situation. In the case of Greek culture, Heidegger repeatedly emphasizes the central role that religiosity played in this culture as a whole. Rather than being a kind of diversion for personal edification, religion, taken as a body of beliefs and practices, defined the Greek experience of reality at a fundamental level. By including the "godly ones" in his later accounts of "being-in-the-world," Heidegger is clearly recommending something like the Greek model. That is, he is envisioning a way of life that departs radically from the washed-out nature of modernity by allowing religious meaning to form the core of the experience of the meaning of things. As regards his approach to the phenomenology of religion, it will be recalled that Heidegger blends descriptive and normative elements in virtually all of his discussions. That is, beyond simply getting the "facts" about the deep meaning of religious life right, Heidegger is also interested in uncovering this deep structure as a normative *ideal* against which actual, concrete manifestations of religiosity can be weighed.

Here again, by incorporating the "godly ones" into the "fourfold," Heidegger presents a contrast between the deep structure of religiosity and its pale modern instantiations.

This is perhaps best seen in a passage from the 1951 essay "Bauen Wohnen Denken." Here, he sketches in just a few lines an authentic mode of religiosity which sounds a lot like his analysis of Pauline Christianity in WS 1920–1921 and his idealization of "Christianness" in the 1927 piece "Phenomenology and Theology." This passage summarizes the central thrust of Heidegger's lifelong attempts to work out a phenomenological account of religion that would adequately address the modern situation:

> Mortals dwell in that they await the godly ones as godly ones. In hope they hold up to the godly ones what is unhoped for. They wait for hints of their arrival and do not overlook the signs of their absence. They do not make gods for themselves, and do not worship idols. In the very depth of misfortune they wait for the weal that has been withdrawn. (G7 152)

Among the more striking aspects of this passage is its echoing of the famous "golden calf" episode from Exodus 32. Here, the people of Israel have grown impatient in Moses' absence, and so they say to Aaron, "Come, make gods for us, who shall go before us" (Exodus 32:1). That is, in a situation of crisis, of a loss of moral and spiritual anchoring, the temptation is to make one's own gods. The result, in this case, was of course the casting of an idol of a calf or young bull (Exodus 32:2–6). No doubt with this famous story in mind, Heidegger addresses the situation of the present age head on. He suggests that, in the first instance, room be made for the "holy" and for the epiphanies of the divine. He also suggests that the practices whose meaning is grounded in religion be preserved and nurtured, even in the face of growing meaninglessness. Above all, Heidegger suggests that cultural crisis cannot be met with the erection of a new "table of values," but rather with the reinvigoration of the tradition and the criticism of the present age. This, in the end, is the central message of Heidegger's phenomenology of religion from start to finish.

Conclusion

The preceding discussion has shown that, despite the oftentimes fragmentary and scattered nature of Heidegger's explorations, he has a substantive
and stable position on the philosophy of religion. This position is best understood as being a species of the *phenomenology* of religion. That is, to borrow
a distinction from Merold Westphal, Heidegger's primary concern is with the
meaning of religious life rather than with the *justification* of religious beliefs.[1]
Beginning in the final years of World War I, and continuing virtually up until
his death in 1976, Heidegger attempts to uncover and explicate the basic
structural features of religious life as it has been manifested in Christianity,
in ancient Greece, and in Hölderlin's poetic vision of a post-nihilistic future.
The first goal of such a project is simply to *understand* what religious life
actually *is*, to grasp its *meaning*. As Heidegger makes clear, for example, in
his WS 1920–1921 lecture course and in "Phenomenology and Theology,"
this goal is subsumed under a further one, namely, that of opening up the
possibility of informed religious commitment. That is, phenomenology of
religion does not finish with a *theory* of what religion is, but points beyond
this to the possibility of an existential decision. In Heidegger's case, this *practical*
aim is itself part of a still broader concern, the criticism of culture. The phenomenology of religion, by uncovering and explicating the deep structural

---

1. See Westphal (1987): 9–15.

features of religion, is meant to provide, at least in outline, a normative standard for assessing contemporary manifestations of the religious impulse.

All of these interlocking goals can be detected throughout Heidegger's examinations of religion. Between 1917 and 1921, he articulates his view of the basic structural features of religion through a series of detailed explorations of historic Christianity, both in its earliest forms and in later instantiations. The view worked out during this period turns on the idea that religion is a mode of "being-in-the-world," of pre-reflectively inhabiting a sphere of meaning that opens up possibilities for acting in certain ways and for conceiving of reality in certain ways. To be religious is to inhabit a sphere of *religious* meaning, a sphere that is not constructed or projected by human subjectivity, but is instead *given* and then preserved in communal practices and traditions. This basic position, which I have labeled "ontological realism," remains in place, more or less unchanged, throughout Heidegger's long career. In the 1940s and 1950s, he endeavors to uncover this same structure in the religious life of ancient Greece.

Alongside his articulation of this basic position, Heidegger also makes it clear that his work aims at "leading" one into a "situation of religious decision." Like his friend and colleague Rudolf Bultmann, and like his hero Kierkegaard, Heidegger's aim in depicting the fundamental contours of religious life is to open it up as a live possibility for actual men and women in the modern world. Part of this project involves clearing the way for a reinvigoration of theological reflection, for theology, as Heidegger stresses time and again, has as its aim the sustenance of religious life. Perhaps one way to understand this aspect of Heidegger's phenomenology of religion is to think of his goal as being the grounding of "informed consent." That is, his intuition seems to be the valid one that a meaningful religious commitment should be based on an understanding of just what it is that one is committing oneself to. Despite the prevalence of readings to the contrary, this goal remains in place in Heidegger's later discussions of religion. At the conclusion of his Parmenides lectures from WS 1942–1943, he suggests that his discussion of Greek religion, and his criticism of the "Roman" interpretation of religion, can be fruitfully appropriated by theologians and by others who are interested in offering an intelligent case for religious belief. At the end of 1945, Heidegger appeals to Kierkegaard's distinction between "Christendom" and "Christianity," as if to say that his old mentor's concerns are still alive and well in his own thought. Perhaps more telling is the fact that, in the 1950s and 1960s, Heidegger reconnected with Bultmann and with other theologians, and actively encouraged the attempt to develop his insights within the context of a faith-community.

Even while he was a university student, Heidegger evidenced a profound concern with contemporary culture. Like many in his generation, he was deeply aware of the crisis of value and meaning that seemed to afflict European civilization in the twentieth century. This concern runs like a "red thread" through all of Heidegger's work, linking his lectures on university reform (1919), his infamous and shameful involvement with the Nazis as rector of Freiburg University (1933–1934), his participation in the nuclear disarmament movement (1940s and 1950s), and his later writings on the dangers of technological modernity (1950s and 1960s). For Heidegger, this crisis is the symptom of the deep framework that, for modern people, grounds the intelligibility of things. For moderns, meaning and value are located within subjectivity. Rather than putting a claim on human projects, normativity derives from these projects themselves. Heidegger was well aware that, in such a situation, religion begins to make less and less sense as a viable option. At most, religion becomes yet another "world-view," yet another possibility for escape from the drab uniformity of modern life. For moderns, the gods have fled. The ultimate, overriding concern that unifies Heidegger's efforts in the phenomenology of religion is precisely the cultural situation of modernity. It is a situation that, for Heidegger, presents a deep planetary danger. The subjectivization and marginalization of religion are unmistakably (and deeply troubling) symptoms of this larger danger. Heidegger's philosophy is *explicitly* meant to confront this whole situation head on, to critically expose its historical roots, and to "formally indicate" (to use a term from Heidegger's work in the 1920s) an alternative. With respect to religion, he tries to achieve this goal, in the first instance, by undermining theories of religion that are rooted in modern "philosophy of culture." Second, his efforts to explicate the deep structure of religious life are meant to show that, at the heart of religion, there lies the understanding that religious meaning and normativity derive *not* from human decisions, but rather from a transcendent source. Religion, at its roots and in its essence, actually represents a spirit totally alien to that of technological modernity. Based on an understanding of being as "the holy," as overwhelming and awesome, religious patterns of life represent a concrete historical instantiation of a radical alternative to the conceptual paradigms of late modernity. It is no wonder, then, that religion plays such a central role in Heidegger's philosophy as a whole.

That Heidegger achieved something in the philosophy of religion, then, seems hard to deny. But what does this achievement mean for us *today*? How ought we to evaluate it? First of all, Heidegger provides us with a clear, consistent exemplification of what it means to approach the philosophy of religion in a *phenomenological* way. That is, Heidegger's work maps out a model for one of the ways in which one can do the philosophy of religion. This is not to say, of course, that this is the *only* or *best* way of doing the philosophy of religion. The approach typified by recent Anglo-American or "analytic" work in this field certainly has plenty to recommend it. But, the phenomenological approach is still alive and well, and what Heidegger offers is a clear model for what this approach should look like. The hallmark of the phenomenological approach is the effort to suspend prior commitments to explanatory frameworks that often have little more to recommend them than the inertia of tradition. Moreover, phenomenology of religion is not about merely *describing* what naïve religious people think and do. Instead, the aim is to uncover the deep structures that make religion a distinctive domain of human life. The results of a phenomenology of religion, therefore, might diverge in significant ways from the surface-level aspect of religious phenomena. As a result, such work can be a rich stimulus to reflection.

The phenomenology of religion comprises a key piece in the overall edifice of philosophical theology. As D. Z. Phillips has pointed out, discussions in the philosophy of religion are often hampered by a failure to achieve antecedent clarity regarding the subject.[2] Phenomenology of religion is specifically designed to redress this shortcoming. Its place is to help philosophers to get a grip on what it is that they are talking about *before* the business of talking about it begins in earnest. But the phenomenology of religion is not *merely* about defining one's terms. Instead, when faced with a detailed, systematic account such as the one Heidegger offers, one must also hold open the possibility that a deeper understanding of the meaning of religious life will have profound effects on the conceptual apparatus used to explicate and defend it. What would arguments for the existence of God look like if, for example, one tailored one's conception of God to Heidegger's ontological realism? What happens to theodicy, or to religious ethics, once the deeper patterns of religious life are made objects of explicit attention? Naturally, answering these sorts of questions is beyond the scope of the present discussion. Still, Heidegger's phenomenology of religion provides the kind of detailed theoretical groundwork that, if adopted even in part, could hardly fail to have an effect on the broader discipline of the philosophy of religion.

Another positive aspect of Heidegger's achievement is that he attempts to reoccupy territory that has largely been abdicated by contemporary philosophers of religion, i.e., cultural criticism. One of the undeniably fruitful elements of the contemporary Anglo-American approach is its focus on specific problems, on the careful construction (and reconstruction) of arguments, and on the rigorous explication of concepts. However, partisans of this approach have by and large passed over broader social, cultural, and historical issues in the philosophy of religion. What is the religious situation of today, and what, if anything, can philosophers do to address it? This is a question that rarely gets asked, but which, as I have shown above, almost

---

2. See Phillips (1970).

obsessively occupied Heidegger. For Heidegger, the only really worthwhile reason to do philosophy is, in fact, to effect some change, however subtle and imperceptible, in the way people perceive cultural realities. Given that religion is one of the deepest concerns of most human beings throughout most of human history, it stands to reason that one of the things philosophers can and should do is to reflect about the position of religion in contemporary culture. In particular, what Heidegger suggests is that the resources of religious traditions like Christianity remain largely *unrealized,* and that these resources provide a basis for sober critical responses to dominant cultural trends. One of Heidegger's favorite phrases was, "higher than actuality stands possibility." Applied to religion, this suggests that it be viewed not as a relic or a historical curiosity, but as a challenge. By uncovering the deep meaning of religious life, Heidegger intends (1) to indicate an alternative to late modernity, and (2) to stimulate internal dynamism within religion itself. Ultimately, for Heidegger, we "are" history. Religion is therefore constitutive of our identities, and has the potential to be a powerful force in shaping new post-technological, post-nihilistic identities.

Finally, Heidegger's phenomenology of religion supplies a powerful weapon to the apologetic arsenal. Anti-realist theories of religion — Marxist, Freudian, Neo-Kantian, Nietzschean — had become, by the time Heidegger began to work out his own ideas, a virtual orthodoxy. Such theories still prevail in fields like sociology, where religious life is analyzed into social expedients, with virtually no mention of God or even of belief. Wittgensteinian theories of religion, though perhaps less prevalent than they once were, still represent a powerful current of anti-realism. Heidegger's phenomenology of religion offers strong reasons to be suspicious of such theories. Heidegger's suggestion is that these theories are motivated not by a sober look at the phenomena of religious life, but rather by antecedent commitments to particular explanatory schemes. Heidegger argues that these commitments can be traced back to Enlightenment — and particularly, idealist — theories of culture. To the extent that one has reason to find these theories dubious, one therefore has reason to doubt the trenchancy of the theories of religion derived from them.

Of course, it is an open question as to whether proponents of anti-realist views would be convinced by Heidegger's account. It must be recalled that his target is *semantic* anti-realism, i.e., the view that the *meaning* of religious assertions and practices derives entirely from human cognitive and volitional capacities. For Neo-Kantians and Nietzscheans, religion was never *really* about God, but rather about human (all too human!) values. Heidegger's claim is that rigorous phenomenological analysis exposes the falsity, or, at least, the dubitability, of such views. But phenomenological analysis lacks the tight premise–premise–conclusion structure of traditional philosophical argument. Instead, it rests its case upon interpretive fit between the results of the analysis and a naïve, pre-reflective familiarity with the subject matter. Moreover, as Heidegger famously points out in *Being and Time,* justification in phenomenology is *circular.* Phenomenological analysis does not lead to iron-clad certainties, but rather to more or less plausible reconstructions of the phenomena in question. It the present case, it remains open to the semantic anti-realist to dispute the conclusions of Heidegger's analysis. Since phenomenology does not generally involve *internal* criticism of an opposing view (at least not as part of the phenomenological analysis per se), one could hardly expect definitive refutations of opponents' views. Heidegger could, however, console himself with the recognition that such refutations, and the sorts of arguments needed to generate them, are as rare in every interpretive discipline as they are in everyday life.

Such considerations naturally lead one to reflect on the limitations of Heidegger's approach to the philosophy of religion. Like most phenomenological approaches to the philosophy of religion, Heidegger's lacks any positive apologetic. Despite the power of his explication of the structure of religion, Heidegger seems simply uninterested in offering any reasons for why one might adopt a life that has this structure. He simply "brackets" these traditional philosophical concerns. He has his reasons for this lack of interest. In the early 1920s, he seems to have adopted a quasi-Barthian view of the deep incompatibility between philosophy and theology, and he seems also to have held onto this view throughout the remainder of his career. Similarly, Heidegger also shared the traditional Continental suspicion of so-called "natural theology," which generally plays a large role in positive apologetic. This is an aspect of Heidegger's philosophy of religion that has received extensive comment.[3] Heidegger is famous for making the (somewhat unfortunate) term "onto-theology" into a buzzword in Continental philosophy and contemporary theology. Aligning himself with a long tradition, Heidegger is deeply suspicious of the "God of the philosophers," the God of classical theistic metaphysics. His view is that (unlike religious meaning as such) such a God *is* very much a conceptual construction aimed at grounding a comprehensive theoretical framework. "God" is a name for the *archē,* the metaphysical first principle, that has been on the philosophical agenda since Thales. To assimilate the God of religious devotion to this abstraction is, for Heidegger, to force to God work on human terms, to force God into a role in our Promethean project of achieving totally conceptual mastery over reality as a whole. Unfortunately, this "God of the philosophers" is generally the *terminus ad quem* of some of the more impressive apologetic arguments

---

3. The best reading to date is Westphal (2001).

currently on offer. It is certainly true that, at least in some cases, the "God of the philosophers" is just that—a term in a philosophical explanation. But Aquinas, Descartes, and Leibniz would all, no doubt, be surprised to learn that the God for Whom they argue is something other than the "God and Father of Our Lord Jesus Christ." Heidegger, unfortunately, seems simply to *assume* that there is *always* a difference here. He therefore bequeaths to the philosophy of religion a troubling dichotomy. Philosophers who other- wise agree about religion (e.g., are Christians) largely ignore one another as "onto-theologians" or "fideists" respectively. Combined with the famous (and largely vacuous) divide between "Continental" and "analytic" approaches to philosophy, this in effect forecloses the possibility of Heidegger's own partici- pation in contemporary discussions.[4]

Heidegger was also reticent about the pedantry involved in investing par- ticular world-views with philosophical authority. As he envisioned the task of the philosopher, this task was to "make things hard," to persevere in relent- less questioning, rather than to offer people comfort. The criticism of onto- theology and this particular conception of the pedagogic role of philosophy may, in the last analysis, all be good reasons for being suspicious of rational apologetic as it is usually practiced. However, this suspicion also limits the acceptability of Heidegger's theories.

As I have argued throughout, the core of Heidegger's position on the phenomenology of religion is a kind of *realism*. That is, Heidegger argues that religious meaning is *given* rather than *created*. Given that this is, in fact, a correct understanding of the structure of religious belief and practice, there is still a large question left over. The question is, *why* does religion have this structure, given that it does? Why does religion put a normative claim on human beings, rather than the other way around? These are ques- tions that Heidegger's work simply lacks the resources to answer. Indeed, he seems quite content to leave them open. For Heidegger, the fact that we inhabit a meaningful world at all is something that can be explicated, but not *explained*. There is an irreducible element of *mystery* when it comes to meaning. For most, however, this conclusion will hardly be satisfactory. One might still want to know *why* it is the case that religious meaning seems to "come from beyond," as it were. Here, it seems that a religious hypothesis, such as theism, can fill the breach. Religious meaning and value transcends

---

4. This mutual incomprehension is plain, for example, in Alvin Plantinga's discussion of Heidegger in Plantinga (2000). Plantinga maintains (following Rorty) that Heidegger's view is opposed to classical theism since Heidegger expresses a kind of "guilt" over having not been the originator of the world (Plantinga 2000: 423). He misses the fact that Heidegger's criticisms of Nietzscheanism are actually quite congruent with his own.

subjectivity because it actually derives from a personal deity that exists independently of the conditions of human understanding. If this explanation is to be convincing, however, there must be some positive apologetic. That is, there must be a case made for plausibility of the religious hypothesis. As I have pointed out above, Heidegger's debunking of the anti-realist fruits of the "hermeneutics of suspicion" can play an important role in the overall case for theism. But, beyond that, Heidegger's suspicions of rational apologetic impede his ability to mount a rational case for theism.

While this is a very real limitation, it by no means precludes a generally positive assessment of Heidegger's achievement in the philosophy of religion. In the last analysis, Heidegger offers a way of looking at religion that is worth defending and certainly worth developing further. The rigor of his phenomenological methods, the consistency of his conclusions, and the intuitive force of much of his account all commend his theory. If Heidegger's work is taken seriously as a contribution to our understanding of religion, then this book will have fulfilled its purpose. Heidegger's challenge to an entrenched way of viewing religion is a serious one; his challenge to the attitudes and assumptions that ultimately anchor this point of view is salient and compelling. Heidegger raises questions about religion to which advocates of anti-realist views must have a response. To take Heidegger seriously on these points is to give a place to an insistent, powerful, and even disturbing voice in a conversation that remains as urgent today as when Heidegger wrote.

Bibliography

Anderson, Elizabeth. 1988. "Values, Risks, and Market Norms." *Philosophy and Public Affairs* 19 (1990): 71–92.

———. 1993. *Value in Ethics and Economics.* Cambridge, Mass.: Harvard University Press.

Anderson, R. Lanier. 2005. "Neo-Kantianism and the Roots of Anti-Psychologism." *British Journal for the History of Philosophy* 13 (2): 287–323.

Bambach, Charles R. 1995. *Heidegger, Dilthey, and the Crisis of Historicism.* Ithaca, New York: Cornell University Press.

———. 2003. *Heidegger's Roots: Nietzsche, National Socialism, and the Greeks.* Ithaca, New York: Cornell University Press.

Barash, Jeffrey. 1988. *Martin Heidegger and the Problem of Historical Meaning.* Dordrecht: Martinus Nijhoff.

Beiser, Frederick C. 2002. *German Idealism: The Struggle Against Subjectivism 1781–1801.* Cambridge, Mass.: Harvard University Press.

———. 2003. *The Romantic Imperative: The Concept of Early German Romanticism.* Cambridge, Mass.: Harvard University Press.

Boulton, David. 1997. *A Reasonable Faith: Introducing the Sea of Faith Network.* Loughborough, U.K.: Sea of Faith.

Breuer, Stefan. 1993. *Anatomie der Konservativen Revolution.* Darmstadt: Wissenschaftliche Buchgesellschaft.

Burkert, Walter. 1997. "From Epiphany to Cult Statue: Early Greek *Theos*," in Alan B. Lloyd, ed., *What Is a God? Studies in the Nature of Greek Divinity*, 15–34. London: Duckworth.

Byrne, Peter. 2003. *God and Realism.* Aldershot: Ashgate.

Callicott, J. Baird. 1989. *In Defense of the Land Ethic: Essays in Environmental Philosophy*. Albany: SUNY Press.

Caputo, John D. 1993a. *Demythologizing Heidegger*. Bloomington and Indianapolis: Indiana University Press.

———. 1993b. "Heidegger and Theology," in Charles B. Guignon, ed., *The Cambridge Companion to Heidegger*, 270–288. Cambridge: Cambridge University Press.

———. 1994. *"Sorge* and *Kardia*: The Hermeneutics of Factical Life and the Categories of the Heart," in Theodore Kisiel and John Van Buren, eds., *Reading Heidegger From the Start: Essays in His Earliest Thought*, 327–344. Albany: SUNY Press.

Cassirer, Ernst. 1955. *The Philosophy of Symbolic Forms*, 3 vols. Vol. 2: *Mythical Thought*. Ralph Manheim, trans. New Haven and London: Yale University Press.

Crowe, Benjamin D. 2005. "Heidegger's Romantic Personalism." *History of Philosophy Quarterly* 22 (2): 161–176.

———. 2006. *Heidegger's Religious Origins: Destruction and Authenticity*. Bloomington and Indianapolis: Indiana University Press.

Crowell, Steven G. 1994. "Making Logic Philosophical Again (1912–1916)," in Theodore Kisiel and John Van Buren, eds., *Reading Heidegger From the Start: Essays in His Earliest Thought*, 55–72. Albany: SUNY Press.

———. 2001. "Neo-Kantianism: Between Science and Worldview," in Steven G. Crowell, *Husserl, Heidegger, and the Space of Meaning*, 23–36. Evanston, Ill.: Northwestern University Press.

Cupitt, Don. 1980. *Taking Leave of God*. London: SCM.

Dahlstrom, Daniel O. 2001. *Heidegger's Concept of Truth*. Cambridge: Cambridge University Press.

Dreyfus, Hubert L. 2005. "Heidegger's Ontology of Art," in Hubert L. Dreyfus and Mark A. Wrathall, eds., *A Companion to Heidegger*, 407–419. Oxford: Blackwell.

Edwards, James C. 1997. *The Plain Sense of Things: The Fate of Religion in an Age of Normal Nihilism*. University Park: University of Pennsylvania Press.

Feenburg, Andrew. 2005. *Heidegger and Marcuse: The Catastrophe and Redemption of History*. London: Routledge.

Fehér, István M. 1995. "Heidegger on the Atheism of Philosophy: Philosophy, Religion and Theology in His Early Lectures up to *Being and Time*." *American Catholic Philosophical Quarterly* 69 (2): 182–228.

Frank, Manfred. 1982. *Der kommende Gott: Vorlesungen über die neue Mythologie*. Frankfurt am Main: Suhrkamp.

Frischmann, Bärbel. 2002. *Vom transzendentalen zum frühromantischen Idealismus: J. G. Fichte und Fr. Schlegel*. Paderborn: Schöningh.

Fritsche, Johannes. 1999. *Historical Destiny and National Socialism in Heidegger's Being and Time*. Berkeley: University of California Press.

Gadamer, Hans-Georg. 1987. "Die religiöse Dimension," *Gesammelte Werke 3: Neuere Philosophie: Hegel, Husserl, Heidegger*. Tübingen: J. C. B. Mohr (Paul Siebeck).

Green, Michael Steven. 2001. *Nietzsche and the Transcendental Tradition*. Urbana: University of Illinois Press.

Hardenberg, Friedrich von. 1960. *Novalis: Schriften 3: Das philosophische Werke II,* Richard Samuel, Hans-Joachim Mähl, and Gerhard Schulz, eds. Stuttgart: W. Kohlhammer.

Hebblethwaite, Brian. 1988. *The Ocean of Truth: A Defense of Objective Theism.* Cambridge: Cambridge University Press.

Heinz, Marion. 1997. "Die Fichte-Rezeption in der südwestdeutschen Schule des Neukantianismus." *Fichte-Studien* 13: 109–129.

——. 2000. "Philosophy and Worldview: Heidegger's Concept of Philosophy and the Baden School of Neokantianism," in Tom Rockmore, ed., *Heidegger, German Idealism, and Neo-Kantianism,* 209–238. Amherst, New York: Humanity.

Helting, Holger. 1999. *Heideggers Auslegung von Hölderlins Dichtung des Heiligen: ein Beitrag zur Grundlagenforschung der Daseinanalyse.* Berlin: Durcher and Humboldt.

Hemming, Lawrence Paul. 2002. *Heidegger's Atheism: The Refusal of a Theological Voice.* Notre Dame: Notre Dame University Press.

Henrich, Dieter. 1992. *Der Grund im Bewußtsein: Untersuchungen zu Hölderlins Denken (1794–1795).* Stuttgart: Klett-Cotta.

——. 1997. *The Course of Remembrance and Other Essays on Hölderlin,* ed. Eckhart Förster. Palo Alto, Calif.: Stanford University Press.

Herf, Jeffrey. 1986. *Reactionary Modernism: Technology, Culture and Politics in Weimar and the Third Reich.* Cambridge: Cambridge University Press.

Homann, Harald. 1994. "Die 'Philosophie der Kultur.' Zum Programm des 'Logos,'" in Helmut Holzhey and Ernst Wolfgang Orth, eds., *Neukantianismus: Perspektiven und Probleme,* 88–112. Würzburg: Königshausen and Neumann.

Husserl, Edmund. 1968. *Logische Untersuchungen, Zweiter Band, II. Teil: Untersuchungen zur Phänomenologie und Theorie der Erkenntnis.* 5th ed. Tübingen: Max Niemeyer.

Ibáñez-Noé, Javier A. 1995. "Heidegger, Nietzsche, Jünger, and the Interpretation of the Contemporary Age." *Southern Journal of Philosophy* 33: 57–81.

——. 2002. "Nietzsche and Kant's Copernican Revolution: On Nietzsche's Subjectivism." *New Nietzsche Studies* 5: 132–149.

Kant, Immanuel. 1996. *Religion and Rational Theology,* ed. Allen Wood. Cambridge: Cambridge University Press.

Kisiel, Theodore. 1988. "War der frühe Heidegger tatsächliche ein 'christlicher Theologe'?" in Annemarie Gethmann-Siefert, ed., *Philosophie und Poesie: Otto Pöggelerzum 60. Geburstag,* 59–75. Stuttgart: Frommann-Holzboog.

——. 1993. *The Genesis of Heidegger's Being and Time.* Berkeley: University of California Press.

——. 1994. "Heidegger (1920–21) on Becoming a Christian: A Conceptual Picture Show," in Theodore Kisiel and John Van Buren, eds., *Reading Heidegger From the Start: Essays in His Earliest Thought,* 175–193. Albany: SUNY Press.

——. 2000. "Heidegger—Lask—Fichte," in Tom Rockmore, ed., *Heidegger, German Idealism, and Neo-Kantianism,* 239–270. Amherst, New York: Humanity.

——. 2002. "Why Students of Heidegger Will Have to Read Emil Lask," in Alfred Denker and Marion Heinz, eds., *Heidegger's Way of Thought: Critical and Interpretive Signposts,* 101–136. New York: Continuum.

Kluge, Friedrich. 2002. *Etymologisches Wörterbuch der deutschen Sprache*, ed. Elmar Seebold. 24th ed. Berlin: Walter de Gruyter.

Koehnke, Klaus. 1991. *The Rise of Neo-Kantianism: German Academic Philosophy between Idealism and Positivism*. Cambridge: Cambridge University Press.

Kovacs, George. 1994. "Philosophy as Primordial Science in Heidegger's Courses of 1919," in Theodore Kisiel and John Van Buren, eds., *Reading Heidegger From the Start: Essays in His Earliest Thought*, 91–110. Albany: SUNY Press.

Larmore, Charles. 2000. "Hölderlin and Novalis," in Karl Ameriks, ed., *The Cambridge Companion to German Idealism*, 141–160. Cambridge: Cambridge University Press.

Löwith, Karl. 1998. *Martin Heidegger and European Nihilism*, ed. Richard Wolin. Trans. Gary Steiner. New York: Columbia University Press.

Lyne, Ian. 2000. "Rickert and Heidegger: On the Value of Everyday Objects." *Kant-Studien* 91: 204–225.

Moore, Andrew. 2003. *Realism and Christian Faith: God, Grammar, and Meaning*. Cambridge: Cambridge University Press.

Orth, Ernst Wolfgang. 1992. "Martin Heidegger und der Neukantianismus." *Man and World* 25: 421–441.

———. 1994. "Die Einheit des Neukantianismus," in Helmut Holzhey and Ernst Wolfgang Orth, eds., *Neukantianismus: Perspektiven und Probleme*, 13–30. Würzburg: Königshausen and Neumann.

Otto, Walter F. 1965. *Dionysius: Myth and Cult*. Trans. Robert B. Dalmer. Bloomington and Indianapolis: Indiana University Press.

Phillips, D. Z. 1970. *Faith and Philosophical Enquiry*. London: Routledge.

Pinkard, Terry. 2002. *German Philosophy 1760–1860: The Legacy of Idealism*. Cambridge: Cambridge University Press.

Plantinga, Alvin. 1980. "The Reformed Objection to Natural Theology." *Proceedings of the American Catholic Philosophical Association* 54: 49–62.

———. 1981. "Is Belief in God Properly Basic?" *Nous* 15: 41–52.

———. 2000. *Warranted Christian Belief*. Oxford: Oxford University Press.

Poellner, Peter. 1995. *Nietzsche and Metaphysics*. Oxford: Clarendon Press.

Reinach, Adolf. 1989. *Sämtliche Werke: Textkritische Ausgabe in 2. Bänden*. Vol. 2: *Die Werke*, ed. Karl Shuhmann and Barry Smith. Munich: Philosophia Verlag.

Richardson, William J. 2003. *Heidegger: From Phenomenology to Thought*. New York: Fordham University Press.

Rickert, Heinrich. 1921. *System der Philosophie, Erster Teil: Allgemeine Grundlegung der Philosophie*. Tübingen: J. C. B. Mohr (Paul Siebeck).

———. 1999a. "Die Heidelberger Tradition und Kants Kritizismus (Systematische Selbstdarstellung)," in Rainer A. Best, ed., *Philosophische Aufsätze*, 347–411. Tübingen: J. C. B. Mohr (Paul Siebeck).

———. 1999b. "Lebenswerte und Kulturwerte," in Rainer A. Best, ed., *Philosophische Aufsätze*, 37–72. Tübingen: J. C. B. Mohr (Paul Siebeck).

Rosemann, Philipp W. 2002. "Heidegger's Transcendental History." *Journal of the History of Philosophy* 40 (4): 501–523.

Rudd, Anthony. 2003. *Expressing the World: Skepticism, Wittgenstein, and Heidegger*. Chicago and La Salle: Open Court.

Rush, Fred. 2001. "The Availability of Heidegger's Later Thought." *Inquiry* 44: 201–222.

Schleiermacher, Friedrich. 1996. *On Religion: Speeches to Its Cultured Despisers.* Trans. Richard Crouter. Cambridge: Cambridge University Press.

Sheehan, Thomas. 1986. "Heidegger's 'Introduction to the Phenomenology of Religion,' 1920–1921," in Joseph J. Kockelmans, ed., *A Companion to Heidegger's* Being and Time, 40–62. Washington, D.C.: Center for Advanced Research in Phenomenology and University Press of America.

———. 2001a. "A Paradigm Shift in Heidegger Research." *Continental Philosophy Review* 34: 183–202.

———. 2001b. "*Kehre and Ereignis:* A Prolegomenon to *Introduction to Metaphysics,*" in Richard Polt and Gregory Fried, eds., *A Companion to Heidegger's Introduction to Metaphysics,* 3–16. New Haven: Yale University Press.

Sluga, Hans. 2001. "'Conflict is the Father of All Things': Heidegger's Polemical Conception of Politics," in Richard Polt and Gregory Fried, eds., *A Companion to Heidegger's Introduction to Metaphysics,* 205–225. New Haven: Yale University Press.

Small, Robin. 2001. *Nietzsche in Context.* Aldershot: Ashgate.

Taylor, Paul. 1986. *Respect for Nature: A Theory of Environmental Ethics.* Princeton: Princeton University Press.

Tenbruck, Friedrich. 1994. "Neukantianismus als Philosophie der modernen Kultur," in Helmut Holzhey and Ernst Wolfgang Orth, eds., *Neukantianismus: Perspektiven und Probleme,* 71–87. Würzburg: Königshausen und Neumann.

Thomson, Iain D. 2003. "The Philosophical Fugue: Understanding the Structure and Goal of Heidegger's *Beiträge.*" *Journal of the British Society for Phenomenology* 34 (1): 57–73.

———. 2004. "Ontology and Ethics at the Intersection of Phenomenology and Environmental Philosophy." *Inquiry* 47 (4): 380–412.

———. 2005. *Heidegger on Ontotheology: Technology and the Politics of Education.* Cambridge: Cambridge University Press.

Travers, Martin. 2001. *Critics of Modernity: The Literature of the Conservative Revolution in Germany, 1920–1933.* New York: Peter Lang.

Troeltsch, Ernst. 1922a. "Wesen der Religion und der Religionswissenschaft," *Gesammelte Schriften* 1: *Zur religiösen Lage, Religionsphilosophie, und Ethik,* 452–499. Tübingen: J. C. B. Mohr (Paul Siebeck).

———. 1922b. "Zur Frage des religiösen Apriori," *Gesammelte Schriften* 1: *Zur religiösen Lage, Religionsphilosophie, und Ethik,* 754–768. Tübingen: J. C. B. Mohr (Paul Siebeck).

Van Buren, John. 1994. *The Young Heidegger: Rumor of the Hidden King.* Bloomington and Indianapolis: Indiana University Press.

———. 1995. "The Ethics of *Formale Anzeige* in Heidegger." *American Catholic Philosophical Quarterly* 69 (2): 157–170.

Westphal, Merold. 1987. *God, Guilt, and Death: An Existential Phenomenology of Religion.* Bloomington and Indianapolis: Indiana University Press.

———. 2001. *Overcoming Onto-Theology: Towards a Postmodern Christian Faith.* New York: Fordham University Press.

———. 2005. "Continental Philosophy of Religion," in William J. Wainwright, ed., *The Oxford Handbook of Philosophy of Religion,* 472–493. Oxford: Oxford University Press.

Williams, Stephen N. 1995. *Revelation and Reconciliation: A Window on Modernity.* Cambridge: Cambridge University Press.

Williamson, George S. 2005. *The Longing for Myth in Germany: Religion and Aesthetic Culture from Romanticism to Nietzsche.* Chicago: University of Chicago Press.

Windelband, Wilhelm. 1911a. "Kulturphilosophie und transzendentaler Idealismus," in *Präludien: Aufsätze und Reden zur Einführung in die Philosophie,* 4 Aufl., vol. 2, 256–271. Tübingen: J. C. B. Mohr (Paul Siebeck).

———. 1911b. "Das Heilige: Skizze zur Religionsphilosophie," in *Präludien: Aufsätze und Reden zur Einführung in die Philosophie,* 4 Aufl., vol. 2, 272–309. Tübingen: J. C. B. Mohr (Paul Siebeck).

———. 1920. *Einleitung in die Philosophie,* 2 Aufl. Tübingen: J. C. B. Mohr (Paul Siebeck).

Woods, Roger. 1996. *The Conservative Revolution in the Weimar Republic.* London: Macmillan.

Wrathall, Mark A. 2003. "Between Earth and Sky: Heidegger on Life After the Death of God," in Mark A. Wrathall, ed., *Religion After Metaphysics,* 69–87. Cambridge: Cambridge University Press.

Young, Julian. 1995. "Being and Value: Heidegger Contra Nietzsche." *International Studies in Philosophy* 27 (3): 105–116.

———. 2001. *Heidegger's Philosophy of Art.* Cambridge: Cambridge University Press.

———. 2002. *Heidegger's Later Philosophy.* Cambridge: Cambridge University Press.

Zimmerman, Michael E. 1990. *Heidegger's Confrontation with Modernity: Technology, Politics, and Art.* Bloomington and Indianapolis: Indiana University Press.

———. 1994. *Contesting Earth's Future: Radical Ecology and Postmodernity.* Berkeley: University of California Press.

Index

BENJAMIN D. CROWE teaches in the philosophy department at the University of Utah. He is author of *Heidegger's Religious Origins* (Indiana University Press, 2006).

Lightning Source UK Ltd.
Milton Keynes UK
UKHW020249260921
391056UK00014B/560